SELECTED WORKS OF MODERN CHINESE LEARNING

THE FINANCING OF PUBLIC EDUCATION IN CHINA

A FACTUAL ANALYSIS OF ITS MAJOR PROBLEMS OF RECONSTRUCTION

Ronald Yu Soong Cheng

2015 · BEIJING

First Edition 2015

All rights reserved. No part of this publication may be reproduced or transmitted in any form or by any means, electronic or mechanical, now known or to be invented, without permission in writing from the publishers, except for brief quotations by reviewers.

ISBN 978 - 7 - 100 - 11074 - 7
© 2014 The Commercial Press

Published by
The Commercial Press
　36 Wangfujing Road, Beijing 100710, China
　www.cp.com.cn

Ronald Yu Soong Cheng

(1899—1992)

Editorial Note

One hundred years ago, Zhang Zhidong tried to advocate Chinese learning by saying: "The course of a nation, be it bright or gloomy, the pool of talents, be it large or small, are about governance on the surface, and about learning at the root." At that time, the imperialist powers cast menacing eyes on our country, and the domestic situation was deteriorating. The quick infiltration of Western learning made the long-standing Chinese tradition come under heavy challenge. In those days, Chinese learning and Western learning stood side by side. Literature, history and philosophy split up, while many new branches of learning such as economics, politics and sociology were flourishing, which made many Chinese dazed. However, there appeared a vital and vigorous learning climate out of the confusing situation. It was at this critical moment that modern Chinese scholarship made the transition—by exchanging views, basing on profound contemplation and even with confrontation of idea and clash of views, the scholarship made continuous progress, bringing up a large number of persons of academic distinction and creating numerous innovative works. Changes in scholarship and in general modes of thinking made transition in all aspects of the society possible, thus laying a solid foundation for revitalizing China.

It's over a century since the journey of modern Chinese learning started, during which various schools of thought stood in great numbers, causing heated discussions. The journey sees schools of thought as well as relevant arguments rising and falling, waxing and waning instantly, leaving complicated puzzles to followers. By studying and reviewing the selected works, one may gain new insights into that journey; and it is the editor's sincere hope that readers would ponder over the future by recalling the past. That's why we have compiled "Selected Works of Modern Chinese Learning". The effort includes masterpieces of celebrated scholars from diverse fields of study and different schools of thought. By tracing back to the source and searching for the basis of modern Chinese learning, we wish to present the dynamics between thought and time.

The series of "Selected Works of Modern Chinese Learning" includes works (both in Chinese and in foreign languages) of scholars from China—mainland, Hong Kong, Macau, and Taiwan—and from overseas. These works are mostly on humanities and cover all fields of subjects, such as literary theory, linguistics, history, philosophy, politics, economics, jurisprudence, sociology, to name a few.

It has been a long-cherished wish of the Commercial Press to compile a series of "Selected Works of Modern Chinese Learning". Since its foundation in 1897, the Commercial Press has been privileged to have published numerous pioneering works and masterpieces of modern Chinese learning under the motto of "promoting education and enlightening people". The press has participated in and witnessed the establishment and development of modern Chinese learning. The series of "Selected Works of Modern Chinese Learning" is fruit of an effort to relay the editorial legacy and the cultural propositions of our senior generations. This series, sponsored by National Publication Foundation, would not be possible if there were no careful planning of the press itself. Neither would it be possible without extensive collaboration among talents of the academic circle. It is our deeply cherished hope that titles of this series will keep their place on the bookshelves even after a long time.

Moreover, we wish that this series and "Chinese Translations of World Classics" will become double jade in Chinese publishing history as well as in the history of the Commercial Press itself. With such great aspirations in mind, fearing that it is beyond our ability to realize them, we cordially invite both scholars and readers to extend your assistance.

Editorial Department of the Commercial Press
December 2010

INTRODUCTION BY DR. MA YEN-CH'U

It is gratifying to know that some one has dared to tackle the problem of educational finance, which, in China, is still an unexplored field on the borderland between the science of education and the so-called dismal science. The unusual difficulty in making this type of study is evident, especially when it is attempted in a foreign country. The background needed does not only involve a thorough knowledge and wide experience of educational administration and other activities as well as, at least, an intelligent grasp of the fundamentals of public finance and economics, but it also demands a knowledge of the bearings of many branches of the social science including some mastery of the tools of research. It is a wonder that Dr. Cheng has done a pioneer work so well. I have no doubt that this solid piece of work will be recognized as highly valuable by those engaged in the cause of public education in China and by those leaders in the government who are laboring to lift China out of her desperate slough of poverty and ignorance.

When I graduated from Columbia University, my dissertation was on New York Finance. After my return, I found that it had little practical use for my work. It was only after I became a serious student of the actual conditions in China that I began to turn my Western knowledge into account in meeting the outstanding economic and financial problems. I have often thought of the problem of educational finance in China and I am convinced that it needs very careful consideration on the part of our political leaders, though it is very difficult to tackle. The pressure of many other important issues upon my attention have prevented me from making a thorough study of it. Therefore I have much sympathy for the author of this book for directly tackling a key problem of China and applying the methods of American experts. His courage and patience and industry alone deserve commendation. I heartily endorse his work and recommend it highly to the public.

MA YEN-CH'U,
*Chairman of the Finance Committee
and Member of the Legislative Yuan,
National Government of China.*

*Nanking,
June 3, 1935.*

INTRODUCTION BY DR. SHUANG-CHIU TAI

About twenty-two hundred years ago, the philosopher Shiun Tze said that chaos is the result of inaccuracy and order is fulfilled by detailed information (荀子：亂生於差治盡其詳). Lord Kelvin once said that he who can tell something in numbers knows something about it. Edward L. Thorndike said that whatever exists at all exists in some amount, and therefore can be measured. Therefore facts, their accuracy and measurement, are *sine qua non* for any scientific investigation. Chinese scholars and writers have too often indulged in flowery literature, mere ideas, theories, opinions, general impressions, and sweeping generalizations. Such a tradition does not encourage the development of science. It is the duty of the returned student to promote the scientific method and spirit. Years ago I foresaw its importance and tried my part in the field of education with the desire of making education a science in China. My doctoral dissertation was on "Objective Measures Used in Determining the Efficiency of the Administration of Schools." But the neglect of accurate facts and statistical data by Chinese educational workers has made it difficult to push forward this movement. The development of educational finance as an applied science has barely begun in China. Government reports have not as yet provided sufficient pertinent data for scientific analysis. There have been many obstacles in attempting to make a school survey. Therefore all my writings so far on the problems of increasing the educational budget, fiscal independence, equalization of burden, and the like are based upon meager data available. Although the fundamental principles of school support have been developed and recognized by leaders in educational administration in China, yet their realization in practice awaits more complete and accurate information and the development of procedures and techniques through research and survey. The appalling economic crisis at present has brought about serious shrinkage in government revenues and consequently widespread retrenchment in school budget. The traditional ideology that education comes after prosperity has caused public opinion less in favor of increasing school support in times of crisis. To talk about educational finance at such times requires courage and vision, a courage to break away with tradition and the "favor of the crowd," and a vision to see the economic effects of education.

Dr. Cheng is to be congratulated for making a very significant contribution in this field. It is the first comprehensive study of its kind. It is, first of all, a piece of scientific work of high quality. The amount of data collected and the detailed documentation exhibited and the careful analysis reveal his unusual pluck in overcoming difficulties, his habits of scientific procedure, his patience and zeal in the cause of public education. He has made the following outstanding contributions:

1. All available outstanding facts concerning the major aspects of financing education in China have been assembled for the first time in one volume. It is a source book of information.

2. "Facts are more forceful than vehement arguments." He has raised loud protests in silent numbers which would convince any conscientious politician on the side of retrenchment in education.

3. Although his modesty has prevented him to make definite recommendations for financing a comprehensive educational program, he has actually shown the possibility of a solution of the problem.

Introduction ix

4. A pattern for research in educational finance has been laid down. The study of Hupeh Province and the lines of research recommended throw much light on the future research in local educational finance.

5. Numerous methods and techniques or statistical procedures have been applied. He has shown how objective measures and graphic methods should be developed and used. Personal equation has been eliminated as much as possible.

The following improvements or additions to the study or methods of study in educational finance in China are noticed:

(1) A broader viewpoint of the problem through understanding the economic and social setting and in relation to wealth and income.

(2) The equated Chinese dollar in devising the index of educational expenditure which shows that expenditure has not kept pace with enrollment.

(3) The cubical method of presenting facts on the extent of educational opportunities for various groups of the population.

(4) A tentative method of estimating the ratio of population in various age-groups to total population.

(5) A mathematical formula for estimating the total cost of the public educational system of China, and a method of estimating the total cost of education borne on three government levels.

(6) A new method for comparing the relation of education cost to national budget in various countries (see Table 35).

(7) The application of Tai's 8 criteria in analysing the local educational fiscal control.

(8) A more rational classification of local sources of school revenue.

(9) A detailed analysis of local sources of school revenue in Hupeh and their graphic presentation.

(10) A suggested refinement in the method of estimating the probable future cost of a program of universal education.

(11) A tentative method for measuring the economic ability of local districts and for ranking the economic ability of the provinces.

(12) A suggested approach to a documentary study of the history of Chinese school land.

A word must be said about the question of reliability of Dr. Cheng's primary data. Here the principle of relativity must be applied. Social science is still very young and has been said to be two hundred years behind the exact sciences. Physics can measure one millionth of an inch but finance in its pioneer stage must be contented with the present products of variable human nature largely dealing with trends and probabilities. It is the relative reliability of data and the open-mindedness we are after. It is true that the figures reported by some local governments are mere guesswork. But, relatively speaking, with these figures it is better than without. The habits of accuracy of the research student tend to stimulate accuracy in future reports and surveys. Hence Dr. Cheng's work is to be appreciated. It is natural that the professors of Columbia University think highly of this study. Professor John Dewey wrote to Dr. Hu Shih that this is a solid illuminating piece of work which will be highly valuable to China. Professor George D. Strayer wrote that this study is not only a challenge to educational administrators in China but also will be recognized as an important contribution by educators of the world. Professor McCall said that this is one of the most significant dissertations ever produced in Teachers College, Columbia University and it has been defended in an exceptionally brilliant manner.

Introduction

Just at this time the National Government has taken a progressive step in announcing its $957,184,006 budget for the fiscal year 1935–36 by increasing the Central educational budget as well as the budget for industry by three and half million dollars while decreasing the budgets of many other government functions. A ten-year program of universal education beginning with June, 1935, has been launched and sources of support have been allocated. This will stimulate the provinces to take similar action. The Ministry of Finance is also initiating the inheritance tax and income tax with the hope of equalizing the burden of the population. But the problem of adequate and stable support of education has not been solved. Dr. Cheng's book meets the need for research admirably. I wish that he will put it in the Chinese language as soon as possible and make further progress in research along the lines he has proposed.

TAI SHUANG-CHIU,
Dean, College of Education,
Great China University.

Shanghai,
The Dragon Boat Festival,
June 5, 1935.

TO
THE MEMORY OF HIS MOTHER
THIS BOOK IS AFFECTIONATELY DEDICATED BY
THE AUTHOR

ACKNOWLEDGMENTS

The author is deeply grateful for the constant encouragement and help which he received from his sponsor, Professor George D. Strayer and for criticisms and suggestions given by his advisers, Professor Paul R. Mort and Professor John K. Norton. He is indebted to Professor Robert M. Haig for his training in public finance, to Professor N. L. Engelhardt and Professor Carter Alexander for his training in school finance and business administration, to Professor Harold Rugg and Professor H. F. Clark for his understanding of the economic and social foundations of school finance. He also acknowledges his indebtedness to his professors of statistics and comparative education, and to Professor Goodrich of the Chinese Department.

To the following persons the author acknowledges his gratitude for financial assistance or its equivalent during the critical stages of this difficult study: Mr. Frederick V. Field, Professor George D. Strayer, Professor Milton C. del Manzo, Dr. Charles D. Hurrey of the North American Y.M.C.A., Dr. Sheyting C. Wang, Minister of Education, Mr. Chang Chun, Chairman of the Hupeh Provincial Government, Dr. S. C. Tai, and Mr. Chih Meng. Dr. S. T. Leo has given the author constant guidance.

To the following persons and institutions the author is grateful for assistance in assembling data and reference work: Mr. Ma Ho-tian of the Examination Yuan, former Commissioner of Education of Kansu Province, Dr. S. C. Tai, Dean, College of Education, Great China University, Mr. T. V. Soong, former Minister of Finance through his secretary, Mr. Chin Yin-chun,

Mr. Chin Fen, Secretary-General of the National Economic Council, Mr. Chia Sze-yi, Commissioner of Finance of Hupeh Province, Mr. Chu Kia-hua, former Minister of Education, now Minister of Communications, Mr. Chen Pu-lei, Commissioner of Education of Chekiang Province, Mr. Kao Tan-shan of the Hupeh Provincial Department of Education, friends of the Shensi Department of Education and many other provincial departments of education, Professor Thomas T. Wang of Kiangsu College of Education, Mr. Ding U. Doo, Librarian of Chiao Tung University, Dr. Alfred K. M. Chiu of the Harvard Chinese Library, Mr. Wang Chang-pin of the Columbia Chinese Collection, Mr. Rachel Gambert of the Bureau International d'Education, Geneva, Dr. J. F. Abel of the United States Office of Education, Dr. Paul Monroe, Mrs. Nancy Reger, Messrs. Kao Jo-fu, James Huang, Chang Lung-tu and many others, and especially the Library of Congress and the library of the American Council, Institute of Pacific Relations.

The author is also grateful to Miss Ethel Spore and her sister for typing, checking, and rechecking the tables, to his American friend, Gordon MacCloskey for reading over the English, to the Bureau of Publications of Teachers College for editorial reading, and to Miss Horton for statistical assistance.

To all authors and publishers from whom the author makes quotations, he wishes to acknowledge deep gratitude. He is especially grateful to Mr. Y. W. Wong, general manager of the Commercial Press, the largest publisher in the Orient, for publishing this costly study.

R. Y. S. C.

CONTENTS

CHAPTER	PAGE
I. INTRODUCTION	1
STATEMENT OF THE PROBLEM	1
THE NEED FOR RESEARCH IN EDUCATIONAL FINANCE IN CHINA	1
SOURCES OF DATA	6
PROCEDURE	7
II. THE EDUCATIONAL PROGRAM OF CHINA	9
A BRIEF RETROSPECT	9
THE PRESENT ADMINISTRATIVE SET-UP FOR THE PROGRAM	10
THE PRESENT ORGANIZATION OF THE EDUCATIONAL PROGRAM OF CHINA	16
THE GROWTH OF THE EDUCATIONAL PROGRAM	21
THE EXTENT OF EDUCATIONAL OPPORTUNITIES	26
III. THE COST OF THE EDUCATIONAL PROGRAM	31
THE CURRENT COST OF THE SCHOOLS AND INSTITUTIONS	31
TRENDS IN SCHOOL COSTS	47
RISING SCHOOL COSTS EXPLAINED	50
THE CAPITAL COST	55
THE VARIATION OF COSTS BORNE BY THE PROVINCES AND SPECIAL MUNICIPALITIES	56
IV. THE PRESENT EDUCATIONAL COST FURTHER ANALYZED	60
ANALYSIS OF COSTS BY CHARACTER	60
THE COST OF TEACHERS' SALARIES	62

CHAPTER	PAGE
The Per Pupil Costs of Education in China	66
The Cost of Education Per Capita of Population	73
V. THE COST OF EDUCATION AND OTHER GOVERNMENT COSTS COMPARED	**78**
The Cost of Education and the Government Budget	78
China Compared with Other Countries in the Proportion of Governmental Expenditure Devoted to Education	85
The Cost of Education and Military Expenditures Compared	91
VI. HOW THE PRESENT EDUCATIONAL PROGRAM IS SUPPORTED	**94**
Fiscal Control	94
VII. HOW THE PRESENT EDUCATIONAL PROGRAM IS SUPPORTED (*Continued*)	**104**
The Sources of Educational Revenue	104
The Nontax Sources of Educational Revenue in China as a Whole	112
Tax Sources of Educational Revenue of the Central and Provincial Governments	117
Tax and Nontax Revenue	122
A Case Study of the County Sources of Educational Revenue in Hupeh Province	128
VIII. THE FINANCIAL IMPLICATIONS OF THE NEW EDUCATIONAL POLICY	**137**
Financial Implications of the Emphasis on Productive Education	152

CHAPTER	PAGE
IX. THE ABILITY OF CHINA TO SUPPORT EDUCATION	155
The Economic Foundations	155
China's Present Economic Crisis	156
Sources of the Wealth of China	163
Estimates of China's National Wealth and Income	169
China Compared with Other Countries in Per Capita Wealth and Income	170
The Ability of China to Support Education, Considered in Relation to Estimates of Her National Wealth and Income	173
X. THE ABILITY OF CHINA TO SUPPORT EDUCATION	177
The Financial Foundations	177
The Financial Ability of the Central Government	179
China's Foreign and Domestic Indebtedness	181
The Financial Ability of the Local Governments	185
What the Government Has Done in the Reconstruction of the Revenue System of China	188
The Effects Upon Educational Support and What Education Can Expect	197
Needed Readjustment and Education's Expectation	200
APPENDIX—A STATISTICAL ANALYSIS OF SCHOOL SUPPORT IN HUPEH PROVINCE AND ITS PROBLEMS OF RECONSTRUCTION	225
The Position of Hupeh Province	225
The Rank of Hupeh in Educational Opportunities Among the Provinces and Special Municipalities	229

Contents

	PAGE
THE COST OF THE PRESENT PROGRAM AND TRENDS IN TOTAL AND PER PUPIL EXPENDITURE . . .	232
TRENDS IN THE EXPENDITURES OR COSTS OF PROVINCIAL AND COUNTY EDUCATION	234
THE SUPPORT FOR THE EDUCATIONAL PROGRAM OF HUPEH	237
THE ABILITY OF HUPEH TO SUPPORT EDUCATION	250
MAJOR PRACTICAL PROBLEMS IN THE RECONSTRUCTION OF THE SYSTEM OF PUBLIC SCHOOL SUPPORT IN HUPEH.	256

BIBLIOGRAPHY 263

LIST OF TABLES, DIAGRAMS, AND MAP

TABLE	PAGE
1. Fundamental Statistics Concerning the Present Public and Private Educational Program of China, 1930–31	15
2. Status of Social Education Institutions Other Than Schools, 1930–31	21
3. The Growth of Enrollment by Three Levels of Schooling and in Teacher-Training Institutions of All Levels, 1907–31	22
4. The Part Played by Productive Education, As Shown by Enrollments, 1907–31	23
5. Ministry's Figures on the Trends in School Enrollment in China, 1907–31	24
6. Growth in Total School Enrollment Including Higher Education and Private Schools, Compared with the Status of Population Since 1902	25
7. Percentage of Children of School Age (6–12) in School, by Administrative Units, 1929–31	27
8. Proportion of Population in School in China, Compared with Other Countries	29
9. Current Cost of Education in Chinese Silver Dollars According to School Organizations, 1930–31	33
10. Distribution of the Current Expenditure of Public Schools and Institutions by Three Government Levels, 1930–31	36
11. Percentage That Expenditure for Elementary Education Is of Total Provincial Government Educational Expenditure	38
12. Percentage That Expenditure for General Control Is of Total Provincial Government Educational Expenditure, 1928–33	40

List of Tables, Diagrams, and Map

TABLE		PAGE
13.	Percentage That Expenditure for General Control Is of Total County Government Educational Expenditure, 1928–32	42
14.	Per Cent That Expenditure for Overhead Activities Other Than General Control and for Grant-in-Aid Is of Total Educational Budget of the Government	44
15.	Distribution of the Total Current Cost of the Entire Educational System of China—An Estimate for the Year 1930–31	47
16.	Trend in Educational Expenditure, Public and Private, Central and Local, Inclusive, in All China	48
17.	Trends in Expenditure for Three Levels of Schooling	49
18.	Percentage Distribution of Various Items of School Property and Funds, 1907–09	55
19.	Variation in Elementary and Secondary Educational Revenues and Expenditures in the Provinces and Special Municipalities, 1929–30	57
20.	Total Educational Expenditure by Administrative Units, 1929–30	58
21.	Percentage Analysis of Costs of Education by Character Classification in the United States	60
22.	Percentage Classification of Higher Education Expenditure by Character, 1930–31	61
23.	Total Educational Expenditures Classified According to Uses in 23 Provinces Reporting, 1907	62
24.	Frequency Distribution of Mid-Points Between Maximum and Minimum Monthly Salaries of Teachers Under the Statutes of Various Educational Authorities as Effective, 1934	64
25.	Trends in School Per Pupil Costs in China as a Whole, 1912–32	68

TABLE	PAGE
26. Variation of Average Per Pupil Costs of Elementary Education in Different Provinces and Special Municipalities, 1929–30	69
27. Variation of Average Per Pupil Costs of All Secondary Education in Different Provinces and Special Municipalities, 1929–30	70
28. Comparison Between Average Per Pupil Costs in Provincial or Urban and County or Rural Schools from Available Data, 1930–31	71
29. Ratio Comparisons of Per Pupil Costs, 1930–31. . .	72
30. The Burden of Educational Expenditure Per Capita of Population in the Provinces and Special Municipalities, 1929–30	74
31. Per Capita Burden of Educational Expenditure in China Compared with Other Countries	76
32. Proportion of Central Government Expenditures for Educational and Military Purposes Compared, 1911–34	79
33. Educational Expenditures Under Central Government Authorities Other than the Ministry of Education, 1931–32	81
34. Proportion of Provincial Governmental Expenditure for Education and Military Purposes Compared (Budget) . . . . *Facing*	82
35. Relation of Education Cost to National Budget in Various Countries	86
36. Per Cent Educational Budget or Expenditure Is of Total State or Provincial Government Budget or Expenditure, China Compared with Certain Other Countries	87
37. Per Cent Educational Budget or Expenditure Is of Total Municipal or City Budget or Expenditure, China Compared with United States	89
38. Percentage That Educational Expenditures Are of Total Local Budgets	90

TABLE		PAGE
39.	Summary of the Central Expenditure Budget, China	91
40.	Percentage That Military Budget Is of Total National Budget, China Compared with Other Countries .	93
41.	The Present Status of Educational Fiscal Control in the Various Provinces and Special Municipalities and Counties of China, Analyzed According to Eight Factors or Criteria of Fiscal Independence . . . . *Facing*	100
42.	Administrative Units Classified According to Policies of Fiscal Control, 1934	100
43.	Proportion of Various Sources of Education Revenue 1907–09	106
44.	The Proportions of Various Sources of Higher Education Revenue in All China, 1931–32	108
45.	Classification of Educational Revenue Budget of Kiangsu Province, 1929–30	108
46.	Classification of Revenue Budget of Honan Provincial Educational Program, Prepared by the Honan Educational Funds and Property Administration Bureau, 1929–30	109
47.	Distribution of Government-Owned School Land, 1753	113
48.	Tuition Fees Paid by Chinese Students, 1922–23, 1925–26	117
49.	Sources of Revenue Supporting Education Indirectly under the Appropriation Policy, in Order of Their Importance in the Provinces and Special Municipalities, 1931–32	120
50.	Earmarked Tax Sources of Educational Revenue under the Allocation and Independence Policies .	123
51.	Sources of County Education Revenue in Shantung Province, 1932–33	125
52.	Sources of County Education Revenue in Kiangsu Province, 1927–28	126

List of Tables, Diagrams, and Map xxv

TABLE		PAGE
53.	Sources of Educational Revenue in 58 Counties of Hupeh Province, 1932–33	127
54.	A General Classification of Sources of County and Local Educational Revenue in Hupeh, Hunan, Honan, Shantung, and Kiangsu Provinces	129
55.	Frequency of Each Type of Revenue in Counties of Hupeh, Hunan, Honan, Shantung, and Kiangsu, and in Certain Local School Districts of Honan and Hunan	131
56.	Types and Names of Sources of Revenue Further Classified	132
57.	Sources of Educational Revenue Compared with the Same Sources of County Government Revenue in Hupeh Province, China ...... *Facing*	134
58.	Estimated Cost of the Twenty-Year Plan of Educational Expansion and Improvement, According to the Second National Conference on Education	141
59.	Average Number of Lower Elementary School Pupils Per Teacher in the Provinces and Municipalities, 1929–30	148
60.	Size of Lower Elementary Schools in the Provinces and Municipalities, 1929–30	149
61.	Number of Pupils Per Teacher in China and in Other Countries Compared	150
62.	Estimates of China's Land Area in Millions of Mow, in Order of Their Recency and Acceptability	163
63.	The Status of China's Raw Materials . . *Facing*	166
64.	Statistical Contrasts Between China and the United States in the Extent of Industrialization	166
65.	Summary of Ku You-chuan's Energy Estimate of China in Kilowatt Hours	168
66.	Corrected Estimates of China's Wealth in Millions of Unit Currency	170

List of Tables, Diagrams, and Map

TABLE		PAGE
67.	A Comparison of Estimated Wealth in China and in Other Countries in Millions of Chinese Dollars	171
68.	A Comparison of the Estimated Income of China and Other Countries in Millions of Chinese Dollars	172
69.	Proportions of National Income and of Taxes Devoted to Public Education in the United States and China	175
70.	Status of Central Finance under the Peking Government, 1916–22	180
71.	Trend of Outstanding Indebtedness of Chinese Central Government, Including Foreign and Domestic Secured and Unsecured Loans and Indemnities	182
72.	Relation Between Debt Service and National Indebtedness in Various Countries, 1932–33	184
73.	Financial Situation in Nine Provinces Reporting for the Fiscal Year, 1931–32	185
74.	Indebtedness of Eight Provinces and Five Municipalities, Including Some Special Loans, 1927–32	186
75.	Indebtedness of Twelve Provinces and Municipalities, According to Purposes of Loans, for the Calendar Year 1932	186
76.	Status of Boxer Indemnity Remissions and the Amount Available for Education	*Facing* 204
77.	Estimated Amount of Boxer Indemnity Remissions Proposed for Rural Education	205
78.	Enrollment in New Institutions for Training Cadres in Soviet Russia	216
79.	Budget Estimates of the Various Industrial Plans	217
80.	Trend in Modern School Enrollment, Public and Private, Hupeh Province, 1902–32	226
81.	Rank of Hupeh Province in Educational Opportunities Among Twenty-Nine Provincial Units and Seven Municipalities, 1929–30	229

List of Tables, Diagrams, and Map xxvii

TABLE	PAGE
82. Trend in Total Actual Educational Expenditure, Public and Private, Provincial and Local, Inclusive, in Hupeh	232
83. Trend in Per Pupil Expenditure in Hupeh Province, China	Facing 232
84. The Variation of Total County Educational Expenditures	235
85. Summary of Statistics Concerning School Lands and Funds in Hupeh Province, 1355–1896	238
86. Hupeh Provincial Government Revenue for Fiscal Years 1914–15 to 1932–33	241
87. Total Tax Burden of People of Hupeh Province	246
88. Educational Expenditure Per Capita of Population in Hupeh Province	247
89. Rank of Hupeh Province in Economic Ability in Normal Years	Facing 250
90. Derived Data—Economic, Financial, and Educational—in All Counties, Hupeh Province	Facing 252
91. Population of Hupeh Province	261

DIAGRAMS

DIAGRAM |
---|---
1. The Educational Program of China as Organized Under the Statutes Effective 1934 with Age Periods and Proportional Enrollments for 1930–31 | 14
2. Showing the Needed Educational Program in Proportion to Total Population | 28
3. Percentage Increase in School Costs and School Enrollments Compared, China, 1912–31 | 51
4. Showing Relative Importance of Various Sources of Education Revenues | Facing 118
5. Showing Earmarked Sources of School Revenue Compared with County Government Revenues | Facing 134

xxviii   List of Tables, Diagrams, and Map

DIAGRAM   PAGE
   6. Showing the Scope of a Needed Dynamic Educational Program for Hupeh Province . *Facing* 226
   7. Showing Method of Estimating the Proportion of Chinese Population in Each Age Group *Facing* 261

MAP

MAP
   1. Showing the Expenditure Levels and Extent of Educational Opportunities in Hupeh Province . . . . *Facing* 226

CHAPTER I
INTRODUCTION

STATEMENT OF THE PROBLEM

This study is an attempt to make a factual analysis of the problem of financing public education in China. Because of the limitation of available data, the study attempts to answer only the following questions:

1. What are the facts concerning the costs of the present educational program?

2. What is the probable cost of a defensible program of universal education?

3. How is the present educational program supported and what are the facts concerning the sources of educational revenue?

4. What are the facts concerning China's ability to support a defensible program of universal education?

5. What are the available financial resources hitherto untapped?

Answers to the above questions are sought for the purpose of throwing some light upon the solution of the problem of securing adequate and stable support for public education.

THE NEED FOR RESEARCH IN EDUCATIONAL FINANCE IN CHINA

Further progress in education in China depends upon the solution of the various problems of financial support. At present these problems probably constitute the key problems in contemporary Chinese education. Since the establishment of the modern school system in 1902–03,[1] no comprehensive and stable financial plan has been carried out. There has been no national survey and little scientific research in any phase of educational finance. The scarcity of literature dealing with the subject indicates the neglect of research in this field. In China, the *Bibliography on Education* and the *Periodical Index* contain altogether only 145 magazine articles on educational finance written during the period 1909–33.[2] By way of contrast, in the United States the *Bibliography on Educational Finance*, 1924, listed no fewer than 1,900 titles on school finance studies up to January, 1923.[3] The *Bibliography* for 1923–31 listed no fewer than 6,800 titles under 66 topics.[4] In China, of 18 outstanding books on educational administration and general problems of education, only two give 136 out of 542 pages and 139 out of 452 pages respectively to school finance. Thirteen of them give fewer than 30 pages to this subject.[5]

Chinese writers in the field of educational administration treat the subject of school finance through statements of principles and policies and descriptions of actual conditions, but sufficient substantiating data are seldom provided. So far as the writer can discover, only three books have been written upon the subject of educational finance exclusively, namely, Kan Yu-yuan's *Educational Finance in the Counties of Kiangsu Province*, (1928), Tai Shuang-chiu's *The Problem of Using Temple Property for Schools* (1929), and Hoh Yam-tong's *The Boxer Indemnity Remissions and Education in China* (1933, in manuscript).

[1] Ministry of Education, *The First Education Year Book of China*, p. 23.
[2] Tai, S. C., and Others, *Bibliography on Education, passim; Periodical Index of Human Culture Monthly, passim;* Unpublished Document No. 1.
[3] Alexander, Carter, *Bibliography on Educational Finance* (number calculated on basis of 8 titles per page for 244 pages).
[4] Alexander, Carter, and Covert, Timon, *Bibliography on School Finance*, 1923–31 (number calculated on basis of 20 titles per page for 343 pages).
[5] See books listed in Unpublished Document No. 2.

The Influence of the Literati Tradition

The neglect of fiscal studies in general and in school finance in particular has an underlying cause. Certain teachings of Confucianism and the tenets of Taoism and Buddhism lay undue emphasis upon the nonmaterial side of life.

"Under the influence of Confucius, the public financiers of different dynasties have been unfavourably criticized. The term, 'collecting imposts' has been an odious term. The Chinese have carried this point too far and it has retarded the science of finance. . . .

"Since the Chinese scholars are afraid of talking about money-making, even for public use, China is hampered in the natural development of her financial system."[6]

Taoism, according to the teachings of Lao-tze, would abolish government and education entirely and return to nature. Like Taoism, Buddhism is too spiritual, disregarding material welfare.

"Under its influence, the scholars of the Sung, the Yuan, the Ming, and even the Tsin Dynasty, were little concerned about economic problems."[7]

The Aversion to Numbers and Statistics

There is another aspect of the literati tradition which discourages the science of numbers. The emphasis upon flowery literature and abstract concepts gave rise to the tradition of sweeping generalizations and an aversion to numbers. Hence, huge inaccuracies in measurement and the absence of statistical procedures in the administration of practical affairs are commonplace. President Lo Kia-lun of the National Central University, in an address at the Central Party Headquarters, said:

[6]Chen Huan-chang *The Economic Principles of Confucius and His School*, pp. 628–29.
[7]*Ibid.*, p. 718.

"The Chinese people have always shown a dislike for numbers. Such phrases as 'in general' and 'about' are often their shibboleths. The secondary school students at large all show a tendency of aversion to mathematics. Allured by belles-lettres, they neglect the study of mathematics under the pretext of temperament. This is certainly a most dangerous phenomenon. Modern science is built upon mathematics. When mathematics penetrates learning, it then can become science with certainty. . . . In recent years, college entrance examinations show that out of a thousand papers on mathematics, more than five hundred bear the mark of zero. If scholarship in mathematics is so low, it is futile to talk about scientific research."[8]

The Shifting of Responsibility

Still another tradition exerts its influence to discourage a rational attack upon the problems of school finance. According to the Confucian ideology, "He who is not in any particular office has nothing to do with plans for the administration of its duties."[9] Many Chinese educators maintain that school finance belongs in the field of public finance, and hesitate to delve into the subject.

"Everybody sweeps himself the snow at his door and never minds the frost on somebody else's roof," says a common proverb. Such a tradition develops only a minimum of public spirit on the part of the people and fails to encourage desirable forms of coördination and coöperation among the various governmental departments.

The Need for Facts on Educational Finance

Almost every year since the establishment of the Republic in 1912, there has been either major or minor internecine warfare.[10] Previous to the establishment

---

[8]Lo Kia-lun, "The Crisis of Chinese Higher Education," *Hupeh Education Monthly*, No. 5, p. 18, January, 1934.

[9]Legge, James (translator), *The Chinese Classics* (second edition, revised), Volume I, Book VIII, Chapter XIV, p. 213.

[10]Wen Kung-chih, *A History of Chinese Military Strife*, 1930, *passim*; Unpublished Document No. 3.

of the National Government in Nanking in 1927, the school system had been kept in an impoverished state because of the drainage of public funds by the war lords.[11] The movement for stabilizing educational support and for fiscal independence under professional leadership began to arouse public opinion early in 1915 with the first national conference of the National Federation of Provincial Educational Associations.[12] Protests, strikes, and clashes with the government were frequent. The National Association for the Advancement of Education was the most powerful force in the movement.[13]

The Nanking government called two national conferences on education in which detailed plans for reconstruction of the system of public school support were proposed.[14] Schemes of free universal education had been repeatedly proposed since 1912,[15] but the movement failed to move the reactionary régime to action. The resulting clamor and inaction seemed to arise from a lack of a deep understanding or a thorough grasp of the facts and techniques of fiscal science. There has been only a vague knowledge of the extent to which school support is inadequate, of the amount of school costs in relation to total government costs, the amount of available school revenues, and the facts on expenditure in relation to economy and efficiency. The solution of the problem of financing public education in China therefore, requires,

[11]Hsu Hsing-chen, *Chinese Educational Directory*, for the years 1925 and 1926. Sections on "School Finance."
[12]"Proceedings of the National Conferences of the Educational Associations," p. 132, as quoted by Hsu Hsing-chen in his *History of Modern Educational Thoughts in China*, 1929, p. 259.
[13]*New Education*, May, 1922, pp. 953-58; October, 1922, pp. 589-91; October, 1923, pp. 51-58; September, 1924, *passim;* September, 1925, p. 209.
[14]First National Conference on Education, *Proceedings*, 1928, Section B, "Educational Finance," pp. 223-92; Second National Conference on Education, *Proceedings*, 1930, pp. 1-73.
[15]Unpublished Document No. 4.

first, accurate factual knowledge of its present status and its trends. Armed with such knowledge, those concerned can proceed to map policies and launch strategic schemes of action.

Sources of Data

The annual reports, bulletins, separate statistical reports, and budgets of the Ministry of Education and various Provincial Departments of Education, and yearbooks, along with other published or unpublished documents secured through questionnaire and correspondence, furnish the chief primary sources of the data used in this study. These are listed in the Bibliography. In some cases, the figures reported in the news section of the educational periodicals and in the largest Chinese newspapers are used.

Lack of Reliable Statistics

Emphasis upon statistics is only a recent development in China. An intelligent understanding of educational finance evidently depends upon adequate and accurate facts. The inadequacy and dearth of pertinent statistical information, as well as the writer's inability to secure certain existing data, have been the source of much difficulty during the course of this study. For example, in many cases there is no accurate census. Many unit measures and estimates in this study have been derived on the assumption that the population figures concerned are accurate and reliable. Furthermore, the data available often have had to be transformed and re-tabulated and re-calculated. There is lack of standardized or uniform categories of classification or equal units of measure in a few cases. Occasionally errors have been disclosed and corrected.

Collection of Data

At the close of 1932, a questionnaire blank was sent to the Ministry of Education and to all Provincial Departments of Education in China proper. After a period of six months, only four replies had been received. The study was almost abandoned. Through indirect means, private correspondence, and trips to various libraries, the data presented in this study were finally secured by the end of 1933.

Method of Attack

The principal method of attack is simple statistical analysis and appraisal of facts. The quality as well as the quantity of the data do not warrant the use of elaborate statistical techniques.

The questionnaire blank now on file[16] was not successful in securing satisfactory returns.

The sampling method has been relied upon by the writer for determining certain trends in the country as a whole from data in government documents.

Certain of the techniques developed and used by American experts in school surveys have been employed in this study; for example, the index technique, the equated dollar, the graphic method of presenting facts, and the like.

Correspondence with certain governmental departments and prominent professional authorities, and interviews have been used to secure expert advice.

PROCEDURE

The procedure employed in this study was as follows:

1. A comprehensive plan of readings in the economic and social fields was carried out for the purpose of noting trends by which to orient the problem in hand.

[16]On file in the office of Professor George D. Strayer, Teachers College, Columbia University, New York, N. Y.

2. Then an outline of the problems of educational finance in China was prepared as a guide in securing data.

3. A questionnaire was prepared and distributed, and government documents were collected.

4. Available data relating to educational finance were selected, re-tabulated, and evaluated on the basis of comparable data from similar studies of other countries.

5. A comprehensive documentary study was made. It comprised more detailed study of the historical, theoretical, and statistical aspects of the major problems in the reconstruction of public school support in China.

6. Finally, this single aspect—a factual analysis of the present status and future prospect—was selected for more thorough and concise treatment.

CHAPTER II

THE EDUCATIONAL PROGRAM OF CHINA

A Brief Retrospect

The extent of public education in China in the past has been well characterized in the following quotations from Chu Yu-kuang and Kuo Ping-wen respectively:

"The whole idea of popular education as a government function was lacking in the ideology of the statesmen."[1]

"Indeed, it may be said that the popular education was almost left entirely to private enterprises and public charity, the government contenting itself with gathering the choicest fruits and encouraging their production by rewards in the way of degrees, official titles, and other public recognition."[2]

Modern education with government support began in the year 1862 with the establishment of Tung Wen Kuan, the college for training translators.[3] The comprehensive modern school system was first introduced in 1902.[4] The old examination system was abolished in 1905 and the Hsueh Pu, Board of Learning or Ministry of Education, was officially established in 1906.[5] Since 1912, public school administration and organization has several times undergone modifications. School enrollment in all China has increased from 6,912 in 1902 to 12,611,942 in 1931.[6]

---

[1] Chu Yu-kuang, *Some Problems of a National System of Education in China*, 1933, p. 53.
[2] Kuo Ping-wen, *The Chinese System of Public Education*, 1917, pp. 62–63.
[3] Ministry of Education, *The First Education Year Book of China*, 1934, p. 23; Hsu Hsing-chen, *Historical Source Materials of Modern Education in China*, 1928, Volume I, p. 7.
[4] Ministry of Education, *The First Education Year Book of China*, p. 23.
[5] *Ibid.*, pp. 27–28.
[6] See Table 6, page 25 of this study.

The Present Administrative Set-Up for the Program

Political

At present the National Government at Nanking is under the control of the Kuomintang or Nationalist Party, which functions through the Central Executive Committee and the Central Supervisory Committee which derive their powers from the National Party Congress.[7] The Central Political Council is the highest policy-determining or legislative body elected by the Central Executive Committee.[8] The latter appoints the President of the National Government and members of the State Council, as well as the President and the Vice President of each of the five Yuans or councils directly under the National Government.[9] During the Political Tutelage Period the National Government also exercised powers derived from the Provisional Constitution which was established by the National People's Convention in 1931.[10] This period, 1930 to 1935, was devoted to the training of citizens in the exercise of political power and in taking part in the reconstruction program.[11]

The Executive Yuan is one of the five Yuans and is the highest executive organ of the National Government. Under it there are ten Ministries and nine Commissions.[12] There are 28 provincial governments, 4 territory governments, and 5 special municipal governments, 1939 Hsien or county governments, 44 special

---

[7] "Constitution of the Party," adopted in 1924 and amended in 1926 and 1929. Tyau, M. T. Z., *Two Years of Nationalist China*, 1930, p. 23; *Central Party Affairs Bulletin* (Monthly) No. 40, "Chart of Organization," p. 2606.
[8] *Ibid*.
[9] "Organic Law of the National Government of the Republic of China," Chap. 1, Article 10; *Shun Pao Year Book*, 1934, p. 212.
[10] *Shun Pao Year Book*, 1934, p. 207.
[11] Tyau, M. T. Z., *op. cit.*, 1930, p. 34.
[12] *Shun Pao Year Book*, 1934, "Organization of the National Government," pp. 218–22.

county governments, and 14 city governments, including the four lost provinces.[13]

Educational

Public education is administered on four levels of educational authority:[14]

1. The Ministry of Education under the Executive Yuan.
2. The Provincial Departments of Education and the Special Municipal Bureaus of Education.
3. The Hsien or County Bureaus of Education and some City Bureaus of Education.
4. The School District Committeeman (Hsueh Chu Chiao Yu Wei Yuan).

The Ministry of Education is headed by the Minister of Education, who is assisted by the Political Vice Minister and the Standing Vice Minister, all appointed by the President of the National Government at the instance of the President of the Executive Yuan.[15] The Minister of Education has the power to control the administrative affairs of education and culture of the nation, and to direct and supervise the highest administrative heads of the local governments with respect to education.[16] The Central Research Yuan or Academia Sinica is independent of the Ministry of Education.[17]

[13]*Shun Pao Year Book*, 1934, "The Latest Administrative Divisions of China," to end of 1933, p. 97.
[14]Ministry of Education, *The First Education Year Book of China*, 1934, "Chart of Present Educational Administrative System," p. 56.
[15]Woodhead, H. G. W., *China Year Book*, 1933, pp. 398–400, "Revised Organic Law of the National Government of the Republic of China," promulgated December 27, 1932.
[16]Ministry of Education, *The First Education Year Book of China*, 1934, Section B, pp. 1–2, "Revised Organic Law of the Ministry of Education," promulgated April 22, 1933, Articles 1 and 2.
[17]Kwo, Wei, *A Complete Collection of Administrative Laws of China*, 1933, p. 1840, "Organic Law of the Academia Sinica," promulgated November 9, 1928.

The latter is organized into the following departments and organizations:[18]

1. General Affairs (including finance and business administration).
2. Higher Education.
3. General Education.
4. Social Education.
5. Mongolian and Tibetan Education.
6. The Secretariat.

The Provincial Department of Education is headed by the Commissioner of Education who is one of the members of the Provincial Government Commission appointed by the National Government.[19] The Special Municipal Bureau of Education is headed by the Director of Education. The Executive and minor legislative powers are concentrated in the person of the Commissioner and Director who are responsible to their respective government commissions and, at the same time, directly responsible to the Ministry of Education.[20] The organization of the Provincial Department of Education and the Special Municipal Bureau of Education varies somewhat in different provinces. In general, it consists of three or four divisions in addition to the Secretariat, the Supervisors, and Advisory Experts and various committees.[21] For instance, the Hupeh Provincial Department of Education consists of the following four divisions:[22]

[18]Ministry of Education, *The First Education Year Book of China*, 1934, Section B, pp. 1-2, ''Revised Organic Law of the Ministry of Education,'' promulgated April 22, 1933, Articles 4-18.
[19]Kwo, Wei. *A Complete Collection of Administrative Laws of China*, 1933, pp. 96-101, ''Revised Organic Law of the Provincial Government,'' promulgated March 23, 1931, Article 16.
[20]*Ibid.*, Article 17.
[21]Ministry of Education, *The First Education Year Book of China*, 1934, Section A, p. 50.
[22]Hupeh Department of Education, *Present Laws and Regulations of the Department of Education of Hupeh Provincial Government, March*, 1932, pp. 1-4, ''Statute of Organization of the Department of Education of Hupeh Provincial Government,'' Articles 5-9.

1. First Division, in charge of records, personnel, finance, and business administration.
2. Second Division, in charge of general education on all levels.
3. Third Division, in charge of social education.
4. Fourth Division, in charge of auditing, editing, publicity, and statistics.

Where there is educational fiscal independence, as in Honan, an independent Educational Finance Administration is established with a legislative committee and a supervisory committee as a complete unit.[23]

The Hsien or County Bureau of Education is headed by the County Superintendent or Director of Education, appointed by the Provincial Commissioner of Education on recommendation by the County Magistrate from a list of candidates who passed the professional examination.[24] The County Director is thus made immediately responsible to the County Magistrate and, at the same time, acts as the agent of the Provincial Department of Education. Sometimes when the county is small, the County Bureau becomes a mere division in the county government.[25] The County Bureau of Education is organized into two or three divisions with one or two school supervisors. Often there is an educational finance committee.[26]

Ordinarily a county is divided into several local school districts, each in charge of one Education Agent or Committeeman who is responsible to the County Bureau of Education.[27]

---

[23]Honan Department of Education, *Special Bulletin on the Educational Funds and Property of Honan Province*, 1930, Section on Laws and Regulations, pp. 1-6, ''Statute of Organization of Honan Educational Funds and Property Administration.''

[24]Kwo, Wei, *A Complete Collection of Administrative Laws of China*, 1933, pp. 70-74, ''Statute of Organization of the Hsien Government,'' promulgated July 6, 1931, Articles 4, 13, 14, 17, 18, 20.

[25]Hsia Chen-fung, *Modern Educational Administration*, 1932, p. 415.

[26]Ministry of Education, *The First Education Year Book of China*, 1934, Section A, p. 54.

[27]*Ibid.*, Section A, pp. 51-52, ''Statute of Organization of County Bureau of Education of Chekiang Province,'' Article 13.

DIAGRAM 1

THE EDUCATIONAL PROGRAM OF CHINA AS ORGANIZED UNDER THE STATUTES EFFECTIVE, 1934 WITH AGE PERIODS AND PROPORTIONAL ENROLLMENTS FOR 1930-31

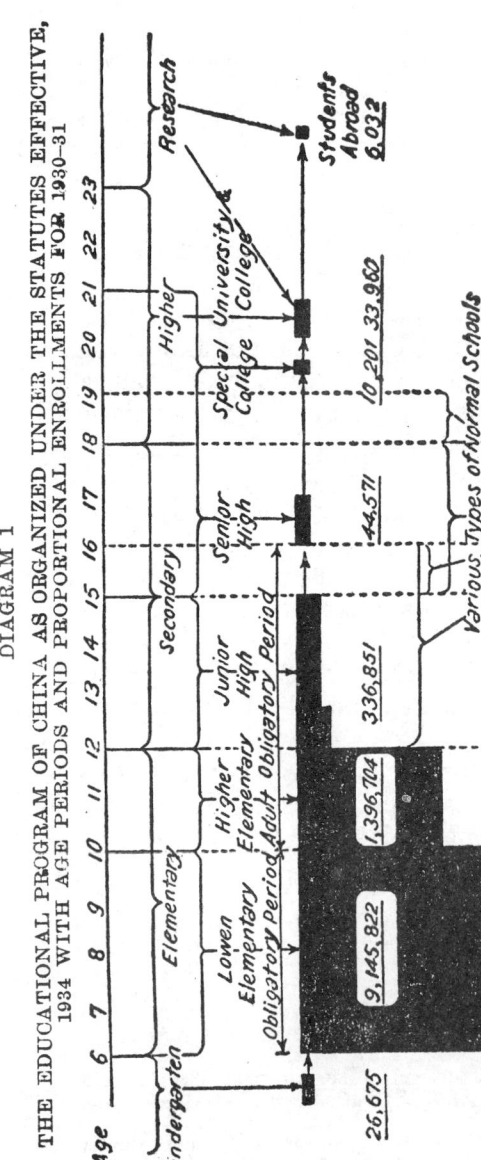
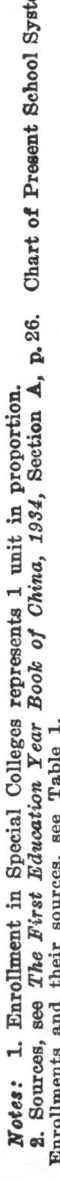

Notes: 1. Enrollment in Special Colleges represents 1 unit in proportion.
2. Sources, see *The First Education Year Book of China, 1934*, Section A, p. 26. Chart of Present School System. Enrollments and their sources, see Table 1.

TABLE 1
FUNDAMENTAL STATISTICS CONCERNING THE PRESENT PUBLIC AND PRIVATE EDUCATIONAL PROGRAM OF CHINA, 1930-31

Type of Education	Number of Institutions	Number of Teachers and Officers	Enrollment				Total 100 Per Cent
			Public		Private		
			Number (1)	Per Cent (2)	Number (3)	Per Cent (4)	
Elementary Education. . . .	250,840	568,484	8,267,701	75.5	2,589,612¶	23.6	10,948,979
Kindergarten. .	630	1,376	19,380		7,295		26,675
Lower elementary . . .	222,545	455,533	7,037,127		2,108,695		9,145,822
Higher elementary . . .	18,008	88,475	1,080,234		54,795		1,396,704
Others . . .	676	2,085	22,099		8,124		30,223
Secondary Education	2,992	58,919	325,967	63.5	188,642	26.5	514,609
High schools . .	554	19,724	86,625		92,456		44,571
Junior high . .	1,320	23,030	137,089		80,778		336,851
Normal schools .	846	10,321	78,620		4,189		93,540
Vocational schools	272	5,844	23,633		11,219		39,647
Higher Education .	103	7,053	22,564	49.8	27,635	50.2	50,199
University and college . . .	73	6,183	19,986		19,416		33,960
Special colleges .	30	870	2,010		2,755		10,201
Students abroad .	—	—	568	9.0	5,464*	91.0	6,032†
Social Education .	70,166	110,178	892,935	80.9	211,252	19.1	1,104,187
TOTAL	324,101	744,634	9,509,167	75.5	3,017,141	24.5	12,611,942
Total Excluding Social Education.	253,935	634,456	8,616,232		2,805,889		11,507,755
Total Elementary and Secondary Education . .	253,832	627,403	8,593,668	75.0	2,778,254	25.0	11,463,588

Sources of Data:
1. *Shun Pao Year Book,* 1934, pp. 1042–1115, separate tables on each type of education selected from the latest statistical reports for the year, 1930–31 of the Ministry of Education, not available to writer.
2. Ministry of Education, *Higher Education Statistics in All China,* 1931–32, *passim,* 1933.
(1), (2), (3), (4)—Freshly calculated from separate original tables.
¶—Error in original table.
* See Unpublished Document No. 5.
† Figure for 1928–29.

THE PRESENT ORGANIZATION OF THE EDUCATIONAL PROGRAM OF CHINA

This study covers only those phases of the present educational program, both public and private, which are under the direct control or supervision of the Ministry of Education and local educational authorities. The special educational undertakings, such as military schools, institutions for political training, for the training of personnel, and the like, under various other departments of the central and local governments, are not included.[28] Professor Harold Rugg, in an address given before the Chinese Education Club, Teachers College, Columbia University, in May, 1933, quoted from Dr. W. T. Tao, former General Secretary of the Chinese National Association for the Advancement of Education, to the effect that official statistics do not include the enrollment in the old-type tutor schools, which may be as numerous as the modern primary schools in some localities. These tutor schools also are not included in this study.

The present educational system is graphically represented in Diagram 1. Detailed statistics are presented in Table 1 for the year 1930–31.

In 1930–31 there was a grand total of 12,611,942 children and youths enrolled in all grades and types of schools and institutions in the entire country, including those studying abroad. There were 11,507,755 students enrolled in the school system proper. There were 11,463,588 in the elementary and secondary schools combined, with 627,403 teachers and officers. The following discussion is based upon the preceding diagram and table.

[28] See the *National Revenue and Expenditure Budget of the Republic of China*, 1931–32; Cf. Table 33 on page 81 of this study. Chekiang Provincial Department of Education, *Three Years of Education in Chekiang Province*, 1933, pp. 21–32.

The Public School Task Compared with the Private School Task

The public school system enrolls a total of 9,509,167 students, or 75.5 per cent of the public and private school enrollments in the entire country. The task of the private schools is about a quarter (24.5 per cent) of the whole task.[29] There are 8,267,701 children, or 75.5 per cent of the total elementary school enrollment, in the public elementary schools. In public secondary schools there are 325,967 students, or 63.5 per cent of the total secondary school enrollment. In public universities and colleges there are 22,564 students, or 49.8 per cent of the total higher education enrollment. There are 892,935 students in public continuation schools, mass education schools, and other social education institutions, or 80.9 per cent of the total social education group. Both public and private educational institutions are under the supervision of the government.[30]

Obligatory Education

Legally, all children reaching six years of age shall receive "obligatory education," a term used in place of compulsory education in China. As long as the present financial situation exists the compulsory period is only four years—the ages 6 to 10.[31] The beginning age may be delayed to the ages 7 to 9, according to local conditions.[32] A short-term obligatory education is provided for those aged 10 to 16 years.[33] The legal number of days in school session per year for all elementary schools is 281, but when Sundays are excluded there

---

[29] Table 1, Columns (1) to (4).
[30] "Provisional Constitution for the Political Tutelage Period," promulgated June 1, 1931, Chapter V, Article 3. See *The First Education Year Book of China*, 1934, p. 1, Section B.
[31-33] *The First Education Year Book of China*, 1934, pp. 33–34, in Section B, "Administrative Measures for Carrying Out the First Period of the Obligatory Education Program," promulgated June 25, 1932.

remain only 239 days. The short-term obligatory education for the part-time schools requires a period of 540 and 2,800 hours, distributed in one and two years respectively for two types of enrollments.[34]

Kindergarten Education

The kindergartens of China admit children under the age of six. Table 1 shows that there were only 26,675 kindergarten children in the entire country during the year 1930–31. Of these, 19,380 were in public kindergartens.

Elementary Education

The regular elementary school consists of two levels: the lower elementary school, taking children aged 6 to 10 years; and the higher elementary school taking children aged 10 to 12 years. The lower elementary school has the largest enrollment in the school system; it is 74 per cent of the grand total enrollment of all levels of schools.[35]

Secondary Education

Secondary education in China consists of all general, vocational, and normal schools on the secondary level. The junior high school period begins at 12 years and ends at 15. The senior higher school period is a period of three years for the ages 15 to 18 years. The period for either the vocational or the normal school varies slightly (see Diagram 1). The minimum number of successive school days per year is 285, or 243 excluding Sundays. At the present time the junior high schools

---

[34] *The First Education Year Book of China*, 1934, Section B, p. 27, "Elementary School Statutes," promulgated March, 1933.

[35] Computed from Diagram 1.

in China enroll more than seven times as many students as the senior high schools.

There are four types of teacher training institutions, namely, those for the ages 12 to 16 years, 15 to 18 years, 15 to 16 years, and 18 to 19 years. Their enrollment totaled 93,540 for the year 1930–31.

The junior vocational school period begins at the age of 12 and continues for one, two, or three years. The senior vocational school period is five or six years in length, beginning also at the age of 12. There were only 39,647 students enrolled in these schools during the year 1930–31. There has been a definite policy and determination on the part of the Ministry of Education to expend vocational education and limit general education.[36]

Higher Education

The government undertakes only about one-half the task of higher education in all China. The rest is left to private initiative. The university and college period is four or five years in length, beginning at the age of 18. The special college period is two or three years in length, also beginning at the age of 18. There were 50,199 students enrolled in higher education in 1930–31, including 6,032 students studying abroad. About 91 per cent of the latter number are privately supported students, and about 54 per cent of these spent the year in Japan.[37] The minimum number of school days in session is legally 271 per year, or 229 excluding Sundays.[38]

[36]*The First Education Year Book of China*, 1934, Section B, p. 45 *sqq.*, "Vocational School Laws and Statutes."
[37]Unpublished Document No. 5.
[38]*The First Education Year Book of China*, 1934, Section B, p. 91, "Revised Regulations Governing Holidays."

Social Education

Social education[39] in China includes mass education schools for the removal of illiteracy, vocational continuation schools, general continuation schools, people's reading centers, institutions for special education, schools and classes for the training of workers in the social education service, people's educational lyceums, lecture halls, libraries, museums, playgrounds, public theaters and motion picture houses, public tea houses, parks, and the like. The mass education school period extends from the ages of 16 to 50.[40] The period of schooling consists of at least three months, with 12 hours per week.[41] There were 944,289 students enrolled in the mass education schools during the year 1930–31. The vocational continuation school begins at the age of 12. During 1930–31 these schools enrolled 114,588 students. The social education teacher and personnel training schools enrolled 4,738 pupils during 1930–31. Other social education schools enrolled 34,975.

Special education is very meager at present. There were in 1930–31 only 17 schools for blind and deaf students, 25 schools for mental defectives, 60 institutions for orphans and pauper children, and 16 reformatories.[42] All these schools and institutions enrolled only 5,597 students.

The Ministry of Education has recently included agricultural extension service in the program of social education.[43]

---

[39]*The First Education Year Book of China*, 1934, Section B, pp. 101–13, "All Central Laws Governing Social Education."

[40]*Ibid.*, Section B, p. 101, "Administrative Measures for Mass Education Schools," promulgated July 16, 1932, Article 2.

[41]*Ibid.*, Article 10.

[42]*Shun Pao Year Book*, 1934, pp. 1099–1100, "Table on Statistics of Social Education" for the year 1930–31.

[43]*The First Education Year Book of China*, 1934, pp. 108–110, "Revised Regulations Governing Agricultural Extension Service," promulgated March, 1933.

Table 2 presents statistics concerning other social education agencies and institutions in which no regular instruction is directly carried on.

TABLE 2

STATUS OF SOCIAL EDUCATION INSTITUTIONS OTHER THAN SCHOOLS 1930–31

Type of Institutions	Number	Number of Staff Members
People's reading centers	2,838	2,380
Educational Lyceums	645	2,904
Libraries	1,273	2,648
Museums	27	182
Art galleries	24	43
Antique museums	40	99
Public playgrounds	1,440	1,732
Swimming pools	91	33
Popular lecture halls	2,308	3,842
People's newspaper reading halls	12,949	7,468
People's reading and writing inquiry agents	10,609	9,771
People's tea houses	1,810	3,046
Public parks	425	797
Music societies	577	1,304
Physical culture societies	175	957
Theaters	461	4,015
Motion picture theaters	224	1,934
Public recreation grounds	303	1,836
Young people's clubs	61	565
Moral advancement clubs	22	163
Other institutions	432	1,935
Total	36,488	47,744

Adapted from *Shun Pao Year Book*, 1934, pp. 1090–1101, General Table on Status of Social Education in All China for the Year, 1930–31.

THE GROWTH OF THE EDUCATIONAL PROGRAM

The constant growth of China's educational program is a remarkable achievement in view of the tremendous odds her educators have encountered during all the trying years of the past. This factor alone gives some cause for optimism. An analysis of the trend in school enrollment will show this growth in quantity. It is presented in Tables 3, 4, 5, and 6 which follow. The figures vary from the figures recently reported by the Ministry of Education for the years following 1912.[44] This may be due to different methods of classification or to the difference in the omission or inclusion of estimated figures for those administrative units not reporting. Both sets of figures are presented for comparison.

Table 3 shows that elementary school enrollment increased slowly from 926,918 in 1907 to 3,843,455 in 1916-17. In 1922-23 the increase became more apparent, being

TABLE 3

THE GROWTH OF ENROLLMENT BY THREE LEVELS OF SCHOOLING AND IN TEACHER-TRAINING INSTITUTIONS OF ALL LEVELS, 1907-31*

Year	Elementary Education	Index	Secondary Education	Index	Higher Education	Index	Teacher Training	Index
1907	926,918		31,682		14,117		36,608	
1908	1,191,721		36,264		18,629		33,604	
1909	1,531,746		40,468		20,572		29,126	
1912-13	2,793,633	100	98,045	100	41,709	100	39,909	100
1913-14	3,485,807	125	117,333	119	40,086	96	37,124	90
1914-15	3,921,727	140	119,057	121	34,554	83	28,755	72
1915-16	4,140,066	148	126,455	128	27,730	67	30,332	76
1916-17	3,843,455	138	111,078	113	19,921a	48	26,957	63
1922-23	6,601,802	236	182,804	187	34,880	84		
1929-30	8,882,077b	318	341,022	348	53,410	123	65,695	165
1930-31	10,948,979c	393	514,609	525	50,199	120	93,540	232

*Huang, Y. P., "An Appraisal of Twenty-Five Years of Chinese Educational Statistics" (C), *Human Culture Monthly*, Vol. IV, No. 5, pp. 1-28, June 16, 1933 (rearranged).
(a) Including 4,020 in missionary schools.
(b) 1929-30. From sources, J1-J4, see Bibliography.
(c) 1930-31, see sources in Table 1 of this study.
Note: Enrollments in normal schools and vocational schools are included in secondary school enrollment.

[44] See Table 5, Ministry's Figures on Trends in School Enrollment in China, 1907-1931.

TABLE 4

THE PART PLAYED BY PRODUCTIVE EDUCATION, AS SHOWN
BY ENROLLMENTS, 1907–31

Year	Enrollment in Productive Education, Including All Levels of Technical and Vocational Schools	
	Number	Index
1907	8,835	
1908	13,778	
1909	16,823	
1912–13	31,615	100
1913–14	34,772	110
1914–15	36,423	115
1915–16	36,021	114
1916–17	33,561	106
1928–29	21,323(+147,732)*	68
1929–30	36,768	116
1930–31	55,226	175

*J2 does not include the continuation vocational schools, in parenthesis, which do not require graduation from higher elementary schools for entrance. For example, see pp. 24–25. Cf. J4, Table 9 (26,659).
Source: Same as Table 3 of this study.

236 per cent over 1912–13. In 1930–31 the increase was 393 per cent over 1912–13. Secondary school enrollment increased at a greater rate than elementary school enrollment. In 1930–31 there were 514,609 secondary school students enrolled in contrast with 98,045 in 1912–13. The increase was 525 per cent in 1930–31 over 1912–13. According to the Ministry's figures, the increase was 764 per cent. Higher education enrollment has increased at the slowest rate, the increase being only 120 per cent in 1930–31 over 1912–13. But if the Ministry's figures are correct, which is questionable, the increase during the same period would be 2,230 per cent. The difference between these two enrollment figures for higher education is explained in the footnotes to Table 5. As the writer has checked his figures with the

TABLE 5

MINISTRY'S FIGURES ON THE TRENDS IN SCHOOL ENROLLMENT IN CHINA, 1907-31

Year	Elementary		Secondary		Higher		Total	
	(1) Number	(2) Index	(3) Number	(4) Index	(5) Number	(6) Index	(7) Number	(8) Index
1907	918,586		30,734					
1908	1,192,921		25,006					
1909	1,532,746		38,881					
1912-13	2,793,633	100	52,100	100	1,976	100	2,747,709	100
1913-14	3,485,807	125	57,980	111	3,084	156	3,546,871	129
1914-15	3,921,727	140	67,254	129	3,208	162	3,392,189	123
1915-16	4,140,066	148	69,770	134	3,458	175	4,214,294	187
1916-17	3,843,455	137	60,924	117	3,609	182	3,907,988	142
1922-23	6,601,802	236	130,385	250				
1925-26			129,978	250	21,483	1090		
1928-29			188,700	363	31,253	1580		
1929-30	8,820,777	313	248,668	479	34,938	1768	9,104,383	331
1930-31	10,788,582	386	396,948	764	41,966	2120	11,227,496	409
1931-32					44,805	2230		

Sources: The First Education Year Book of China, 1934, Section C: Column (1), on pp. 423-24; original table without notes. Column (3), on pp. [93-94; original table without notes. Column (5), on pp. 22-23; original able with following notes:

> 1912-17 figures from the fifth Report of Educational Statistics and Charts for the year, 1916-17.
> 1925-26 figures from statistics published by the National Association for the Advancement of Education.
> 1928-31 figures from Higher Education Statistics in All China for the year, 1931-32, published by the Ministry of Education, 1933.

Columns (2), (4), (6), (7), (8), freshly calculated.

Notes: Column (5) varies a great deal with the figures of this study. Upon checking with original sources, it is found that these figures for 1912-17 do not include enrollment in the provincial colleges. Other columns differ slightly, perhaps owing to the different method of classification of schools and to the inclusion and exclusion of certain estimated figures for those administrative units not reporting for that particular year, etc.

original tables found in the Library of Congress, Washington, D. C., the data presented with respect to this point may be relied upon.

TABLE 6

GROWTH IN TOTAL SCHOOL ENROLLMENT INCLUDING HIGHER EDUCATION AND PRIVATE SCHOOLS, COMPARED WITH THE STATUS OF POPULATION SINCE 1902

Year	Enrollment	Index	Population	Per Cent of Population in School — China	Per Cent of Population in School — U. S.
1902	6,912(1)	0.24	439,947,271 (2)	0.002	
1903	31,428(1)	1	(439,947,271)	0.01	
1904	99,475(1)	3	(439,947,271)	0.02	
1905	258,876(1)	9	(439,947,271)	0.06	19.94
1906	468,220(1)	16	(439,947,271)	0.16	
1907	1,024,988(A)	35	(439,947,271)	0.23	
1908	1,300,739(B)	44	439,405,000 (3)	0.30	
1909	1,639,641(C)	86	(439,405,000)	0.37	
1910			438,373,680 (4)		
1912–13	2,933,387(D)	100	(438,373,680)	0.67	
1913–14	3,643,206(E)	124	(438,373,680)	0.83	
1914–15	4,075,338(F)	139	(438,373,680)	0.93	
1915–16	4,294,251(G)	146	(438,373,680)	0.98	19.63
1916–17	3,974,454(H)	—	(438,373,680)	—	
1920			434,063,000 (5)		20.40
1921–22	4,987,647(I)	170	(434,063,000)	1.15	
1922–23	6,819,486(I)	232	436,094,953 (6)	1.56	
1926			451,842,000 (7)		21.4 (1925)
1928			474,418,700 (8)		
1928			485,508,838 (9)		
1929–30	10,312,669(J2)	352	(485,508,838)	2.12	24.35(1930)
1929–30			450,500,560 (10)	2.29	
1929–30			474,787,386 (11)	2.17	
1930–31	12,611,942	430	488,304,025 (12)	2.58	
1934	12,611,942		473,537,335 (13)	2.67	

(1) Chuan, C. H., "Thirty Years of Chinese Modern Education." *Educational Research*, 2:2, March, 1928 (original source quoted).
(2) Official estimate. See Woodhead, H. G. W., *The China Year Book*, 1933, p. 2.
(3) Maritime Customs estimate. (4) Ministry of Interior Census.
(5) Post Office estimate. (6) *China Year Book*, 1933, p. 2.
(7) Customs estimate.
(8) Ministry of Interior Census for 15 provinces, plus estimates.
(9) Post Office estimate; *The China Year Book*, 1933, uses it for the ar 1926, which is incorrect according to Chuan-Shih Li
(10) Customs estimate with correction for Manchuria. See *China Year Book*, 1933, p. 3.
(11) Ministry of Interior estimate, published in September, 1932.
(12) Shun Pao's revision in 1933, based upon direct reports and documents of the provinces, census and geographies of the latest kind.
(13) Population for 1934, see *Shun Pao Year Book*, 1934, p. 168.
1916–17 (H) Kwangsi, Kweichow, and Szechwan provinces not reporting.
Note: (A) to (J2) refer to their respective sources, see Bibliography.

Increase in the number of students in teacher training institutions of all levels has not kept pace with the increase in enrollment in the school system as a whole. A limited proportion of the students enrolled in all schools has been interested in vocational education, as shown in Table 4. The 1930–31 increase over that of 1912–13 in teacher training and in vocational school enrollment is 232 per cent and 175 per cent respectively.

The grand total of enrollments is presented in Table 6. It shows that the total enrollment in the modern school system increased 86 times in 1909 over that of 1903. The greater amount of increase has occurred since 1912–13, following the establishment of the National Government. The increase in 1930–31 over 1912–13 is 430 per cent.

The Extent of Educational Opportunities

The extent of educational opportunities in relation to the population and the number of children of school age is shown in Table 7 and in Diagram 2. They are self-explanatory.

Table 7 shows that on the average elementary education has reached 5.06 per cent more of the children of school age in 1930–31 than during the previous year. About 22.07 per cent of the 49,116,060 children of school age are now attending schools. China falls far behind Japan and the United States. Japan has 99.51 per cent of her children 6 to 14 years of age in school, while the United States has 81.3 per cent of her children 5 to 17 years of age in school.

Diagram 2 shows that the task of educating 38,258,767 more children of school age awaits China. About 33.4 per cent of her boys of school age are in school, while only 7.6 per cent of her girls of school age attend.

TABLE 7

PERCENTAGE OF CHILDREN OF SCHOOL AGE (6–12) IN SCHOOL, BY ADMINISTRATIVE UNITS 1929–31

PERCENTAGE	NUMBER OF PROVINCES AND MUNICIPALITIES	
	A—1929–30	B—1930–31
65–70		1 (Shansi)
60–65	2	1 (Weihaiwei)
55–60		1 (Shanghai)
50–55		1
45–50		1
40–45	1	1
35–40		1
30–35	2	5
25–30	4	3
20–25	1	3 (All China)
15–20	3	3
10–15	7	2
5–10	3	4 (Hupeh)
1– 5	4	6
less than 1		1 (Sikang)
Number of Cases	27	34
Median	14.64%	21.7 %
Average:		
China	17.1 %	22.07%
Japan	99.51% (6–14 years, 1931)	
U. S. A.	81.3 % (5–17 years, 1930)	

A—Adapted from Source J1, Table 5.
B—*Shun Pao Year Book*, 1934, p. 1096, adapted.
Japan—See *A General Survey of Education in Japan*. Tokyo: Department of Education, 1933, p. 1 sqq.
U. S. A.—See *Biennial Survey of Education*, 1928–30, p. 41.

China Compared with Other Countries

In comparing China with other countries, it is apparent how far China lags behind. The best measure adapted as a basis of comparison operates in terms of the total population, since the school ages in different countries vary. The trend in per cent of total population in school has been shown in the last column of

28 The Financing of Public Education in China

DIAGRAM 2

SHOWING THE NEEDED EDUCATIONAL PROGRAM IN PROPORTION TO TOTAL POPULATION

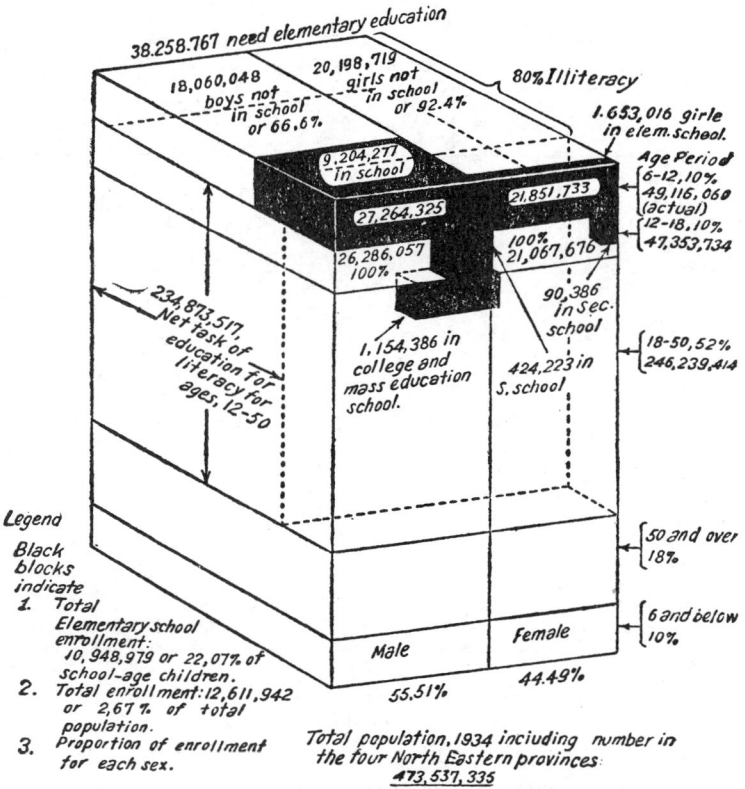

Sources: 1. Shun Pao Year Book, 1934, population for 1934, see p. 168. Reported school census for ages, 6–12, see p. 1096 sqq.
2. Enrollment figures for 1930–31, see Table 3 of this study.
3. Method of estimating population of different age-groups, see Diagram 7.

Table 6. The task of eliminating illiteracy is also illustrated in Diagram 2. The proportion of total population in school in other countries is presented in Table 8.

TABLE 8

PROPORTION OF POPULATION IN SCHOOL IN CHINA, COMPARED WITH OTHER COUNTRIES

Country	Year	Percentage of Total Population in School on All Levels (A)	Percentage of Total Population Aged 6–14 (B)	Percentage of Total Population Aged 14–18 (C)	Percentage of Total Population Illiterate (D)
China	1930–31	2.67 (f)			
China	1929–30	2.12 (f)			80 (f)
Albania	1930	3.12 (f)			
British India	1930	3.54 (f)			92.53 (1921)
Turkey	1928	4.11			
Portugal	1928	6.21			68
Lithuania	1929	7.68			44.1 (1921)
Yugoslavia	1929	9.09			
Estonia	1928	11.32	15.00	8.00	3 (1926)
Latvia	1929	11.36	14.00		14.72
Spain	1929	11.45	16.00		53.7 (1920)
Rumania	1928	11.92	18.00		60.16
Soviet Russia	1931	12.14	16.50	8.00	10 (1932)(f)
Soviet Russia	1932	19.5 (f)			
France	1929	13.01	11.00	6.10	8.2
France	1931	15.8 (f)			
Greece	1928	13.01	18.00		57.2 (1907)
Bulgaria	1928	12.54	16.00	8.50	55.5 (1920)
Italy	1931	13.15	17.00	7.50	27 (1921)
Poland	1929	13.53	16.70	8.00	24.2 (1921)
Finland	1929	14.14	15.00		1 (1920)
Denmark	1930	15.03	17.00	8.00	
Austria	1930	15.31	12.00	8.00	4
Czechoslovakia	1929	15.43	16.00	9.00	2.7 (1921)
Hungary	1930	15.81	14.00		23.6 (1920)
Sweden	1930	16.00	14.40	7.40	
Norway	1929	16.02	18.00	7.50	1
Belgium	1928	16.67	11.60	7.20	9.3 (1920)
Germany	1927	17.13	12.00	8.00	0.03 (1927)
England & Wales	1931	17.20 (f)			0.345
Holland	1929	18.92	16.80	7.00	
Japan	1931	19.65 (f)	15.46		0.7 (1927)
Switzerland	1929	20.99	14.30	7.70	
Australia	1930	19.60 (f)			15.2 (1921)
New Zealand	1930	20.30 (f)			1 (1916)
Irish Free State	1929–30	20.30 (f)			11.9 (1911)
Scotland	1930–31	21.60 (f)			0.26
Canada	1531	21.80 (f)			7.64 (1931)
U.S.A.	1930	24.35	25.71 *(5–17)		4.3 (1930)

Med.15.5 Med.8.64
N=22 N=15

Sources of Data: Columns A, B, C from Percy, Eustace, ed.: *The Year Book of Education*, London: Evans Brothers, Ltd. 1933. Table 58, p. XCVIII. With the following exceptions:

1. Soviet Russia, 1932, from *Summary of the Fulfillment of the First Five-Year Plan*. Moscow: Society for Cultural Relations with Foreign Countries, 1933.
2. Japan, 1931, from a *General Survey of Education in Japan*. Tokyo: Department of Education, 1933.
3. U.S.A. from *Biennial Survey of Education*, 1928–30.
4. France, England and Wales, Scotland, Canada, Australia, New Zealand, India, China, and Irish Free State. Freshly calculated. Population figures taken from *The Statesman's Year Book*, 1932.

D from *World Almanac*, 1933 with exception of (f).
*5 to 17 years of age.

Table 8 shows that in China in 1930–31 only 2.67 per cent of the total population was in school. This percentage was the lowest among the 36 countries selected. Thirty countries have more than 10 per cent of their population in school, and twenty countries have more than 15 per cent of their population in school. Six countries have more than 20 per cent of their population in school. The United States leads with 24.35 per cent of her population in school.

China has approximately 80 per cent illiteracy in her total population.[45] Among the countries for which more recent data are available, Soviet Russia has only 10 per cent illiteracy (1932); the United States, 4.3 per cent (1930); Canada, 7.64 per cent (1931); Japan, 7 per cent (1927); and Germany, .03 per cent (1929). Thus, China has the largest percentages of illiteracy among the civilized countries (India excluded). Diagram 2 shows that she faces a task of educating 234,873,517 people at the ages of 12 to 50 years for the mere purpose of removing "letter-blindedness," as Chinese educators term it.

[45] *Ministry of Education Bulletin*, Volume II, No. 7. See "Plan on Removal of Illiteracy."

CHAPTER III

THE COST OF THE EDUCATIONAL PROGRAM

THE CURRENT COST OF THE SCHOOLS AND INSTITUTIONS

To make a scientific study of the cost of the entire educatinoal program of China is difficult for the following reasons:

1. The expenditures for various types of schools and institutions reported by the Ministry of Education are the totals obtained from the annual expenditure of each school and institution. The term, "annual expenditure" (Sui Chu) in the reports is the actual cash disbursement each year.[1] Therefore the expenditures for "General Control" or administrative overhead costs and certain coördinated activities and the like are not included in the total.

2. There is no adequate classification of expenditures. Only totals classified by organizations are available for this study. The Reports of Educational Statistics and Charts for the years 1907–09, made by the Ministry of Education, did classify expenditures, but later reports give only the totals, with the exception of the reports on higher education from 1928 to 1931–32.[2] Nor do they give figures on the government educational budgets. These data are scanty in published forms and seldom have standardized or uniform classifications.

---

[1]Sources J1, J2, J3, J4, in Bibliography. Tables on annual expenditures of each type of school and institution.

[2]Ministry of Education, *Higher Education Statistics in All China*, for the years 1928–31 and 1931–32. published in 1931 and 1933 respectively.

3. The "accrued economic charge"[3] is not determinable. By this is meant not the amount of money paid but the money's worth used up by the school plants. The reports of 1907–09 give one single item, the total value, of school funds and property (Tzu Ch'an) combined. Since 1916, the only similar data available are for higher education for the years 1928–31, and for elementary education for the year 1930–31.[4] The value of the school plant is included in this total but is not classified as in the reports of 1907–09. The value of school buildings, sites, and equipment constituted an average of 57.43 per cent of the total for these three years.[5] The other 42.57 per cent was the value of school lands and other profit-bearing property and school funds. This is not an accrued economic charge.

Furthermore, without accurate basis it is impossible to estimate the amount of annual depreciation. The rate must vary to quite an extent among different types of plants and equipment.

Hence, only the total current cost of all schools and institutions is available as a means of estimating the total current cost of operating the entire school system of China.

Table 9 presents the actual current costs of all public and private schools and institutions in China for the year 1930–31. As the original sources listed therein show plainly, these totals do not include the costs of administration and certain overhead costs, such as the expenses of special committees, athletic meets, and medical and health service and the like, borne by

[3]Strayer, G. D., and Haig, R. M., *The Financing of Education in the State of New York*, 1923, p. 35.
[4]Sources A, B, and C in Bibliography. *Shun Pao Year Book*, 1934, p. 1092.
[5]*Higher Education Statistics in All China*, 1931–32, Tables 61 and 63. *Ibid.*, 1928–31, Tables 3 and 77. *Note:* The cost of school building is not included and is not available.

TABLE 9
CURRENT COST OF EDUCATION IN CHINESE SILVER DOLLARS ACCORDING TO SCHOOL ORGANIZATIONS, 1930-31

Type of Education	Cost of Public Schools (1)	Per Cent (2)	Cost of Private Schools (3)	Per Cent (4)	Total Cost: 100% (5)	Per Cent for Each Type of Ed. (6)
Kindergarten					468,329	
Lower elementary					57,580,494	
Higher elementary					28,331,750	
Others					447,812	
Total, elementary	70,639,412	79.0[1]	18,777,565	21.0[1]	89,416,977	48.1
High school					20,540,210	
Junior high					14,791,711	
Normal school					8,419,140	
Vocational school					4,961,996	
Total, secondary	31,251,653	64.2	17,461,404	35.8	48,713,057	26.2
University					31,582,507	
Special college					1,936,730	
Students abroad[2]	2,600,000[3]	6.0	7,328,000[3]	74.0	9,928,000[2]	
Total, excluding students abroad	19,528,576	58.1	14,090,661	41.9	33,619,237[4]	18.1
Total, including students abroad	22,128,576		21,418,661		43,547,237	
Social education	6,653,674	47.4	7,374,817	52.6	14,028,491	7.6
Grand Total,	$		$		$	
A. Excluding students abroad	128,073,315	69.0	57,604,447	31.0	185,777,762	100%
B. Including students abroad	130,673,315	66.9	64,932,447	33.1	195,705,762	100
C. Elementary and secondary	101,891,065	64.5	36,238,969	35.5	138,130,034	100

Sources: (5) from same sources as enrollment, see Table 1 of this study. (1), (2), (3), (4), (6), freshly calculated except two minor cases.

Notes: [1]Proportion for 1929–30, see source J1, Table (3), as no data for such separation are available now for 1930-31.

²Figure for 1929–30. See source J3, Table 1.
³Method of segregating the total into public and private, see Unpublished Document, No. 5.
⁴Figure for 1931–32. See *Higher Education Statistics in All China, 1931–32,* 1933. Section 111, p. 2, Table 2.
(2) and (4) refer to the proportion of public and private costs.
(6) refers to the proportion of each type of education that is of China's total cost of all schools and institutions.

? Most probably the cost of "general control" or administrative overhead cost is not included as seen from the nature of the original sources.

the Ministry of Education and all departments and bureaus of education.

The cost of students abroad and the ratio between the cost of public elementary schools and that of private elementary schools are based upon 1929–30 data, so that the grand total may be secured. (See footnotes in Table 10.)

Table 9 shows that at present China is spending $130,673,315 annually for her public schools and institutions of all levels, and $64,932,447 for her private schools and institutions of all levels. The grand total cost of all these schools and institutions is $195,705,762, including the cost of students abroad, or $185,777,762 excluding the cost of students abroad. The ratio between the cost of all public schools and institutions and the cost of all private schools and institutions, including the cost of students abroad is 66.9 per cent to 33.1 per cent.

The cost of all elementary schools is $89,416,977, of which about 21 per cent is the cost of public elementary schools. The cost of all secondary schools is $48,713,057, of which about 64.2 per cent is the cost of public secondary schools. The cost of all higher education institutions is $33,619,237, of which about 58.1 per cent is the cost of public universities and colleges. The cost of all social education institutions is $14,028,491, of which about 47.4 per cent is the cost of public institutions. The public elementary and secondary schools together spend only $101,891,065

The Cost of the Educational Program

The elementary schools are responsible for 48.1 per cent of the grand total cost of all schools and institutions of China. The secondary schools are responsible for 26.2 per cent; the higher education institutions for 18.1 per cent; and the social education institutions for only 7.6 per cent of the grand total cost of all schools and institutions in China.

The Current Costs of Public Schools and Institutions Under the Control of the Three Levels of Government

Table 10 presents the distribution of the current expenditure or cost of public schools and institutions by the three government levels. The method of distribution is explained in the footnotes to the table. As the National or Central Government supports almost no elementary schools directly from its budget, the distribution of elementary school cost is only between the provincial and special municipal government level and the county local government level. The amount of money spent by the provincial and municipal government for elementary schools is estimated.[6] How this is estimated is explained on page 38 of this study.

Table 10 shows that the proportion of the total cost of all public schools and institutions borne by the Central Government is 11.05 per cent; by the provincial and municipal governments, 28.25 per cent; and by the county local governments, 60.70 per cent. Public education in China, therefore, is largely supported by local governments and communities.

About 92 per cent[7] ($64,975,533) of the total cost of public elementary schools is borne by the counties. About 63 per cent ($19,722,825) of the total cost of public secondary schools is borne by the provincial and

---

[6] See Table 10, p. 36, of this study.
[7] This percentage and all that follow in this section are read from the slide rule and are based upon figures in Table 10.

36 *The Financing of Public Education in China*

TABLE 10

DISTRIBUTION OF THE CURRENT EXPENDITURE OF PUBLIC SCHOOLS AND INSTITUTIONS BY THREE GOVERNMENT LEVELS, 1930-31

	TOTAL	NATIONAL	PROVINCIAL AND SPECIAL MUNICIPAL	COUNTY LOCAL
	$	$	$	$
Elementary education	70,639,412	..	5,663,879(4)	64,975,533(9)
Secondary education	31,251,653	809,966(1)	19,722,825(5)	10,718,862(10)
Social education ..	6,653,674	..	3,139,419(6)	3,514,255(11)
Higher education ..	22,128,576	13,615,603(2)	5,912,973(7)	..
Students abroad ..	2,600,000	34,000(3)	2,566,000(8)	..
Grand total	$130,673,315	14,459,569	37,005,096	79,208,650
Per Cent	100 %	11.05 %	28.25 %	60.70 %

Notes: (1), (5), (10) Original distribution, see *Shun Pao Year Book*, 1934, Table on pp. 1165-66.

(2), (7) Original distribution, see *Higher Education Statistics in All China*, Section III, p. 2, Table 2.

(3), (8) (3), see *The National Revenue and Expenditure Budget of the Republic of China*, 1931-32, p. 179. (8), total—(3).

(4) 12.21% of total estimated educational expenditure of all provinces, $42,016,059 for 1929-30 (see Table 34, column 11, of this study) and that of 5 special municipal districts, $4,371,155 for 1931-32 (see Directorate of Budgets and Statistics, *Budget Estimates for the Provinces and Municipalities*, 1931-32, pp. 1-3 and Unpublished Document No. 7). For 12.21% see Table 11 of this study.

(9) Total—(4) Compare total estimated educational expenditure for all provincial and municipal governments: $46,387,214 (42,016,059+4,371,155) with the actual total of $43,258,876 for the fiscal year, 1933-34. (See Kiangsu Provincial College of Education, *Education and the Masses Magazine*, Volume V, No. 6, February, 1934, p. 1068. From actual reports of 26 provinces and special municipalities.)

(6) By adding the actual social education expenditures of 26 provincial and municipal governments for the year, 1930-31. Survey made by Department of Social Education, Ministry of Education. See Source J4, appendix.

(11) Total—(6).

Totals and grand total, see Table 9 of this study. All blanks represent very insignificant amounts which do not affect the distribution.

municipal governments. The Central Government is responsible for only about 2.6 per cent of the total cost of public secondary schools. The cost of public social education institutions is almost equally divided between the provincial and municipal governments and the county local governments.

The Central Government spends $13,615,603 for higher education institutions. This is approximately 61.6 per cent of the total cost of public higher education institutions, or 94.5 per cent of the total Central Government expenditure for all public schools and institutions.

The cost of public higher education institutions, therefore, is borne largely by the Central Government; the cost of public secondary schools by the provincial and municipal governments; and the cost of public elementary schools by the county local governments and communities.

The Total Cost of Elementary Schools Borne by the Provincial and Special Municipal Governments in China—An Estimate

In order to arrive at the estimated total cost of elementary schools borne by the provincial and special municipal governments as presented in Table 10.

Table 11 has been prepared to show the percentage that expenditure for elementary education is of the total provincial government expenditure for education, or the total provincial education budget. Seventeen samples have been taken, five for 1930–31 and twelve for 1928–29. This table reveals that the five selected provincial governments spent $1,909,114 for elementary education in 1930–31, which is 13.8 per cent of their combined educational budget. Twelve selected provincial governments spent $2,523,377 for elementary education in 1928–29, which is 11.50 per cent of their combined educational expenditures. The aggregate mean percentage that

TABLE 11

PERCENTAGE THAT EXPENDITURE FOR ELEMENTARY EDUCATION IS OF TOTAL PROVINCIAL GOVERNMENT EDUCATIONAL EXPENDITURE

Province	1930–31 (1) %	Province	1928–29 (2) %
1. Hupeh	36.80	1. Hupeh	61.80 b
2. Hunan	3.75 a	2. Hunan	5.20
3. Honan	5.73	3. Honan	12.90
4. Kiangsi	6.17	4. Kiangsi	6.56
5. Anhwei	5.42	5. Anhwei	4.40 c
		6. Kiangsu	9.15
Aggregate Mean:		7. Liaoning	23.40
For Elementary Education		8. Chekiang	9.07
$ 1,909,114	13.80	9. Yunnan	9.79
$13,707,500 for total		10. Kansu	2.30
Provincial Educational		11. Kirin	1.88
Expenditure.		12. Heilungkiang	13.30
		Aggregate Mean:	
		$2,523,377	11.50
		$22,025,299	

Aggregate Mean of all 17 cases above:
$4,432,491 for elementary education .. 12.40%
$35,732,799, total provincial educational expenditure
Mean of distribution of 17 cases 12.21%
        Standard deviation 8.75%
        P. E. (mean) 1.48%

Sources: (1) From Hupeh Department of Education, *A Glimpse of Recent Education in Hupeh*, 1932, pp. 12–13.
(2) From *The Statistical Monthly*, Vol. I, No. 10, Dec., 1929, p. 45.
a. 1929–30.
b. Original error corrected by figure in Table 34 of this study, Column (5).
c. Original error replaced by figures taken from Anhwei Department of Education, *Anhwei Educational Statistical Tables and Charts* for the year 1929–30, 1930, p. 3.

elementary education expenditure is of the total educational expenditure of all 17 cases combined is 12.4 per cent. The mean of the distribution of these 17 percentages is 12.21 per cent, with a probable error of 1.48 per cent.

By taking 12.21 per cent of $46,387,214, which is the total educational expenditure of all provincial and municipal governments combined, one arrives at an estimate of $5,663,879 as the total cost of elementary schools borne by all provincial and municipal governments.[8]

The Proportion of the Total Provincial and Municipal Educational Expenditure for Administrative Expenses or General Control

In estimating how much China spends for educational administration or general control on all government levels in operating the educational system, the best method is to find from available samples, the average percentage that this item of expenditure is of the total educational budget, and then to use this percentage in relation to the total current cost of all public schools and institutions.

Table 12 presents all available samples of the percentage that expenditure for general control is of the total provincial educational expenditure, and one sample for the municipal government, for the fiscal years 1928-29 to 1932-33.

This table shows that the range of all 25 averages used is from 3.6 per cent to 14.2 per cent. The aggregate mean of these 25 averages is 6.84 per cent, which is obtained by dividing $4,366,692, the combined expenditure for general control, by $64,012,133, the combined total educational expenditure. Column (2) shows such aggregate mean percentages for each of the eleven provinces with available data. The mean of this distribution is 6.4 per cent, with a probable error of .583 per cent. This 6.4 per cent is accepted as the fair proportion of the total expenditure for general control in relation to the total educational expenditure of all provincial and municipal governments of China.

[8]See Table 10, Note (4).

TABLE 12

PERCENTAGE THAT EXPENDITURE FOR GENERAL CONTROL IS OF TOTAL PROVINCIAL GOVERNMENT EDUCATIONAL EXPENDITURE, 1928–33

Province	Unknown %	(1)					Aggregate (2) Aver %
		1928–29 %	1929–30 %	1930–31 %	1931–32 %	1932–33 %	
Hupeh			5.70 a	4.70 b	4.75 c	6.55 d	5.27
Honan				3.60 g	4.78 h		3.80
Hunan		7.20 i	4.22 j				5.16
Kiangsi		5.10 k			5.00 l		5.05
Anhwei		3.65 m	5.40 n		8.22 o		6.06
Kiangsu		4.60 p			4.06 q		4.25
Chekiang	9.03 r		8.13 s	7.30 t	7.80 u		7.40
Kwangsi		13.90 v			14.20 w	13.00 x	13.60
Yunnan		5.70 y					5.70
Kirin		5.03 z					5.03
Kansu		? 21.40					
Heilungkiang		? 22.90					
Liaoning		? 29.60					
Municipality							
Hankow			7.80 f				7.80

N: Total number of individual cases—25. Total number of aggregated cases (2)-11

Aggregate average from 24 cases except Hankow.... $4,237,266 .... 6.7 %
            $63,284,663

Aggregate average from 25 cases including Hankow.... $4,366,692 .... 6.84 %
            $64,012,133

Central tendency and variability of 11 aggregate averages in Column (2):

Median: 5.70 %
Mean : 6.399% or 6.40%+ .583, PE.
Standard deviation: 2.874 % or 2.87 %

Sources: a, b, c, d, h, j, l, o, q, r. Hupeh Department of Education, *A Glimpse of Recent Education in Hupeh*, 1932, pp. 1, 11–12 of Section 1. a, b, d, freshly calculated.

 f. Hankow Special Municipal Government, *Hankow Special Municipal Statistical Year Book*, 1929. 1930, p. 362.

 g. Honan Department of Education, *Honan Educational Year Book*, 1930. Kaifeng, 1931, p. 304.

 i, k, m, p, y, z, and ?, ?, ?. *The Statistical Monthly*, Vol. 1, No. 10, Dec. 1929, p. 45, "Table on the Distribution of 12 Provincial Governments'

Educational Expenditure for the Year, 1928–29;" Survey made by Hunan Department of Education. 2 errors corrected and 2 cases without desired data. ??? are questionable extremes not considered in this study.
All %'s freshly calculated.

n. Anhwei Department of Education, *Anhwei Educational Statistical Tables and Charts*, 1930–31, p. 3.

s, t, u. Chekiang Department of Education, *Three Years of Education in Chekiang Province*, 1929–32. 1933, p. 33.

v, w, x. Kwangsi Department of Education, *Educational Status in Kwangsi Province*, 1931–32, p. 5.

Note: The total educational expenditure of the above 13 provincial governments constitutes 61% of that of all provinces reporting for 1929–30, see Table 34 of this study, column 11.

The Proportion of the Total County Government Educational Expenditure for General Control

Table 13 presents two sets of samples: (1) the aggregate mean percentages that expenditure for general control is of the total county government educational expenditure in 7 selected provinces having available data; and (2) random samples of individual counties in three selected provinces having available data. The first of these samples have been obtained by dividing the sum of the expenditures for general control by the sum of the total educational expenditures of all counties in each province. The aggregate mean of these aggregate means in Kiangsi, Liaoning, Kirin, Kiangsu, and Chekiang provinces is 14.30 per cent, and the mean of the distribution of all seven aggregate means is 11.68 per cent, with a probable error of 1.11 per cent.

Table 13 indicates that the random samples in the three selected provinces range from 7.3 per cent to 28.3 per cent, and the means are respectively 14.64 per cent, 11.73 per cent, and 13.01 per cent. The average of all medians in this table is 12.16 per cent, and the average of all means is 12.77 per cent. The latter percentage is accepted as a fair representative figure for all counties of China.

TABLE 13

PERCENTAGE THAT EXPENDITURE FOR GENERAL CONTROL IS OF TOTAL COUNTY GOVERNMENT EDUCATIONAL EXPENDITURE, 1928–32

Aggregate Means of All Counties Reporting			Random Sampling		
Province and Number of Counties and Some Cities Reporting	%	Year	Province and Size of Sample	%	Central Tendency and Variability
1. Shantung: 108	11.47	1932–33	8. Hupeh: 5		
2. Hunan: 68	10.08	1928–29	1933–34	19.10	Median: 14.49
60	9.75	1929–30		18.60	Mean: 14.64±1.29 PE
46	10.03	1930–31		14.80	Sigma: 4.26
3. Kiangsi: 40?	20.50	1928–29		13.40	
4. Liaoning: 59	20.35	"		7.30	
5. Kirin: 41	8.28	"	9. Honan: 11		
6. Kiangsu: 61	8.00	"	1930–31	22.20	
7. Chekiang: 76	6.66	"		14.10	
N 559				13.20	
				12.40	
Median 11.25				12.00	Median: 11.49
Mean of distribution 11.68		± 1.11 PE.		11.60	Mean: 11.73± .81 PE.
Sigma 4.93				10.00	Sigma: 3.99
PE. in terms of 559 . .014				9.75	
Aggregate average of 3, 4, 5, 6, 7:				8.65	
$ 3,625,470 . . . . 14.30				7.63	
$25,397,090				7.45	
			10. Anhwei: 11		
			1928–30	28.30	
				20.07	
				15.60	
				15.40	
				11.34	Median: 11.17
				11.20	Mean: 13.01±1.26 PE.
				11.05	Sigma: 6.20
				7.72	
				7.66	
				7.66	
				7.34	

Average of all means above (except 14.30%) . 12.77
Average of all medians above 12.16

Sources: 1. Shantung Department of Education, *County Local Educational Budgets in Shantung for the Fiscal Year, 1932–33,* Chart 3, p. 1128.
2. Hunan Department of Education, *Hunan Educational Administration Documentary Bulletin,* No. 5, April, 1930, appendix and No. 10, Oct.–Dec., 1930, appendix. Hunan Provincial Government, *Hunan Political Year Book,* 1930, p. 422.

3, 4, 5, 6, 7. *The Statistical Monthly*, Vol. I, No. 10, December, 1929, p. 47.

8. Meng Kwang-peng, Commissioner of Civil Affairs of Hupeh Provincial Government, *Reports of Tour in the Counties of Anlu, Kwan, Hua, Tsao Yang, Sian-yang and I-cheng*, 1933.

9. *Honan Educational Year Book*, 1930, Part II.

10. Anhwei Department of Education, *One Year of Anhwei Education*, 1930, Part II.

The Proportion of Expenditure for Overhead Activities Other than General Control

A careful examination of the educational budgets of all governments with data available reveals that, in addition to the expenditures for all schools and institutions under their control and the expenditures for general control (which is termed "Administrative Expenses" in the budgets), there are other overhead expenses itemized separately.[9] In order to find the proportion of this item of expenditure, Table 14 has been prepared from data available in nine provinces.

Table 14 shows that the mean percentage that expenditure for overhead activities other than general control is of the total educational budgets of nine provincial governments from 1928–29 to 1931–32, is 5.04 per cent. On the county government level, this figure is, on the average, 5.66 per cent. These two percentages are accepted as representative in China as a whole.

The grant-in-aid constitutes, on the average, about 5.02 per cent of the provincial government educational budget. This item is presented merely to show the extent of government subsidy. The amounts of government subsidy granted the schools and institutions are already included in the total current cost of all schools and institutions.

[9] See all budgets available in sources listed in Table 12.

TABLE 14

PER CENT THAT EXPENDITURE FOR OVERHEAD ACTIVITIES OTHER THAN GENERAL CONTROL AND FOR GRANT-IN-AID IS OF TOTAL EDUCATIONAL BUDGET OF THE GOVERNMENT

Province	Year	Provincial Government		County Governments	
		Overhead Activities Per Cent	Grant-in-Aid Per Cent	Overhead Activities Average Per Cent	Aid
1. Kiangsu	1929–30	4.20 %			
	1930–31	2.14	3.37 %		
2. Kiangsi	1928–29	15.70		5.30 %	
	1930–31	2.75	3.63		
3. Hupeh	1929–30	.65	1.73		
	1931–32	.47	2.30		
	1933–34		2.25	2.30 a	3.05 %
4. Hunan	1928–29	17.70		5.89	
	1929–30	1.89	12.80	7.06	
	1930–31			8.12	
5. Liaoning	1928–29	3.08		.03	
6. Anhwei	1928–29	7.95			
	1929–30	4.50		5.25 b	11.30
	1930–31	4.55			
	1931–32	.62	3.63		
7. Chekiang	1928–29	2.64			
	1929–30	3.21	7.22		
	1930–31	4.20	7.00		
	1931–32	4.86	6.22		
8. Honan	1928–29	4.10			
	1931–32	10.59			
	1930–31			9.10 c	
9. Kirin	1928–29			7.85	
Number of cases		19	10	9	
Mean of distribution		5.04	5.02	5.66	
Sigma of distribution		4.66	3.22	2.75	
P. E. of mean		.72	.69	.61	

Sources: From same sources in Tables 12 and 13.
Notes: "Overhead activities" include special committee projects, medical service, athletic meets, and the like, and those not classified as administrative expenditures. In arriving at the above figures, all errors and questionable extremes, double-counting, etc., have been either rejected or corrected.

Scholarships for students studying outside the province are in general classified with the expenditure for students abroad. This item is about 10%

of the expenditure for students abroad in Hupeh Province. Taken as a whole for the entire country, it does not affect the total expenditure for education to any significant degree. Its amount is comparatively small.

Grant-in-aid has been accounted for in the total current cost of the individual school accounts. It is probably not significant on the county government level as a whole.

a, b, c, only are from random sampling.

Grants-in-aid or subsidy are mostly for private institutions in China. The Central Government budgets, 1931–32, contains no such item.

An Estimate of the Total Current Cost of the Entire Educational System of China for the Year 1930–31, Including the Costs of Administration and All Overhead Costs

1. *The Cost of Public Education.*

(a) *The Cost Borne by the Central Government.* It is seen from Table 10, Column 2, that the Central Government spends $14,459,569 for all schools and institutions under its control. The budget for general control and the budget for other overhead activities constitute 6.18 per cent and 4.30 per cent respectively of the total budget of the Ministry of Education for the year 1930–31.[10] Let the total cost borne by the Central Government be 100 per cent; then $14,459,569 equals 100 per cent minus (6.18 per cent + 4.3 per cent) or 89.52 per cent of the total cost including the cost for general control and overhead activities. Then the latter equals $14,459,569 divided by 89.52 per cent, multiplied by 100, or $16,152,333.

(b) *The Cost Borne by the Provincial and Municipal Governments.* From Table 10 it is seen that the provincial and municipal schools and institutions spend $37,005,096, and the percentages that the expenditures for general control and overhead activities are of the total educational budgets are 6.4 per cent (see Table 12), and 5.04 per cent (see Table 14). Let the total

---

[10]Calculated from the respective items of the budget of the Ministry of Education, 1930–31. See the *National Revenue and Expenditure Budget of the Republic of China,"* 1931–32, pp. 178–81. The grants-in-aid to the provinces are excluded in the calculation.

cost, including administration and overhead costs, be 100 per cent. Then $37,005,096 is equal only to 100 per cent minus (6.4 per cent + 5.04 per cent) or 88.56 per cent of the total cost. Consequently, 1 per cent of the total cost is $37,005,096 divided by .8856. This quotient times 100 will give the total cost of the entire school system under the control of the provincial and municipal governments, which is $41,785,331.

(c) *The Cost Borne by the County Local Governments.* It is known that the total cost of all schools and institutions under the control of the county local governments is $79,208,650 (see Table 10), and the proportions of costs for general control and other overhead activities are 12.77 per cent and 5.66 per cent respectively (see Tables 13 and 14). Applying the same mathematical procedure as above, we obtain $97,105,124 as the total cost of the public educational system, including the cost of general control and other overhead activities under the control of all county local governments of China.

2. *The Cost of Private Education.*

Nearly all private institutions are independent organizations. Their overhead costs are in general included in the reports of their institutional costs, with the exception, however, of some of the expenses of the missionary educational boards and other private boards and foundations. Therefore, the approximate total cost of the private schools supported entirely by private resources is equal to $64,932,447 (see Table 9), minus government aid, $2,097,624. The latter figure is obtained by taking 5.02 per cent (see Table 14) of $46,387,-214, the total educational expenditure of all provincial and municipal governments combined (see Table 10, Note 4). Therefore the total current cost of the entire educational system of China in 1930–31 would be the sum of all these four totals approximately. This total is shown in Table 15. This table shows that the total

TABLE 15

DISTRIBUTION OF THE TOTAL CURRENT COST OF THE ENTIRE EDUCATIONAL SYSTEM OF CHINA—AN ESTIMATE FOR THE YEAR 1930–31

	Amount	Per cent	Per cent
Public Education:			
National	$ 16,152,333	10.41	
Provincial and municipal	47,785,331	26.96	
County local	97,105,124	62.63	
TOTAL	155,042,788	100.00	71.16
Private Education	62,834,823		28.84
GRAND TOTAL	$217,877,611		100.00

Note: Qualifying statements regarding government aid to private schools are found in the notes to Table 14.

current cost of the entire public school system in China for 1930–31 is approximately $155,042,788. The current cost of private education in China, supported by private sources, is $62,834,823. The grand total cost of the entire educational system, both public and private, is approximately $217,877,611. The ratio between public and private costs is about 71.16 per cent to 28.84 per cent. This is the best possible estimate that this study can offer.

TRENDS IN SCHOOL COSTS

Table 16 shows that in 1907 the total current cost of all schools and institutions was $18,203,716. It increased to $29,667,803 in 1912–13, the first year of the Republic of China, and to $59,424,541 in 1922–23. After the establishment of the National Government, it increased to $159,690,889 in 1929–30 and to $195,705,762 in 1930–31. In terms of 1913 dollars, the increase over 1912–13 was 156 per cent in 1922–23, 354 per cent in 1929–30, and 396 per cent in 1930–31.

Table 17 shows that in terms of 1913 dollars, the increase of elementary school expenditure was only 281 per cent in 1930–31 over 1912–13, while the increase in secondary and higher education expenditure was 458 per cent and 461 per cent respectively 1930–31 over 1912–13.

TABLE 16

TREND IN EDUCATIONAL EXPENDITURE, PUBLIC AND PRIVATE, CENTRAL AND LOCAL, INCLUSIVE, IN ALL CHINA

Year	Total Educational Expenditure (1)	Index of Wholesale Prices (2)	Real Trend in 1913 Dollars (3)	Index (4)	Value of School Property and Funds (5)
	$		$		$
1907	18,203,716	104	17,503,573	63	36,642,951
1908	21,965,061	110	19,968,237	71	60,419,287
1909	25,357,920	111	22,844,973	82	74,103,664
1910		102			
1912–13	29,667,803	106	27,988,493	100	83,041,199
1913–14	35,151,361	100	35,151,361	126	98,087,158
1914–15	39,092,045	100	39,092,045	140	102,680,195
1914–16	37,406,212	116	32,246,734	135	103,274,807
1916–17	39,700,000a	120	33,083,333	118	115,000,000a
1922–23	59,424,541	136	43,694,515	156	No data
1929–30	159,690,889b	161	99,186,888	354	"
1930–31	195,705,762c	177	110,568,233	396	227,260,540d
1931–32		195			
1932–33		173			

Sources: (1) From the same sources of school enrollment.
a. Original figure plus figures for the previous year for the three provinces not reporting.
b. 126,242,541 plus expenditure for social education, including 7 provinces not reporting. This additional expenditure is estimated by the average per pupil expenditure of China and per pupil expenditure of the nearest of similar provinces at 7,468,000 and 6,500,000 respectively.
(2) Wang, Chin-pin, and Others, ed., *The First Chinese Labour Year Book*, Appendix II, pp. 154–56, "Table on Index Numbers of Wholesale Prices of China and Other Countries, 1870–1926"; 1913=100 (in Chinese).
Hsian, Pi-hsien, and Others, ed., *The Second Chinese Labour Year Book*, 1932, p. 207. (See Index Number of Wholesale Prices made by the National Committee on Tax Laws.) 1926=100. The two series are combined.
(4) 1912=100, in order to compare with the trend in enrollment.
(5) From same sources of school enrollment.
c. See Table 9.
d. *Shun Pao Year Book*, 1934, p. 1092; *Higher Education Statistics in All China*, 1931–32, p. 8, Table 4. $220,880,761 for elementary schools and $6,379,778 for higher educational institutions.

TABLE 17

TRENDS IN EXPENDITURE FOR THREE LEVELS OF SCHOOLING

Year	Elementary Education		Secondary Education		Higher Education			
	Amount $	Index No.	Amount $	Index No.	Amount $	Index No.	Amount $	Index No.
1907			1,446,367y Tls.)				(Including students abroad)	
1908			2,291,471y „)					
1909			2,692,950y „)					
1912–13	19,091,109a	100	6,361,962d	100	3,971,361m	100		
1913–14	22,531,124	125	7,448,859e	124	4,172,372n	111		
1914–15	24,899,807	138	8,468,762f	141	5,728,476o	153		
1915–16	23,881,730	114	8,841,619g	127	4,682,963p	108		
1916–17	22,340,084b	105	8,575,059h	119	3,673,155q	82		
1922–23	31,449,963	128	14,024,180i	172	13,950,424r	274		
1925–26			9,540,228?		15,446,338s	278		
1928–29			24,602,366j	262	17,909,810t	305		
1929–30	64,721,025	223	35,988,173k	373	25,533,343u	423	36,793,410x	610
1930–31	89,416,977c	281	48,713,057l	458	29,867,474v	450	43,547,237z	657
1931–32					33,619,237w	461		

Sources: From the same sources as school enrollment. Figures given by the Ministry of Education in the *First Education Year Book of China*, 1934 are at a great variance with the above figures except the unlettered ones. No explanation is given.

Lettered ones are from Sources J1, J2, J3, in Bibliography, *Higher Education Statistics in All China*, 1931–32, and writer's own computation. These have been checked and rechecked and their reliability is supported by actual basis after a thorough search into all possible and available sources.

The different figures given are listed as follows:

a.	19,334,480	*(Education Year Book,* p. 193–4)				
b.	22,840,084	*Ibid.*	m.	4,214,732, (J2), 755,730	*(Year Book)*	
c.	88,510,710	„	n.	822,865,	*(Year Book)*	
d.	3,034,703	„	o.	2,426,911,	*Ibid.*	
e.	3,415,570	„	p.	1,306,058,	„	
f.	4,100,768	„	q.	883,069,	„	
g.	3,917,950	„	r.	From J2		
h.	3,651,870	„	s.	11,473,289,	*(Year Book)*	
i.	6,600,256	„	t.	16,730,621,	*Ibid.*	
j.	18,916,814	„	u.	23,729,430,	„	
k.	24,572,379	„	v.	28,832,912,	,	
l.	35,331,921	„	w.	31,582,507,	„	

x, z. See Tables 9 & J4.

Notes: Index No. is real index in terms of 1913 dollars, see Table 16, notes, sources of data for wholesale price index of China.

The Increase in School Costs and School Enrollments Compared

Data regarding school costs and enrollments are presented in Diagram 3. The following significant facts may be observed:

1. The total expenditure of all schools and institutions has not kept pace with enrollment since 1914. Total expenditure has increased 396 per cent over 1912-13, but enrollment has increased 430 per cent.

2. Since 1914, elementary expenditure has been far behind enrollment and has been the slowest in increase in terms of equated dollars. Higher education expenditure has been far ahead of enrollment, there being a difference of more than 300 per cent increase over 1912-13. Its most rapid increase occurred during the years preceding 1929. Secondary school expenditures have kept comparatively closer to enrollment, but recently have run behind. In 1930-31 the increase in secondary school expenditure over that of 1912-13 was the greatest among all types of expenditure.

RISING SCHOOL COSTS EXPLAINED

One should guard against a false impression of the rapid rise in school costs and the huge sums involved. The reasons for the rapid rise in school costs in recent years can be presented briefly as follows:

1. The Increase in Total School Enrollment. As the school system expands, more teachers and school plants and equipment are needed. These lead to greater cash disbursement and capital outlay.

2. The Factor of More Costly Service in Secondary and Higher Schools. Secondary school enrollment shows a more rapid increase than any other enrollment in the school system. Its service is almost 12 times as expensive as that of the elementary school per pupil.

DIAGRAM 3

PERCENTAGE INCREASE IN SCHOOL COSTS AND SCHOOL ENROLLMENTS COMPARED, CHINA, 1912–1931

Figured on 1912 as a Base from Data in Tables 3, 6, 16, and 17

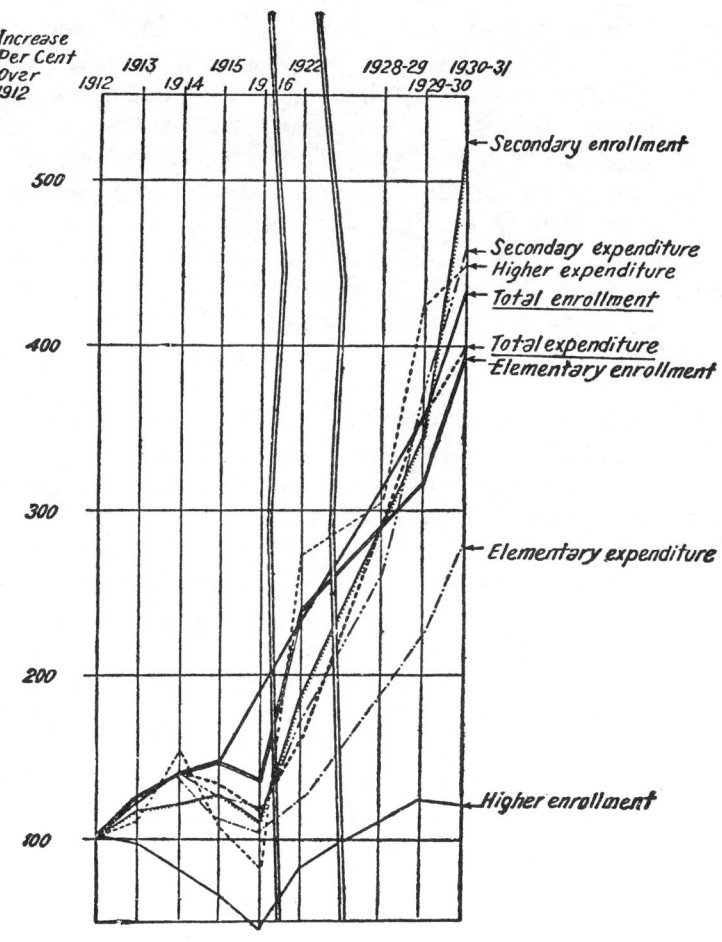

In 1930–31 the average cost per secondary school pupil was $94.66, while the average cost per elementary school pupil was only $8.17 (see Table 25).

University schooling is still more costly than secondary schooling. In 1930–31 the cost per student enrolled in higher education was $693 on the average for all types of universities and colleges. This is 7.3 times the cost per secondary student (see Table 25). It increased to $799.1 per student in 1931–32.[11] Higher education enrollment has increased slowly, but after 1916 expenditures for higher education increased more rapidly than those of other levels of education. This was, therefore, the largest factor in causing the increase in total school costs before that time. (See Diagram 3.)

Each year China sends out thousands of students to study abroad. From 1929 to 1931–32, 3,137 students were sent abroad.[12] On the average each of them costs the nation $1,000 for studying in Japan and $1,770 for studying in other countries.[13] They cause an annual expenditure of approximately $10,000,000 (see Table 9).

Secondary and higher education expenditures constitute about 44.3 per cent of the total expenditure of the entire school program (see Table 9).

3. *The Expansion of Curriculum Offerings and Better Quality of Educational Service.* The modern schools of China offer more varied and richer curricula than heretofore, and these are costly. A survey of the evolution and expansion of China's curriculum lies outside the scope of this study. A description of the present expanded curricula is available in English in the *China Year Book,* 1933.[14] The courses of study of the past have been described by Professor Hsia.[15] The

---

[11]See Table 25 on per pupil cost.
[12]*Higher Education Statistics,* 1931–32, p. 247.
[13]Source J3, p. 1, footnotes.
[14]Woodhead, *China Year Book,* 1933, pp. 530–33 and 525.
[15]Hsia Chen-feng, *Modern Educational Administration,* 1933, pp. 311–33.

number of professionally trained teachers is increasing, and they command higher salaries.

4. *The New Emphasis on Social and Adult Education.* In China there are two foci in the educational system, namely, the child and the adult. The costs of eliminating illiteracy and enlightening adults have increased greatly. The Ministry of Education has issued a ruling that expenditure for social education shall not be less than 20 per cent as a maximum and 10 per cent as a minimum of the total local educational budget.[16] More than a million persons are attending mass education schools and the like (see Table 1). The demands for more libraries, lecture halls, motion pictures, and the recent inclusion of agricultural extension service in the program necessitate greater financial outlays.

5. *The Changed Value of the Silver Dollar.* The actual number of silver dollars spent for education is impressive but misleading. In terms of the equated dollar, those sums have not kept pace with the increase in enrollment.

(a) *The Peculiar Characteristic of the Chinese Silver Dollar.* The value of the silver dollar varies with the value of gold and the prices of commodities. It also varies in different cities and provinces owing largely to the use of the unit of the varying silver tael as a standard of exchange, until its recent abolishment, and also to the inflation of paper money and subsidiary coins. For example, the value of the dollars in Liaoning, Kirin, Yunnan, and so forth, are often far below the value of the Shanghai dollars.[17] The chaotic condition of Chinese currency makes it difficult to compare the exact cost of education both geographically and chrono-

---

[16]*Proceedings of the First National Conference on Education,* 1928, p. 233.

[17]Leavens, D. H., ''Chinese Money and Banking,'' *The Annals of the American Academy of Political and Social Science,* November, 1930, p. 206 sqq.

logically, since the dollar unit as reported has not been explained and corrected in terms of equal value. The reader is reminded, however, that we are dealing with trends and aggregates and that the dollar figures are far more useful than mere guess work without any such figures.

(b) *How the Dollar Is Equated for Various Years.* In order to measure the changing value of the dollar for various years in terms of its power of buying commodities, or "purchasing power," the index of wholesale prices for all China, has been used. In spite of local variations in different parts of China, this aggregate index devised by Chinese economists is adequate to show general trends. One must be warned, however, not to take this index too seriously. Accurate findings must wait until future data for constructing accurate indexes of the cost of living are available and until Chinese currency is standardized. At least the use of the present index shows a method by which the real cost of education in China may be found.

Table 16 shows that the index of wholesale price has increased 161 per cent in 1929–30 over 1913. This means that the value of the dollar has depreciated and the cost of living increased. In 1929, 161 dollars were required to buy what could be bought in 1913 with 100 1913 dollars. In other words, the 1929 dollar was worth only 62 1913 cents. The trend of total educational expenditure in 1913 dollars appears in Column 3 of Table 16. This table shows that approximately 184 per cent of the increase in total educational expenditure in 1929 over 1912 was due to the depreciation of the dollar. In terms of 1913 dollars, the total educational expenditure of $195,705,762 in 1930–31 was really only $110,568,233. Therefore the real increase over 1912 was 396 per cent instead of 660 per cent, and 264 per cent of the increase was due to the depreciation of the dollar.

The Cost of the Educational Program

THE CAPITAL COST

As mentioned above, plant costs of the school system in China have been reported together with school funds and other property as sources of school revenue. The data available are shown in Table 16, Column 5. The proportion of plant value and equipment value included in this item is shown below:

TABLE 18

PERCENTAGE DISTRIBUTION OF VARIOUS ITEMS OF SCHOOL PROPERTY AND FUNDS, 1907–09

Classified Items in Original Reports	Per Cent That Each Item Is of Total Value			
	1907	1908	1909	Average
School buildings, sites, and equipment	48.94	48.59	50.00	49.18
Books, specimens, and apparatus . . .	8.31	8.14	8.30	8.25
School land, forests, and mountains . .	22.61	26.03	25.50	24.71
Other houses and shops owned by schools	2.66	3.18	3.00	2.95
Invested school funds	17.48	14.06	13.20	14.91
Total	100.00	100.00	100.00	100.00

Source: Calculated from original totals in Sources A, B, C, in Bibliography.

The capital cost of the schools in 1907–09 was 57.43 per cent of the aggregate, or about $63,700,000 out of $111,165,902 for the three years combined, being approximately $21,000,000 a year. The aggregate of $227,260,540 for 1930–31 (Table 16, Column 5) is for elementary and higher education only. There is no classified information. Hunan Province reported $12,640,211 for this item. Its classification appears in a bulletin as follows:[18]

[18] Hunan Department of Education, *Hunan Educational Administration Documentary Bulletin*, No. 10, Oct.–Dec., 1931, Appendix, p. 5.

1. School funds $4,843,154
2. Buildings 4,373,847
3. Equipment 1,073,137
4. Value of sites 2,350,073

    TOTAL $12,640,211

Here again it is difficult to tell the value of the school plants in this tabulation because the item of buildings must have included other buildings, such as residential houses and shops which are sources of school revenue.

From the above facts, it may be estimated that China probably spends $100,000,000 for capital cost including school plant and equipment for elementary schools and higher education institutions only.

THE VARIATION OF COSTS BORNE BY THE PROVINCES AND SPECIAL MUNICIPALITIES

Table 20 indicates that there is a wide variation in the gross amounts of educational expenditure in the different administrative units, due to the differences in wealth, density of population, and the degree of modernization. Excluding Mongolia, the province of Kwangtung spent the most money on education, an amount totaling approximately $14,000,000, or more than 300 times the amount spent by Sikiang. Only 10 provinces spent more than $5,000,000. Among the 18 provinces in China proper, Kwangtung spent about 15 times as much as Kweichow. Among the special municipalities, Peiping spent the most, a total of more than $7,000,000, while Shanghai ranked second, spending a little more than $6,000,000. Tsingtao spent the least, or about one thirtieth of the amount spent by Peiping. The other municipalities spent $1,000,000 to $2,000,000.

The provinces which spent the most for elementary and secondary education are, in order according to rank, Kwangtung, Kiangsu, Liaoning, Hopei, Szechwan,

Shantung, Hunan, and Chekiang. Their expenditures range from $6,151,803 to $9,694,410. (See Table 20.)

TABLE 19

VARIATION IN ELEMENTARY AND SECONDARY EDUCATIONAL REVENUES AND EXPENDITURES IN THE PROVINCES AND SPECIAL MUNICIPALITIES 1929–30

Provinces and Municipalities	Revenues $	Expenditures $	Deficit or Surplus
1. Kiangsu	9,603,913	9,582,158	+ 21,716
2. Chekiang	5,937,322	6,151,803	— 214,481
3. Anhwei	3,850,573	3,901,982	— 51,409
4. Kiangsi	2,637,108	2,673,864	— 36,846
5. Hupeh	3,082,685	3,097,604	— 14,919
6. Hunan	5,851,154	6,306,672	— 455,518
7. Szechwan	6,399,592	6,830,325	— 430,733
8. Fukien	2,850,568	2,898,201	— 47,633
9. Yunnan	3,370,469	3,379,481	— 9,012
10. Kweichow	872,745	869,430	+ 3,315
11. Kwangtung	9,320,017	9,694,410	— 374,393
12. Kwangsi	2,622,817	2,653,675	— 30,858
13. Shensi	2,346,860	2,346,860	
14. Shansi	4,655,763	4,626,030	+ 29,733
15. Honan	4,239,929	4,306,434	— 66,505
16. Hopei	6,958,079	7,274,730	— 316,651
17. Shantung	6,500,797	6,430,715	+ 70,082
18. Liaoning	7,404,473	7,435,502	— 31,029
19. Kirin	2,503,066	2,502,894	+ 172
20. Heilungkiang	1,774,745	1,772,138	+ 2,607
21. Kansu	1,441,967	1,417,612	+ 24,355
22. Jehol	316,656	315,625	+ 981
23. Suiyuan	171,308	171,007	+ 301
24. Chahar	891,467	922,571	— 31,104
25. Sinkiang	364,220	364,220	
26. Sikang	37,021	37,021	
27. Chinhai	56,187	54,161*	+ 2,026
28. Ningshia	90,089	95,706	— 5,617
29. Eastern Special	1,780,484	1,775,165	+ 5,319
30. Nanking	759,092	780,278	— 21,186
31. Shanghai	3,222,301	3,274,427	— 52,126
32. Peiping	1,569,168	1,538,369	+ 30,799
33. Tsingtao	293,712	287,977	+ 5,735
34. Tientsin	792,832	794,600	— 1,768
35. Hankow	532,425	532,425	
36. Canton	2,047,955	2,047,955**	
Totals	$107,117,269	$109,218,507	— 2,101,238

TABLE 19 (Continued)

Provinces and Municipalities	Revenues	Expenditures	Deficit or Surplus
Including:			
Original total, elementary	62,631,385	64,721,025	
„ „ secondary	35,976,875	35,988,173	
Elementary estimate for 7 provinces	7,468,000	7,468,000	
Elementary estimate for Canton	1,041,309	1,041,309	

1. By adding totals for elementary and secondary education from Table 12, No. 1, Section B, in J1, and Table 43, Section II in J2. Revenues for secondary education are from the separate Tables 51–86 in J2.

2. Elementary educational revenues and expenditures for provinces Nos. 8, 10, 12, 13, 21, 23, and 26 are estimates of the writer (enrollment x $8, per pupil expenditure of other provinces).

*No data for elementary education. **The amount of elementary education expenditure, $1,041,309 is not included in the total for China ($64,721,025) in the statistical report of the Ministry of Education.

TABLE 20

TOTAL EDUCATIONAL EXPENDITURE BY ADMINISTRATIVE UNITS, 1929–30

Administrative Units	Social Education (1)	University and College (2)	Students Abroad (3)	Total Including Elementary and Secondary (4)
	$	$	$	$
1. Kiangsu	1,608,942	493,004	1,174,000	12,858,104
2. Chekiang	616,764	311,871	1,071,000	8,153,438
3. Anhwei	170,088	291,809	448,000	4,811,879
4. Kiangsi	214,507	240,875	433,000	3,562,246
5. Hupeh	579,256	592,825	514,000	4,783,685
6. Hunan	791,449	267,911	521,000	7,887,032
7. Szechwan	1,057,430	645,739	572,000	9,105,494
8. Fukien	366,973	688,839	473,000	4,427,013
9. Yunnan	175,064	67,194	161,000	3,782,739
10. Kweichow	24,558		21,000	914,988
11. Kwangtung	864,879	1,505,416	1,779,000	13,843,705
12. Kwangsi	175,272('31)	?	91,000	2,919,967
13. Shensi	66,859		89,000	2,502,719
14. Shansi	309,082	441,426	89,000	5,465,538
15. Honan	294,008	311,153	171,000	5,082,595
16. Hopei	432,825	591,986	552,000	8,851,541
17. Shantung	456,062	189,440	253,000	7,329,217

The Cost of the Educational Program 59

TABLE 20 (Continued)

Administrative Units	Social Education (1)	University and College (2)	Students Abroad (3)	Total Including Elementary and Secondary (4)
	$	$	$	$
18. Liaoning	31,204('30)	1,371,436	957,000	9,795,142
19. Kirin	16,408('28)	23,411('28)	167,000	2,709,713
20. Heilungkiang	30,573	13,016('28)	111,000	1,926,727
21. Kansu	128,496	80,726	9,000	1,635,834
22. Jehol	7,209		7,000	329,834
23. Suiyuan	29,257		3,000	203,264
24. Chahar	40,660	60,630	5,000	1,028,861
25. Sinkiang	40,000('31)		4,000	408,220
26. Sikang	4,690		1,000	42,711
27. Chinhai	1,464('30)			55,625
28. Ninghsia	1,308			97,014
29. Eastern Special	874,809			2,649,974
30. Nanking	48,240	575,618		1,404,136
31. Shanghai	2,151,800	1,915,533		7,341,760
32. Peiping	759,661	3,860,914		6,158,944
33. Tsingtao	7,755	?		295,732
34. Tientsin	166,484	240,522		1,201,606
35. Hankow	748,650			1,281,075
36. Canton	?	?	?	2,047,955
37. Mongolia			4,000	4,000
Unclassified			23,000	23,000
Total	13,294,705	14,781,294	9,703,000	146,997,5.6
38. Central Government	?	12,468,383	225,000	12,693,383
Grand Total:				
Ministry's Total	(13,030,337)	(26,869,410)	(9,928,000)	(150,536,945)
New Total	$13,294,705	$27,249,677	$9,928,000	$159,690,889

(1) From J4, Section II, Table 6, and attached Tables 1 and 2.
(2) From J3. Freshly tabulated from figures for separate institutions in Tables 69 and 94. Figures for Central China University, Hupeh, Shantung Christian University, and Chiao Tung College, Liaoning, 1931, are from *Higher Education Statistics*, 1933.
(3) From J3, Tables 101, 106, using Ministry's basis of estimate, $1000 for each student studying in Japan and $3000 for each in other countries. According to prevailing practice, the nativity of students bears close relationship to the number sent from their respective provinces. The Central Party Office in 1929-30 sent 10 students to Japan and 77 to other countries, at a cost of about $241,000 a year. (See Central Executive Committee, *A Survey of Party Members Sent Abroad*, 1931.)

CHAPTER IV

THE PRESENT EDUCATIONAL COST FURTHER ANALYZED

This chapter attempts to discover the available facts concerning the costs of education classified by character as well as the per pupil and per capita costs. China is compared with the United States and certain other countries.

ANALYSIS OF COSTS BY CHARACTER

"Classification by character is the common means for setting forth total costs in public education [in the United States]. Annual reports as a rule compare costs according to this classification. When uniformly followed, it provides the best plan for comparing the costs of one period with those of another."[1]

TABLE 21

PERCENTAGE ANALYSIS OF COSTS OF EDUCATION BY CHARACTER CLASSIFICATION IN THE UNITED STATES

Character	Percentage of Total Cost of Education	
	1929–30 (1)	193? (2)
1. General control	3.4	3
2. Teachers' salaries	54.2	51
3. Teachers' supplies	2.9	3
4. Operation and fixed charges (janitors, supplies, fuel and light, rent and insurance)	19.4	11
5. Maintenance (repairs and replacements)		4
6. Auxiliary agencies (libraries, health service, transportation, and truancy)		4
7. Debt service	4.0	7
8. Capital outlay	16.1	17
Total	100.0	100.0

[1] Engelhardt, N. L., and Engelhardt, Fred, *Public School Business Administration*, 1927, p. 780.

(1) U. S. Office of Education, *Biennial Survey of Education*, 1929–30, p. 78, Table 27, Row 1. Excluding payments of bonds.
(2) Unpublished Document No. 8, "Chart Your Budget Here." Compliments of A. J. Nystrom and Co., Chicago.

The percentage analysis of the total cost of education in the United States is shown in Table 21.

Table 21 shows that in the United States as a whole, in 1929–30, the cost for general control or administration constitutes 3.4 per cent of the total cost of education excluding the payment of bonds; salaries of teachers constitute 54.2 per cent; textbooks and other instructional supplies, 2.9 per cent; the total for instruction, 57.1 per cent; capital outlays, 16.1 per cent; interest, 4 per cent; and miscellaneous expenses, 19.4 per cent.

In China the accounting systems in the elementary and secondary schools have not included any such classification. Only the statistics for higher education provided classified data on the total cost of higher education, as shown in Table 22. This table indicates that salaries and wages in higher education were 55.91 per cent of the total cost of its institutions in 1930–31; operating expenses, 12.42 per cent; and equipment, 19.50 per cent.

TABLE 22

PERCENTAGE CLASSIFICATION OF HIGHER EDUCATION EXPENDITURE BY CHARACTER, 1930–31

Character	Amount in 1930–31	Per Cent
1. Salaries and wages	$18,306,189	55.91
Teachers	(12,142,013)	(37.88)
Officers	(4,699,917)	(14.61)
Workers	(1,106,395)	(3.42)
2. Operation expenses	4,056,108	12.42
3. Equipment	6,379,778	19.50
4. Miscellaneous special expenses	2,566,235	7.85
5. Subordinate institutions	1,412,232	4.32
Total	$33,619,237	100.00

Adapted from *Higher Education Statistics in All China*, 1931–32, 1933, p. 16, Table 8.

62 *The Financing of Public Education in China*

The Reports of Educational Statistics and Charts for the years 1907–09[2] classify China's total educational expenditure in eight categories. For convenience, these are rearranged and shown in seven items in Table 23 for the year 1907. The percentage classification is not comparable with the percentage classification of the total cost of education in the United States except, perhaps, in teachers' salaries and instructional supplies.

TABLE 23

TOTAL EDUCATIONAL EXPENDITURES CLASSIFIED ACCORDING TO USES IN 23 PROVINCES REPORTING, 1907

Uses	Amount Expended	Per Cent of Total
1. Salaries	$ 6,636,833	44.5
Teachers' salaries	(4,779,268)	(32.0)
Officers' salaries	(1,857,565)	(12.5)
2. Wages and board of workmen	831,393	5.6
3. Clothing, board, and supplies	2,705,404	18.3
4. Library books, specimens, instruments, and materials for experimentation	1,007,376	6.7
5. Building and repairs	1,205,473	8.1
6. Rent, interest, and grain taxes	183,515	.9
7. Miscellaneous	2,375,744	15.9
Total	$14,945,738	100.0

Rearranged and calculated from Source A, Table III.

As may be seen from Table 23, salaries and wages constituted 50.1 per cent, instructional supplies and equipment 18.3 per cent, and building repairs 8.1 per cent of the total cost of education in China for 1907.

The Cost of Teachers' Salaries

In the United States as a whole for the year 1929–30, the cost of teachers' salaries constituted 54.2 per cent

[2] Sources A, B, and C in Bibliography.

The Present Educational Cost Analyzed 63

of the total cost of education (see Table 21). In China this item was 44.5 per cent of the total cost of education in 1907, and 50.25 per cent in 1909[3] (see Table 23). The writer has made a study of the expenditure budget of the Hupeh Provincial Department of Education for the year 1933–34. The total budget is $2,066,286, of which 58.76 per cent (49.84 per cent for teachers and 8.92 per cent for officers) is expended for salaries and 6.67 per cent for wages. Excluding administrative expenditure, which is in reality an expenditure for the entire province, the expenditure for students abroad, and provincial aid, the schools and institutions receive $1,694,766. Of this amount, 71.64 per cent is spent on salaries and 8.14 per cent on wages.[4]

In China the expenditure for teachers' and officers' salaries in the elementary and secondary schools legally should not exceed 70 per cent of the total expenditure of these schools.[5] Applying this theoretical percentage, China spends approximately $96,691,024 for salaries of a total of $138,130,034 for the cost of elementary and secondary education. If the actual monthly salaries of all teachers and officers were available, an estimate of the total cost of salaries could easily be obtained. Unfortunately, this is impossible. Table 24 gives an approximate picture of the variation of salary schedules in various administrative units and some actual median salaries based upon very limited data from samplings. It is presented merely for reference.

[3] Freshly calculated from Source C, Table on Distribution of Educational Expenditures According to Uses.
[4] Hupeh Department of Education, "Classified Expenditure Budget of Hupeh Provincial Education for the Fiscal Year 1933–34." Freshly calculated. See Unpublished Document No. 11.
[5] *The First Education Year Book of China*, 1934, Section II, p. 28, "Elementary Education Laws," Article 21, and p. 36, "Secondary Education Laws," Article 17, as promulgated June 25, 1932 and December 24, 1932.

TABLE 24

FREQUENCY DISTRIBUTION OF MID-POINTS BETWEEN MAXIMUM AND MINIMUM MONTHLY SALARIES OF TEACHERS UNDER THE STATUTES OF VARIOUS EDUCATIONAL AUTHORITIES AS EFFECTIVE, 1934

Step Intervals of Mid-points	Number of Cases by Statutes or Administrative Units					
	All Secondary Schools (1)				All Elementary Schools (2)	
	Principals		Teachers		Prin. and Teachers	
	Provincial or Urban	County or Rural	Provincial or Urban	County or Rural	Provincial or Urban	County or Rural
260–265 ..	1					
255–260 ..	1					
250–255 ..	1					
245–250 ..						
340–245 ..	1					
235–240 ..						
225–230 ..						
220–225 ..	1					
215–220 ..	1					
210–215 ..	1					
205–210 ..						
200–205 ..	3		1			
195–200 ..			1			
190–195 ..		1				
185–190 ..						
180–185 ..	1		1			
175–180 ..						
170–175 ..			1			
165–170 ..	1					
160–165 ..		1	1			
155–160 ..			1	1		
150–155 ..	1					
145–150 ..						
140–145 ..			1			
135–140 ..	1	1				
130–135 ..	1	1	1			
125–130 ..						
120–125 ..			1		1	
115–120 ..						
110–115 ..						
105–110 ..						
100–105 ..		1		1		
95–100 ..						
90–95 ...	1				1	
85–90 ...	1		1		1	
80–85 ...						

The Present Educational Cost Analyzed

TABLE 24 (Continued)

Step Intervals of Mid-points	Number of Cases by Statutes or Administrative Units					
	All Secondary Schools (1)				All Elementary Schools (2)	
	Principals		Teachers		Prin. and Teachers	
	Provincial or Urban	County or Rural	Provincial or Urban	County or Rural	Provincial or Urban	County or Rural
75–80	..	1	1	..	..	..
70–75	..	1	..	..	..	..
65–70	..	..	..	1	1	..
60–65	..	..	..	..	3	..
55–60	..	..	1	2	1	..
50–55	..	..	..	..	..	1
45–50	..	..	..	..	2	..
40–45	..	..	..	..	1	1
35–40	..	..	..	..	1	..
30–35	..	..	..	..	1	1
25–30	..	..	..	..	3	1
20–25	..	..	..	..	2	3
15–20	..	..	..	..	3	3
10–15	..	..	..	..	..	4
5–10	..	..	..	..	..	3
Number of Cases	17	7	12	5	21	17
Median	$202.5	$132.5	$150	$67.5	$42.5	$17.5
Mid-points			$135		$25	
Actual (3) Median	140	62.5	79.5	50.4	20.7	
Actual (4) "			94.6		50.2	

Sources:
(1) Unpublished Document No. 9. Calculated from Statutes of Teachers Salary Schedules of various provinces and municipalities. *The First Education Year Book of China*, 1934, pp. 199–304, Section III.
(2) *Ibid.*, pp. 424–510.
(3) Kwo-Nan, "A Survey of the Compensation of Elementary and Secondary School Teachers and Officers." (1008 elementary teachers and officers, and 1609 secondary teachers and officers in selected provinces and counties of China for the year, 1930) *Educational Review*, Volume XXIII, No. 1, January, 1931, pp. 2s1–140, Tables 5, 9, and 10.
(4) Unpublished Document No. 10. *Frequency Distribution of Monthly Salaries and Wages of Educational Workers in the Hupeh Provincial Schools, 1933–34.* Calculated from the Budget.

Notes:
1. Many provinces pay teachers according to the hour system; these administrative units are excluded in the tabulation.
2. Some salary reports are actual conditions for the year, 1930–31.
3. Teachers refer to full-time teachers only.
4. (4) refers to one province only.

Table 24 shows that the mid-points between maximum and minimum monthly salaries as scheduled for secondary school principals in 17 provinces and municipalities vary widely from $70 to $195 in the county schools, and from $85 to $265 in the provincial schools. These salaries for secondary school teachers vary from $50 to $160 in the county schools, and from $50 to $205 in the provincial schools. The medians of these four distributions are respectively $132.5, $202.5, $67.5, and $150.

The corresponding mid-points for elementary school principals and teachers vary from $15 to $120 in the provincial schools, and from $10 to $55 in the county schools. The medians of these two distributions are $42.5 and $17.5 respectively.

The median actual salaries paid to provincial and county secondary school principals, as found from the sample study made for 1930 mentioned in Table 24 were $140 and $62 respectively. Corresponding figures for secondary school teachers were $79.5 and $50.4 respectively; for all elementary school principals and teachers the figure was $20.7.

The Per Pupil Costs of Education in China

Facts concerning per pupil costs of education provide a good basis for evaluating economy and efficiency in a school system. Such facts provide for the comparison of one school with another, one type or level of school with another, or of costs in different periods or localities. Some of the important factors that cause the variation of per pupil costs are:

1. Quality of service.
2. Size of school.
3. Size of class and teacher load.

4. Relative wealth of the community.
5. Communication facilities.
6. Waste or economy.
7. Child-accounting and financial accounting systems, and the like.

A study of the per pupil costs in relation to all these factors would be more desirable if data were available. Unfortunately, the present study can present some facts on only certain phases of this problem. It should be borne in mind that Chinese educational statistics give only the number of pupils enrolled and not those in actual attendance.[6] Therefore the per pupil costs in this study are somewhat deflated or a little lower than the true costs per pupil in average daily attendance. In the United States, the total average daily attendance in 1929–30 was about 83 per cent of the enrollment.[7]

Trends in Per Pupil Costs in China

Table 25 presents the trends in per pupil costs in China as a whole from 1912 to 1932. This table shows that in 1930–31, with the exception of higher elementary and normal schools, per pupil costs for all types of schools in unequated dollars have increased almost uniformly over the 1912–13 level. However, the real per pupil costs in 1913 dollars have been on the decrease since 1912–13, with the exception of the per pupil cost in high schools. The per pupil cost in the lower elementary school in 1912–13 was $3.88 in 1913 dollars. It decreased to $3.75 in 1916–17, but increased to $3.94 in 1929–30, and again decreased to $3.56 in 1930–31. Similar trends in other types of schools may be noted in the table.

[6]See all sources cited on enrollments.
[7]U. S. Office of Education, *Biennial Survey of Education*, 1928–30, p. 37. Enrollment: 25,678,015; average daily attendance, 21,264,886.

TABLE 25

TRENDS IN SCHOOL PER PUPIL COSTS IN CHINA AS A WHOLE, 1912-32

Types of Schools	Average Per Pupil Costs for the Years:									
	1912-13		1916-17		1929-30		1930-31		1931-32	
		1913 Dollars		1913 Dollars		1913 Dollars		1913 Dollars		1913 Dollars
Kindergarten..	—	—	—	—	$12.01	$7.45	$17.56	$9.92		
Lower Elementary	$4.11	$3.88	$4.51	$3.75	6.35	3.94	6.30	3.56		
Higher Elementary	21.72	18.80	29.12	24.20	24.48	15.20	20.28	11.47		
All Elementary Schools..	—	—	—	—	8.15	5.06	8.17	4.62		
High Schools..	58.25	54.90	59.94	49.90	126.81	78.80	114.70	64.90		
Junior High..					77.50	48.10	67.89	38.30		
Normal Schools.	71.33	67.25	123.31	102.50	110.89	68.90	101.67	57.50		
Vocational Schools	81.07	76.50	120.37	100.30	155.16	96.50	142.37	80.50		
All Secondary Schools..	—	—	—	—	105.52	65.60	94.66	53.50		
Universities..	392.77	371.00	—	—	746.00	464.00	693.00	392.00	799.08	410.00
Special Colleges.	274.40	259.00	—	—	386.00	240.00	385.00	218.00	400.41	205.00
Preparatory..	—	—	—	—	—	—	—	—	—	—
All Higher Institutions.	—	—	—	—	664.00	412.00	655.00	370.00	652.00	334.00

Sources: From the same sources as school enrollments. In compiling the data however, much fresh calculation was involved. For index number, see Table 16.

The Variation of Per Pupil Costs in Different Provinces and Special Municipalities

Tables 26 and 27 present a wide variation of per pupil costs in elementary and secondary schools in all provinces and municipalities in China.

Table 26 indicates that the average per pupil cost in 1929-30 was $12.01 for kindergartens, $6.35 for lower elementary schools, $24.48 for higher elementary schools, and $8.15 for all elementary schools in China. The variation extends from this mean of $8.15 to more than $55 as the highest extreme and to $2.50 as the lowest extreme. Other variations are shown in the table.

The Financing of Public Education in China

TABLE 27

VARIATION OF AVERAGE PER PUPIL COSTS OF ALL SECONDARY EDUCATION IN DIFFERENT PROVINCES AND SPECIAL MUNICIPALITIES, 1929–30

Step-Intervals in Dollars	Frequency
$250–259	1
240–249	
230–239	1
220–229	
210–219	1
200–209	
190–199	1
180–189	
170–179	
160–169	2
150–159	2
140–149	1
130–139	1
120–129	2
110–119	5
100–109	6
90– 99	4
80– 89	4
70– 79	1
60– 69	3
50– 59	1
Number of cases	36
Average	$105.52
Median	$103.34

Tabulated from J2, Tables 51–86.

Table 28 shows that the median per pupil costs of provincial or urban secondary schools and county or rural secondary schools for the year 1930–31 are $152 and $64.19 respectively. The ratio is 1 to 2.37. The corresponding figures for urban and rural elementary schools are $23.60 and $12.30 respectively. Their ratio is 1 to 1.92 This means that it costs approximately twice as much to educate a child in the provincial schools or urban areas as in the county schools or the rural areas.

TABLE 26

VARIATION OF AVERAGE PER PUPIL COSTS OF ELEMENTARY EDUCATION IN DIFFERENT PROVINCES AND SPECIAL MUNICIPALITIES, 1929-30*

Cost	Frequency Distribution by Number of Administrative Units			
	Kindergarten	Lower Elementary	Higher Elementary	All Elementary
Above $55	3		2	1
$50–$55				
45– 50			2	
40– 45			1	1
35– 40	2	1	2	
30– 35		1	5	1
25– 30	1	2	4	
20– 25	1	1	8	2
15– 20	7		4	2
10– 15	4	7		7
5– 10	3	12		13
1– 5	2	4		1
No. of Cases	23	28	28	28
Average	$12.01	$6.35	$24.48	$8.15

* Tabulated from Source J1, Tables 1-28.

Table 27 shows that in 1929–30 per pupil costs in the secondary schools ranged from $50 to $259. The mean was $105.42 in all provinces and municipalities. The median was $108.34. Such wide variations can be explained by the seven factors mentioned above (p. 66) Certainly the factor of waste or economy must account for these variations to a large extent.

The Variation of Per Pupil Costs in Provincial or Urban and County or Rural Schools

Table 28 presents the comparison between average per pupil costs in provincial or urban and county or rural schools from available data for the year 1930–31

The Present Educational Cost Analyzed

TABLE 28
COMPARISON BETWEEN AVERAGE PER PUPIL COSTS IN PROVINCIAL OR URBAN AND COUNTY OR RURAL SCHOOLS FROM AVAILABLE DATA, 1930–31

Provinces and Municipalities	Secondary Schools		Elementary Schools		All Secondary Schools	All Elementary Schools
	Provincial or Urban (1)	County or Rural (2)	Provincial or Urban (3)	County or Rural (4)		
	$	$	$	$	$	$
1. Kiangsu	152.00	68.00	47.38	7.08		
2. Chekiang				6.00	111.00	
3. Kiangsi			30.27	12.30	124.00	
4. Hupeh			22.00			
5. Fukien	223.46	66.21	31.80	13.10	125.05	13.80
6. Yunnan	277.00	48.00				19.54
7. Shensi	120.90	90.00				2.50
8. Shansi			25.00		88.22	
9. Honan	89.60	37.00	16.00			
10. Shantung	103.00	72.00	22.20			
11. Chinhai						4.10
12. Kansu	163.00	53.00				10.50
13. Ninghsia	190.00					7.00
14. Liaoning	102.70	69.49	21.08	19.16		
15. Heilungkiang	178.00	120.00				17.00
16. Chahar					145.00	26.00
17. Eastern Special					303.66	81.07
18. Nanking	141.00	96.00				31.64
19. Shanghai					114.00	22.00
20. Peiping						22.50
21. Tsingtao						21.00
22. Weihaiwei						7.64
Number of Cases	11	10	8	5	7	14
Median	$152.00	$64.19	$23.60	$12.30	$124.00	$18.27

Ratio of (2) to (1) = 1:2.37; ratio of (4) to (3) = 1:1.92.

Sources: The First Education Year Book of China, 1934.

1. pp. 199 and 426.
2. pp. 203, 433.
3. pp. 216, 441.
4. p. 444.
5. pp. 232, 447.
6. pp. 234, 451.
7. pp. 250, 457.
8. pp. 253, 459.
9. pp. 258, 461.
10. pp. 269, 465.
11. p. 468.
12. pp. 283, 466.
13. pp. 286, 468.
14. pp. 289, 470.
15. pp. 290, 472.
16. pp. 292, 474.
17. pp. 294, 476.
18. pp. 226, 477.
19. pp. 298, 480.
20. pp. 300, 483.
21. p. 484.
22. p. 485.

Note: The above are the only available comparable figures.

Comparison of Per Pupil Costs of Different Levels and Types of Schools

Table 29 shows the ratio or index of the per pupil costs of all types and levels of schools, with the per pupil cost of the lower elementary schools used as a base ($6.30 in 1930–31). One kindergarten pupil costs 2.79 times as much as one lower elementary school pupil, and one higher elementary school pupil costs 3.18 times as much as one lower elementary school pupil. In other words, the junior high school is 10.76 times as expensive as the lower elementary school per pupil. It takes the cost of educating 18 lower elementary school pupils to educate one student in the general high school for one year. It takes the cost of educating 110 lower elementary school pupils to keep one university student in school for one year.

TABLE 29

RATIO COMPARISONS OF PER PUPIL COSTS, 1930–31
(Per Pupil Cost of Lower Elementary School)

Per Pupil Cost	Ratio Comparisons	
Lower Elementary Schools	1.00	*
Kindergarten	2.79	
Higher Elementary Schools	3.18	
All Elementary Schools		1.00
Junior High Schools	10.76	
Normal Schools	16.15	
High Schools	18.22	
Vocational Schools	22.60	
All Secondary Schools		11.59
Universities	110.00	
Special Colleges	61.25	
All Higher Institutions		108.00

*All elementary school per pupil cost = 1 Unit in Scale of Comparison.

To summarize, the per pupil cost of all secondary schools is approximately 11.59 times the per pupil cost of all elementary schools in China, and the cost per student in higher education institutions is approximately 108 times the per pupil cost of all elementary schools. The ratio of the cost per secondary school pupil to the cost per student in all higher education institutions is about 1 to 9.35. In other words, the cost of one university and special college student is approximately 9 times the cost of one secondary school student.

THE COST OF EDUCATION PER CAPITA OF POPULATION

The cost of education per capita of population indicates how much the average individual citizen is spending for education. One is liable to have an inadequate, if not a false, impression of per capita costs of education if the factors of the composition of the population, the distribution of wealth and tax burden, the distribution of educational opportunities, and the like, are not taken into consideration.

Table 30 reveals the difference in burden borne by the people in the provinces and municipalities.

As shown in Table 30, the average per capita burden for China as a whole is only a little more than 34 cents. Excluding expenditures for private education, it is only about 25 cents. Including expenditures for private education, each person in China spends about 16 cents for elementary education, 8 cents for secondary education, and 11 cents for higher and social education. The burden varies widely among the different administrative units. Considering the per capita burden of total public education expenditure, five of the municipalities pay the largest amounts, ranging from $1.47 to $3.52, while in the provinces the amounts vary from $.0036, the least, in Sikang, to $.734, the most, in Kirin. Among the 18 provinces in China proper, Shansi ranks first, with a per capita burden of $.323, closely followed by Kwangtung, Fukien, Kiangsu, and

TABLE 30

THE BURDEN OF EDUCATIONAL EXPENDITURE PER CAPITA OF POPULATION IN THE PROVINCES AND SPECIAL MUNICIPALITIES, 1929–30

Provinces and Municipalities	Per Capita Elementary Education Expenditure (1)	Per Capita Secondary Education Expenditure (2)	Per Capita Elementary & Secondary Expenditure (3)	Per Capita Total for All Levels and Types of Education Expenditure (4)	
				A	B
1. Kiangsu	$ .20	$ .10	$ .30	$ .40	$ .29
2. Chekiang	.21	.091	.301	.396	.285
3. Anhwei	.11	.07	.18	.222	.16
4. Kiangsi	.05	.078	.128	.175	.126
5. Kupeh	.07	.049	.119	.184	.132
6. Hunan	.14	.061	.201	.250	.178
7. Szechwan	.11	.032	.142	.190	.137
8. Fukien	.17 (e)	.119	.289	.44	.317
9. Yunnan	.17	.075	.245	.274	.197
10. Kweichow	.045 (e)	.014	.059	.062	.045
11. Kwangtung	.21	.096	.306	.44	.317
12. Kwangsi	.143 (e)	.029	.172	.214	.154
13. Shensi	.164 (e)	.035	.199	.212	.153
14. Shansi	.28	.093	.373	.448	.323
15. Honan	.11	.035	.145	.167	.12
16. Hopei	.17	.082	.252	.311	.224
17. Shantung	.15	.079	.229	.259	.186
18. Liaoning	.31	.174	.484	.642	.462
19. Kirin	.74	.212	.952	1.02	.734
20. Heilungkiang	.38	.094	.474	.517	.372
21. Kansu	.177 (e)	.048	.225	.260	.187
22. Jehol	.03	.015	.045	.05	.036
23. Suiyuan	.038 (e)	.043	.081	.095	.068
24. Chahar	.36	.103	.463	.515	.371
25. Sinkiang	.07	.07	.14	.16	.115
26. Sikang	.004 (e)	.0005	.0045	.005	.0036
27. Chinhai	?	.008		.009	.006
28. Ninghsia	.04	.026	.066	.068	.49
29. Eastern Special	.25	.101	.351	.525	.378
30. Nanking	.76	.813	1.573	2.83	2.04
31. Shanghai	1.12	1.06	2.18	4.89	3.52
32. Peiping	.38	.695	.1075	4.29	3.09
33. Tsingtao	.49	.296	.786	.85	.61
34. Tientsin	.35	.221	.571	.875	.63
35. Hankow	.76	.103	.863	2.04	1.47
36. Canton	1.234	1.293	2.527	2.527	1.82
All China	$ .158	$ .077	$ .235	$ .343	$ .247

(1) Items marked "(e)" from estimates.
(2) From Table 48, J2.
(3) Column 1+2.
(4) Including higher education and social education expenditures.
A. Including private education expenditure.
B. Public education expenditure only. Population figures from Section B, Table II, in J1.

Chekiang, while Kweichow ranks last with $.045. Honan ranks seventeenth with 12 cents, and Hupeh ranks sixteenth with only $.126. It may reasonably be expected that the wealthiest provinces, such as Kwangtung, Kiangsu, Chekiang, Hopei, Hunan, and Hupeh, should reach at least the level of the five municipalities mentioned, while other provinces should reach at least the level of the average of China. Whether or not this increase is in proportion to their ability to pay will be discussed later.

A comparison of the per capita burden of educational expenditure of China with other countries, as given in Table 31, shows that the burden of the Chinese people is light, even when the ability to pay is taken into consideration.

Table 31 compares the per capita costs of education in various countries.[8] With the exception of the United States and Japan, whose total educational expenditures are taken directly from their respective government reports, the countries were chosen because their national treasures furnish 100 per cent[9] of the entire cost of education in their respective countries and therefore the educational budgets of their national governments are reported by the International Bureau of Education as representing their total educational expenditures.

It is noted that China spent only 44.6 cents per capita in 1930–31 while the eleven other countries listed in

[8] See Unpublished Document No. 12, A.
[9] Abel, James F., *The Effects of the Economic Depression on Education in Other Countries.* Washington, D. C., 1933, p. 6, "Table on Per Cent of Changes in National Education Funds."

TABLE 31

PER CAPITA BURDEN OF EDUCATIONAL EXPENDITURE IN CHINA COMPARED WITH OTHER COUNTRIES

COUNTRY	BUDGET YEAR	PER CAPITA BURDEN IN CHINESE DOLLARS
Albania	1933	$ 5.85
Bulgaria	1933	8.22
Greece	1932–33	4.64
Costa Rica	1931	17.64
Ecuador	1932	5.82
Guatemala	1932	3.29
Paraguay	1931–32	5.84
Uruguay	1931–32	20.82
New Zealand	1931–32	61.83
United States	1929–30*	62.51
Japan	1930*	11.96 (1)
		6.38 (2)
China	1929–30*	.343 (a)
	1930–31*	.446 (3)
		.408 (4)
		.317 (5)

Sources of total educational expenditure:
Japan—Department of Education, *A General Survey of Education in Japan*, pp. 62–63.
　　Other countries—From International Bureau of Education.
　　Converted from Swiss Francs at mint par of exchange: 1 Swiss Franc equals 19.30 U. S. cents; 1 Chinese dollar equals 29.26 U. S. cents; 1 Japanese Yen equals 49.85 U. S. cents at mint par (1) but only 27.62 at rate quoted. (2) Federal Reserve Board: *Statement for Press*, October 10, 1933. See Unpublished Document No. 12, B.
　　United States—from the *Biennial Survey of Education*, 1928–30, p. 11. Total public and private cost of education, G$3,234,638,567, divided by population, 122,775,046. G$26.35 converted at par of exchange for 1929–30 or 42.15 U. S. cents per Chinese Mexican dollar.
　　China—(a) See Table 30, Cost of Schools and Institutions only.
　　(3) See Table 15, Cost of Schools and Institutions only plus overhead costs.
　　(4) See Table 15, Cost of Schools and Institutions only (population: 488,304,025).
　　(5) See Table 15, Cost of Schools and Institutions public only.
　　* = Actual.

Table 31 spent from $3.29 to $62.51 per capita. Even though the exchange rate varies 50 per cent below the mint par rate of exchange used in the conversion, thus reducing the amount per capita, China would still be far behind other countries. At the mint par of exchange October, 1933, Japan spent about 27 times as much per capita, while at the rate then quoted Japan spent 14 times as much per capita. The United States ranks first among the eleven countries listed in the table. The amount she spent per head of population is about 140 times that of China. China cannot be compared with this wealthiest country of the world, but certainly her citizens should not bear a burden less than that of the Guatemalan or the Greek.

CHAPTER V

THE COST OF EDUCATION AND OTHER GOVERNMENT COSTS COMPARED

The Cost of Education and the Government Budget

Actual revenue and expenditure data are rarely available in China. The available expenditure budgets often show amounts larger than those actually spent. Moreover, governmental authorities other than the educational authorities often conduct schools and training classes of their own, and these expenditures, owing to insufficient data, are not easily separated. Consequently, the total educational cost under all departments of government is indeterminable at present. Here we shall content ourselves with only the cost of education under the educational authorities in comparison with the general budget of the government.

Although the budgets do not represent the actual situation, they at least serve the purpose of showing the emphasis placed upon education by the government.

The Central Government

Table 32 shows that since 1911 educational expenditure, whether in budget or in fact, has never exceeded 3.27 per cent of the total Central expenditure. This percentage occurred in the year 1923–24. The discrepancy between the budget and reality is exemplified in the year 1931–32 when the educational budget was $21,027,268, or 2.36 per cent of the total Central budget, but the actual expenditure was only $11,640,677, or 1.48 per cent of the total Central expenditure. The amounts expended for education since 1911 range from $1,595,814 in 1915–16 to $23,294,556 in 1933–34, which is 2.81 per cent of the total Central budget.

TABLE 32

PROPORTION OF CENTRAL GOVERNMENT EXPENDITURE FOR EDUCATIONAL AND MILITARY PURPOSES COMPARED, 1911–34

FISCAL YEAR	AMOUNT FOR EDUCATION	PER CENT OF TOTAL GOVERNMENTAL EXPENDITURE (CENTRAL)	
		FOR EDUCATIONAL PURPOSES	FOR MILITARY PURPOSES
I. Monarchial Government			
(1) 1911 (Budget)	T 2,747,477.35	0.935	29.4
(2) 1912 (Budget)	$ 2,881,140	1.475	17.7
II. Republican Government			
(3) 1913 (Budget)	$ 6,908,850	1.78	26.9
(4) 1914–15 (Budget)	3,276,904	0.92	39.89
(5) 1915–16 (Actual)	1,595,814	1.15	38.3
(6) 1916 (Old Budget)	12,837,307	2.72	33.82
(7) 1916–17 (New Budget)	5,028,836	1.63	37.1
(8) 1917–18 (Budget)	5,094,436	0.97	36.5
(9) 1918–19 (Budget)	2,761,960	(Military expenditure not included)	
(10) 1919–20 (Budget)	6,763,518	1.05	41.6
(11) 1919–20 (Actual)	2,902,504	2.76	65.1
1920–21	No data existing		
1921–22	No data existing		
1922–23	No data existing		
(12) 1923–24 (Budget)	3,529,981.97	3.27	71.2
1924–25	No data existing		
(13) 1925–26 (Budget)	7,318,852	1.29	48.5
(14) 1925–26 (Budget)	7,711,000	1.22	47
(15) 1926, June–Oct. (Actual)	224,056.6	(6.43)	72
III. Nationalist Government			
(16) 1927–28 (Actual)	2,538,236	1.5	92
(17) 1928–29 (Report)	9,752,013	2.25	48.23
(18) 1929–30 (Report)	14,457,343	2.6	45.5
(19) 1930–31 (Report)	14,901,872	2.1	43.62
(20) 1931–32 (Budget)	21,027,268	2.36	44.4
(21) 1931–32 (Actual)	11,640,677	1.48	37.8
(22) 1932–33 (Budget)	21,027,268	2.39	48.44
(23) 1933–34 (Budget)	23,294,556	2.81	50.14
(24) 1934–35 (Budget)	(19,034,481)a	a(2.45) 2.77	38.80

Sources of Data:

A. *The First China Year Book.* (In Chinese) Shanghai: Commercial Press, 1924.

B. Woodhead, H. G. W.: *The China Year Book*. Shanghai: The North-China Daily News and Herald, Ld., 1928.
C. Woodhead: *The China Year Book*, 1921–22.
D. Woodhead: *The China Year Book*, 1923.
E. Woodhead: *The China Year Book*, 1925.
F. Woodhead: *The China Year Book*, 1926.
G. Lien, D. K.: *China's Industries and Finance*. Shanghai: Chinese Government Bureau of Economic Information, 1927.
H. Chia, S. Y.: *Financial History of the Republic*. (In Chinese) Shanghai: Commercial Press, 1917.
I. *Annual Report for the Fiscal Year July, 1928, to June, 1929*. Nanking: Ministry of Finance, 1930.
J. *Annual Report for the 18th Fiscal Year July, 1929, to June, 1930*. Nanking: Ministry of Finance, 1931.
K. *Annual Report for the 19th and 20th Fiscal Years July, 1930, to 1932*. Nanking: Ministry of Finance, 1932.
L. *The National Revenue and Expenditure Budget of the Republic of China*. (In Chinese) Nanking: The Directorate of Budget and Statistics. Promulgated April 28, 1932.
M. *Proceedings of the National Conference on Finance*. (In Chinese) Nanking: The Secretariat of the Ministry of Finance, 1928.
N. *The Banker's Weekly*, Nov. 28, 1933. Vol. XVII, No. 46. Shanghai: The Banker's Weekly Society.
O. *The Banker's Weekly*, July 4, 1933. Vol. XVII, No. 25.
(24) *Shun Pao*, July 20, 1934, p. 3, Official announcement of Central Political Council.

Page reference to sources:

(1) A: 418–420
(2) A: 422
(3) A: 443–444
(4) B: 541–542
(5) H: 61–66
(6) B: 541–542
(7) B: 541–542
(8) A: 472
(6) A: 473
(10) A: 476–478
(11) C: 234
(12) D: 704–710
(13) E: 712–713a
(14) G: 100–103
(15) F: 544–550
(16) M: Section IV, 3–5
(17) I: 1–2
(18) J: 1–3
(19) K: 2–3
(20) L: 381
(21) N: Section on Domestic News, 1
(22) O: Section on Domestic News, 1–4
(23) O: Section on Domestic News, 4–5

Remarks: 1. All per cent figures are feshly computed. Where there is conflict of report or difference, preference is given to that which is believed as copied directly from the official records.

2. Educational expenditure for the years, 1929–32 is not shown in the Minister's reports. It is included in the total under the item, Expenses for the Executive Yuan and Subsidiary Organs. The figures here given are furnished by the Ministry of Education from correspondence, November, 1933.

3. The yearly expenditure for 1923–24 is derived from the monthly budget by multiplying it by 12.

4. The above references probably constitute all existing sources concerning the Central Government's budgets and actual financial statements and reports in China to date.

a. Not including grant-in-aid which is included in and cannot be separated from the total amount of grant-in-aid to the provinces for all purposes. This amount was $2,474,136 (see Unpublished Document No. 16) for the year, 1933–34. If the same amount is provided for the 1934–35 budget, education would claim $21,508,617 which is 2.77 per cent of the Central budget.

The first budget of the National Government, for the fiscal year 1931–32, as proposed by the Directorate of Budget and Statistics contains estimates for educational expenditures under government authorities other than the Ministry of Education. The budget as approved by the Central Political Council does not show such detailed items. However, an attempt is made here to use these proposed estimates in determining just how much money the other government authorities intended to spend for their own educational undertakings.

TABLE 33

EDUCATIONAL EXPENDITURES UNDER CENTRAL GOVERNMENT AUTHORITIES OTHER THAN THE MINISTRY OF EDUCATION, 1931–32

Ministries	Total Proposed Budget	Proposed for Education	Per cent that Education is of Total
	$	$	
1. Military Affairs and Navy	412,313,673	18,819,485	4.57
2. Interior	7,204,363	201,796	2.80
3. Foreign Affairs	9,874,950	12,000	.12
4. Finance	79,745,628	167,484	.21
5. Justice	2,132,245	62,328	2.96
6. Industry	7,453,462	1,958,062	26.20
7. Communications	4,078,361	240,107	5.90
8. Others		12,484	
Total	522,793,682	21,473,746	4.10
9. Total Central budget estimate	984,266,978	21,473,746	2.20
10. Total Central budget approved	893,335,073	21,473,746	2.40
11. Total Central actual expenditure	682,990,864	?	?
Special Budget			
12. 16 National railways (Actual, 1929)	64,461,489.72	608,159.97	.95
13. Chiao Tung University (Actual, 1929)		655,682.00	
Total estimated educational expenditure by other Central authorities		22,737,588.00	

1-10. See Table, Source I. 1-8 including schools, research, and experimentation.
11. *Ibid.*, Source K, p. 5.
12. Ministry of Railways: *Railway Bulletin*, No. 255, April 19, 1932, Table on "Ten Years of Educational Expenditure of the National Railways."
Woodhead: *China Year Book*, 1933. Table on "Operating Expenses," 1929, p. 291.
13. J3, *Higher Education Statistics*. Table 69.

From the above table it may be seen that the Central authorities other than the Ministry of Education in 1931–32 devoted $22,737,588 to the educational budget. Excluding the special budget, this sum was 2.4 per cent of the total Central budget. The budget under the Ministry of Education for the same year was $21,027,268, or 2.36 per cent of the total Central budget. Thus the proportion of the cost of the Central government caused by all educational purposes would be $42,501,014, or 4.76 per cent of the total Central budget. Including the special budget of the national railways and Chiao Tung University, the total educational budget of all Central authorities would be $43,764,856, or 4.9 per cent of the budget of 1931–32.

The Ministry of Industry provided the largest proportion of its expenditure budget for education and experimentation, i. e., 26.2 per cent. The military authorities provided the largest amount, $18,819,485, for military universities, colleges, schools, training classes, and other educational purposes, including expenditure for sending students abroad. But in comparison with the huge military budget, this amount was only 4.57 per cent of the total.

The Provincial Governments

Table 34 shows that before the Nationalist revolution, public education was universally neglected by the prov-

TABLE 34

PROPORTION OF PROVINCIAL GOVERNMENTAL EXPENDITURE FOR EDUCATION AND MILITARY PURPOSES COMPARED (Budget)

Provinces	(1) 1913-14			(2) 1914-15			(3) 1916-17			(4) 1919-20			(5) 1929-30	
	Amount for Education	Per Cent of Total	Per Cent for Military	Amount for Education	Per Cent of Total	Per Cent for Military	Amount for Education	Per Cent of Total	Per Cent for Military	Amount for Education	Per Cent of Total	Per Cent for Military	Amount for Education (Ministry's Figures)	Per Cent of Total
1. Hupeh	..	..	63.0	175,104	2.6	59.	617,450	6.55	55.5	233,413	2.9	65.5	3,271,893a*	11.1
2. Kiangsu	122,081	.91	58.0	100,000	1.03	50.5	1,261,097	10.2	39.2	599,529	5.1	42.	4,017,552	23.8
3. Chekiang	9,582	.18	44.5	..	..	50.0	734,625	8.7	38.6	53,297	7.3	43.	2,173,585	..
4. Anhwei	35,894	.78	51.0	..	..	61.5	264,096	3.6	57.	35,000	.53	58.	2,845,938	20.1
5. Kiangsi	65,000	1.17	49.0	40,000	.73	59.	421,119	7.8	44.	35,000	.65	45.	2,000,000	..
6. Hunan	70,034	1.3	40.	100,000	1.83	59.	542,956	8.8	51.	35,000	.59	53.5	2,630,532	15.2
7. Szechwan	135,195	1.145	61.5	120,000	1.22	59.	791,306	7.3	55.	170,000	1.8	63.6	..	..
8. Yunnan	..	..	75.	..	..	62.	351,262	5.1	51.	35,000	.67	59.6	252,720	3.2
9. Kwangtung	101,839	.565	68.	63,942	.62	75.	580,891	4.2	58.	306,928	2.5	62.	1,735,357	..
10. Shansi	30,000	.45	57.	100,000	1.88	59.5	440,705	7.75	42.7	140,000	2.96	51.	1,194,709	..
11. Honan	121,233	1.66	54.5	100,000	1.32	61.	495,870	5.4	60.5	40,000	.46	65.	1,611,568.6	..
12. Hopei	314,856	3.2	48.	307,481	3.9	60.	1,249,845	12.5	51.5	414,726	4.6	51.	3,016,314	..
13. Shantung	65,566	.747	56.5	56,928	.730	55.	530,045	5.7	55.5	53,297	1.34	3.5	2,374,839	..
14. Liaoning	..	..	61.	69,013	.7	64.	405,972	4.25	55.0	232,406	2.4	65.	1,151,001	..
15. Kirin	..	..	59.	..	..	64.	280,000	5.3	57.5	235,000	3.7	52.	2,539,264	..
16. Heilungkiang	..	..	64.5	..	..	64.5	174,650	3.	64.5	30,000	.62	62.	480,458	..
17. Jehol	..	..	94.	17,253	1.	70.	17,185	1.03	72.	24,889	1.48	67.	64,320	..
18. Chahar	..	..	64.	10,000	2.1	73.	16,584	2.4	58.	10,958	1.7	63.	213,387	..
19. Sinkiang	..	..	82.	24,347	.52	72.	66,072	1.4	71.7	41,613	.86	73.	..	..
20. Ninghsia	..	..	..	..	..	..	..	..	..	..	..	..	..	..
21. East Special	..	..	..	..	..	..	..	..	..	..	..	..	1,927,584	..
22. Fukien	24,934	.57	52.	..	..	51.	459,317	10.2	42.	35,000	.82	44.	1,549,000	..
23. Kwangsi	33,606	.517	62.	26,458	.45	72.	89,398	1.6	69.	61,250	1.1	70.	..	..
24. Kweichow	..	..	52.	..	..	49.6	158,567	5.46	44.	30,000	1.02	42.5	..	..
25. Shensi	..	..	62.	..	..	71.	282,140	4.75	61.	61,736	1.08	65.	340,702	..
26. Kansu	..	..	63.	..	..	56.	188,247	5.46	50.5	30,000	.58	37.	..	..
27. Suiyuan	..	..	100.	20,000	2.3	70.	20,000	1.94	78.	..	..	77.	..	..
28. Sikang or Chuan Pien	..	..	98.	27,440	1.43	78.	37,384	1.8	73.	37,384	1.8	78.	3,240	..
29. Chinhai	..	..	100.	..	..	..	..	..	..	..	..	..	76,900	..
Total	$1,129,820 N=13	Av. .65 N=13	Av. 61.3 N=32	$1,404,966 N=17	Av. .96 N=17	Av. 61. N=30	$10,528,109 N=26	Av. 6.3 N=26	Av. 54. N=39	$2,991,426 N=26	Av. 1.83 N=26	Av. 55. N=34	$35,464,662 N=22	

Sources of Data:

Column (1) *The First China Year Book.* Shanghai: Commercial Press, 1924, p. 449, Table 13.

(2) *Ibid.*, p. 453, Table 16.

(3) *Ibid.*, p. 469, Table 22.

(4) *Ibid.*, p. 503, Table 30.

(5) For the amount for education, the figures were furnished by the Ministry of Education by correspondence. For the total budgets of the five provinces available, see *Shun Pao Year Book*, 1933, p. M 31.

TABLE 34—(Continued)

PROPORTION OF PROVINCIAL GOVERNMENTAL EXPENDITURE FOR EDUCATION AND MILITARY PURPOSES COMPARED (Budget)

Provinces	(6) 1930-31 Amount for Education (Budget Bureau)	Per Cent of Total	Per Cent for Military	(7) 1930-31 Amount for Education (Ministry's Figures)	Per Cent of Total	(8) 1931-32 Amount for Education (Budget Bureau)	Per Cent of Total	Per Cent for Military	(9) 1931-32 Amount for Education (Ministry's Figures)	Per Cent of Total	(10) 1932-33 Amount for Education (Ministry's Figures)	Per Cent of Total	Per Cent for Military	(11) Estimated Amount of Educational Expenditure Borne by Provinces 1929-30 (Ministry's Figures)
1. Hupeh	$3,865,622	22.6b	39.	$3,893,851	22.	$4,998,862c	17.8	29.6d	$4,260,636e	15.3	$2,466,872f*	13.4*	26.5g	$3,271,893
2. Kiangsu	5,154,184	21.1	17.	4,896,552	20.1	5,123,533	19.6	16.	4,880,000	18.7	4,300,000	..	..	4,017,552
3. Chekiang	2,929,765	13.9	25.	2,531,170	12.	2,959,051	11.2	20.4	2,730,326	10.76	2,427,621*	8.45*	17.9	2,173,585
4. Anhwei	2,763,085	17.1	24.6	2,537,869	15.7	2,771,492	17.8	22.	2,771,492	17.8	2,542,225	..	..	2,845,938
5. Kiangsi	..	..	..	2,000,000	..	..	..	..	2,000,000	11.3	2,000,000*	11.3	19.7	2,000,000
6. Hunan	3,236,348	19.	9.9	3,386,394	19.9	3,231,453	18.9	10.2	3,289,731	13.4	2,475,072	..	..	2,630,532
7. Szechwan	..	..	..	..	..	..	..	..	..	..	..	..	..	2,641,623(Est.)
8. Yunnan	..	..	..	259,615	..	925,800	17.	10.2	875,254	16.1	720,000	..	..	252,720
9. Kwangtung	..	..	..	2,143,753	..	2,273,109	5.3	59.	1,894,149	4.4	1,753,799*	4.6*	52	1,735,357
10. Shansi	1,700,744	11.2	..	1,929,144	12.7	1,647,631	9.3	27.	2,164,372	12.2	1,536,391.4	..	..	1,194,709
11. Honan	1,865,405	12.7	18.4	1,844,766	12.56	1,955,201	10.9	15.1	1,905,624	10.67	2,050,505	..	..	1,611,569
12. Hopei	2,863,878	18.2	4.7	3,373,570	21.2	3,533,962	9.25	2.1	3,321,567	8.75	3,774,365	..	..	3,016,314
13. Shantung	2,746,051	11.6	15.	2,727,549	11.5	3,090,301	12.6	15.6	2,877,549	11.7	3,918,865*	11.9*	16.2	2,374,839
14. Liaoning	1,274,462	..	..	..	..	..	..	..	..	..	..	..	..	1,151,001
15. Kirin	..	..	..	..	..	..	..	..	..	..	..	..	..	2,539,264
16. Heilungkiang	480,458	..	..	..	..	..	..	..	..	..	..	..	..	480,458
17. Jehol	134,259	6.1	32.9	69,876	3.18	143,383	6.1	30.6	75,143	3.2	79,043.6	..	..	64,320
18. Chahar	317,330	15.3	16.8	266,901	12.9	319,989	13.6	14.8	276,389	11.8	276,350	..	..	213,387
19. Sinkiang	710,488	8.45	..	..	..	1,105,627	11.7	..	650,000	7.3	710,000	..	..	710,488
20. Ninghsia	..	..	..	..	..	6,576	2.02	..	6,576	2.02	45,816	..	..	6,576
21. East Special	..	..	..	1,975,726	..	..	..	..	1,840,570	..	..	..	..	1,927,584
22. Fukien	..	..	..	1,549,000	..	1,247,260	3.98	..	1,549,000	5.	1,440,000	..	..	1,549,000
23. Kwangsi	..	..	..	..	..	2,309,835	20.5	..	2,951,316	26.8	2,599,246	..	..	2,309,835
24. Kweichow	..	..	..	..	..	423,139	4.75	18.2	..	..	1,352,519	..	..	423,139
25. Shensi	..	..	..	973,210	..	1,265,957	6.1	2.45	1,257,427	6.05	1,249,687	..	..	340,702
26. Kansu	..	..	..	..	..	..	..	..	259,272	..	231,679	..	..	259,272
27. Suiyuan	..	..	..	..	..	..	..	..	200,464	..	..	..	..	200,464
28. Sikang or Chuan Pien	..	..	..	3,240	..	..	..	..	..	..	..	..	..	3,240
29. Chinhai	..	..	..	76,900	..	109,753	..	..	76,900	..	86,743	..	..	6,900
TOTAL	$30,042,088 N=14 $27,576,680 N=11	Median 14. N=12	Median 18. N=10	$38,139,830 N=19 $26,640,581 N=11	Median 13.75 N=11	$66,369,551 N=20 $39,018,774 N=19	11.42 N=19 Median 10.7	24.1 N=20	$41,152,947 N=23 $36,852,638 N=19		$37,043,107 N=22	Median 10.5 N=5		42,016,059 (80%=33,612,847) N=29

Sources of Data:

(6) *Budgets and Preliminary Estimates of Revenue and Expenditure of the Provinces and Municipalities for the Fiscal Year, 1931-32.* Nanking: The Directorate of Budgets and Statistics. Nov., 1932. Only 14 budgetary figures were available for 1930-31.

(7) The amounts for education were furnished by the Ministry of Education by correspondence. These budgetary figures differ from the corresponding figures of the Budget Bureau or Directorate. Both are given here for comparison.

(8) and (9) From the same sources as (6) and (7).

(10) Furnished by the Ministry of Education. Figures in note below are from the provincial budgets available. See *Shun Pao Year Book*, 1933, pp. M 40-43. These differ and are both given for comparison.

(11) Based upon the Ministry's figures for 1929-30 for education and the total educational expenditure including government and private expenditure for the same year, see J1, J2, J3, J4. Where there is no data for some provinces, the figures are taken from the nearest yearly budgets. For Szechwan, it is estimated by the average ratio between provincial and local expenditure for China after deducting private expenditure.

Note: In column (10) All figures marked with an asterisk (*) are budget amounts. The actual expenditures are as follows:

Hupeh, 1929-30, $3,633,278 for education.
Hupeh, 1932-33, $2,707,283 for education; 14.7 per cent of total; 17.4 per cent for military.
Chekiang, 1932-33, $2,575,816 for education; 8.95 per cent of total.
Kiangsi, 1932-33, $2,000,000 for education.
Kwangtung, 1932-33, $2,997,999 for education; 7.8 per cent of total.
Shantung, 1932-33, $3,156,905 for education; 12.9 per cent of total.

inces, as indicated by the percentages of the budgets provided for education. In 1913–14 the percentage for education was .65 on the average for 13 provinces reporting. This percentage increased to .96 in the following year for 17 provinces, and to 6.3 in 1916–17 for 26 provinces. It decreased to 1.83 in 1919–20 for 26 provinces. After the National Government was established in Nanking, the provinces began to increase their educational budgets considerably. Of the five 1929–30 budgets available, it was found that the percentages devoted to education were 11.1, 23.8, 20.1, 15.2, and 3.2, for Hupeh, Kiangsu, Anhwei, Hunan, and Yunnan respectively. On the average, from 1929 to 1932, Kiangsu led all provinces in providing 23.8 per cent, 21.1 per cent, 20.1 per cent, and 19.6 per cent to education. The world economic depression, internal disasters, and external aggression have checked this upward trend in funds devoted to education. The median percentage decreased from 14 in 1930–31 (in 12 cases) to 10.7 in 1931–32 (in 19 cases). The 1932–33 budgets available for Hupeh, Chekiang, Kiangsi, Kwangtung, and Shantung showed a median of only 10.5 per cent provided for education, but the actual expenditure shown in four reports for the same fiscal year indicates greater percentages of the total expenditure devoted to education:

	Budgeted Per cent	Actual Per cent
Hupeh	13.40	14.70
Chekiang	8.45	8.95
Kwangtung	4.60	7.80
Shantung	11.90	12.90

A further study of the provincial and municipal budgets[1] for the fiscal year, 1931–32, issued by the

[1] Unpublished Document No. 7.

Directorate of Budget and Statistics of the National Government in November, 1932, reveals that the 20 provinces and 5 municipalities reporting had a combined expenditure budget of $388,594,574, of which an aggregate of $70,740,706, or 18.05 per cent, was provided for education. The 20 provinces assigned $66,369,551, or 19.15 per cent, of $348,348,777 for education, while the 5 municipalities assigned $4,371,155, or 10.8 per cent, of the total of $40,245,797 for education. Before the Hankow Special Municipality was taken over by the Hupeh provincial government, Hankow expended $749,880 for education, or 9.87 per cent of the total municipal budget of $7,594,632.32 of 1929–30. The actual educational expenditure for this year was $727,470.23, which was 12.60 per cent of the actual municipal expenditure of $5,775,624.58.[2] All these figures fairly indicate that the government under the Kuomintang placed greater emphasis upon educational support than ever before, in spite of tremendous internal and external odds.

The writer has secured no data concerning educational expenditures under provincial governmental authorities other than the Departments of Education except in Chekiang. The budget of the Chekiang Department of Education for 1931–32 was $2,839,238, while other government departments had a combined educational budget of $847,391, or 29.8 per cent of the regular education budget. This is a considerable sum and should be kept in mind in determining how much the Chinese government is really spending for education.[3]

[2]*Statistical Year Book* of the Hankow Special Municipality for the Fiscal Year 1929–30, pp. 348, 353.
[3]Chekiang Provincial Department of Education, *Three Years of Education in Chekiang Province*, pp. 21–32.

China Compared with Other Countries in the Proportion of Governmental Expenditure Devoted to Education

The Central or National Government

It is very difficult to find strictly comparable data concerning the relation of educational expenditure to the total expenditure of different levels of government in other countries. The International Bureau of Education made an inquiry into the educational budgets of the national governments of 62 countries, mostly for the years, 1932–33.[4] (See Table 35.) Happily, Dr. Abel of the United States Office of Education has made a study of the proportion of the education costs borne by the national treasuries in 52 countries.[5] The national or central governments of 13 countries bear 100 per cent and those of 28 countries bear 50 to 98 per cent of the entire education costs. Since the Second National Conference on Education decided upon the policy that the central government of China should bear 45 per cent of the entire cost of the obligatory education program each year,[6] it is reasonable to compare China with those countries whose central governments bear 50 per cent or less of the entire education costs. Those countries, such as the United States, Canada, and Germany, in which the central government has delegated the educational financial responsibility almost entirely to the states or provinces are not strictly comparable with China. This is shown in Table 35 following.

Table 35 shows that the percentage that the educational budget of the national government is of the national budget in ten selected foreign countries ranges

---

[4] Unpublished Document No. 12, A.
[5] Abel, James F., *The Effects of the Economic Depression on Education in Other Countries*, 1933, p. 6.
[6] *Proceedings of the Second National Conference on Education*, 1930, Section III, p. 9.

TABLE 35

RELATION OF EDUCATION COST TO NATIONAL BUDGET IN VARIOUS COUNTRIES

Countries Whose National Government Bears 13-45 Per Cent of the Entire Educational Costs*		Per Cent Education Budget Is of National Budget	Countries Whose National Government Bears 50-56 Per Cent of the Entire Educational Costs*		Per Cent Education Budget Is of National Budget
Palestine	1931	6.1	Denmark	1933-34	20.6
Turkey	1932-33	3.5	England and		
Austria	1932	3.8	Wales	1933-34	6.15
Japan	1931-32	8.8	Hungary	1932-33	13.2
Colombia	1932	10.0	Latvia	1932-33	16.2
Median for the			Norway	1932-33	14.6
10 countries		9.4	Average for the		
China	1933-34	2.81	10 countries		10.3

U. S. S. R. Unified Financial Plan realized in 4.5 years,
1928-33   11.7

Data for National Budget of U.K. from *Statesman's Yearbook*, 1933.
Data for U.S.S.R. from *Summary of the Fulfillment of the First Five-Year Plan*, 1933. State Planning Commission, Moscow, p. 291, Table No. 28.
*Abel, James F., *Op. cit.*, p. 6.

from 3.5 per cent in Turkey to 20.6 per cent in Denmark. The median is 9.4 per cent and the average is 10.3 per cent. China ranks the lowest among these countries, with only 2.81 per cent of her Central budget for education.

The Provincial Government

The countries whose educational burden is distributed between national, state or province, city and local counties or districts on three levels are chosen for this comparison. The United States is also chosen because the combined educational expenditure of the 48 states constituted only 16.9 per cent of the total educational expenditure of the country in 1930[7], while China has

[7] U. S. Office of Education, *Biennial Survey of Education*, 1928-30, p. 25.

decided upon a policy of requiring the provincial governments to bear at least 10 per cent of the entire cost of the obligatory educational program, in addition to other education costs.[8] Actually the provincial and municipal governments bear approximately 27 per cent of the total cost of education in China according to an estimate in Table 15.

China is compared with four foreign countries in Table 36.

TABLE 36

PER CENT EDUCATIONAL BUDGET OR EXPENDITURE IS OF TOTAL STATE OR PROVINCIAL GOVERNMENT BUDGET OR EXPENDITURE, CHINA COMPARED WITH CERTAIN OTHER COUNTRIES

Country	Year	Per Cent
1. United States (48 States)	1930 (A)	28.3
	1920 (A)	30.1
	1910 (A)	37.6
2. Japan (all local)	1930 (A)	28.1
	1920 (A)	30.0
	1913 (A)	33.9
3. Germany (Prussia)	1933 (B)	18.0
4. Switzerland (5 cantons)	1932–33 (B)	20.7
5. China (20 provinces combined)	1931–32 (B)	19.15
Average per cent (B)		11.42
Median per cent (B)		10.7
Range (B)		2.02–20.5

1. Mort, Paul R., *Op. cit.*, p. 325.
2. Moulton, H. G., *Japan, An Economic and Financial Appraisal*, p. 583, Table 55.
3. See Unpublished Document No. 12.
4. Same as 3.
5. Cf. Table 34, Note (6)
(A) indicates actual expenditure.
(B) indicates budget allowance.

[8]*Proceedings of the Second National Conference on Education*, 1930, Section III, p. 9.

This table shows that the 48 states of the United States have devoted an average of 28.3 per cent to 37.6 per cent of their budgets for education. The figures for Japan include both the second and third levels of government where the educational budget has ranged from 28.1 per cent to 33.9 per cent of the general government budget. Prussia devotes 18 per cent of its government budget to education, while the cantons of Switzerland devote 20.7 per cent of their budget to education. In China, the combined budgets of 20 provinces give 19.15 per cent to education. When individually considered, the Chinese provincial governments devote only a median of 10.7 per cent of their general budget to education, ranging all the way from 2.02 per cent to 20.5 per cent.

The Municipal Government

Table 37 presents the proportion of the educational budgets of American cities compared with those of Chinese special municipalities.

Table 37 indicates that the percentages that the municipalities of China assign to education average only 10.8, while all the cities in the United States of 30,000 population and over show a combined percentage of 36.3. It is generally believed that the largest cities in the United States spend about one third of their budgets for education. Engelhardt[9] showed that seven second-class cities in the State of New York spent a median percentage of 30.3 to 35.1 for education from 1910 to 1920. China should assign at least 25 per cent of the city budgets to education; this would mean that the present amount spent for education should be increased one and one-half times.

[9] Engelhardt, N. L., and Engelhardt, Fred, *Op. cit.*, p. 26.

TABLE 37

PER CENT EDUCATIONAL BUDGET OR EXPENDITURE IS OF TOTAL MUNICIPAL OR CITY BUDGET OR EXPENDITURE, CHINA COMPARED WITH UNITED STATES

Country	Year	Administrative Unit	Amount in Millions		Percentage
			General	Education	
United States	1929 (Actual)	All cities over 30,000	G$3307.5	$307.6	24.4 (1)
	1931 (Actual)	"	Current	expense	37.0 (2)
		Cities of 50,000 and over			31.9
China	1931–32 (Budget)	5 special municipalities	S$40.246	S$4.371	10.8 (3)

(1) *Recent Social Trends in the United States.* Adapted from Tables, pp. 1324–26.
(2) National Education Association, Department of Supervision and Research Service, Circular No. 9, September, 1933, Table on p. 1.
(3) Cf. Table 34, Note (6).

The Local Government

For the local governments or the governments on the third level, some data have been secured, as revealed in the following table.

From the above comparison, it is evident that China must at least double the percentage of county government budget for education in order to reach the United States plane of expenditure, provided the counties of Hupeh give a fair indication of the effort of all other county governments. However, the actual data for 1934 for all 1770 counties cannot be obtained. It is not unfair that education claim 35 to 40 per cent of the county budgets. At present, China falls below the percentages of Japan and of England, Wales and Scotland, even when their second level governments are included in the accounting.

TABLE 38

PERCENTAGE THAT EDUCATIONAL EXPENDITURES ARE OF TOTAL LOCAL BUDGETS

COUNTRIES AND SOURCES OF AVAILABLE DATA	YEAR	PER CENT
United States:		
All local governments other than cities	1929, actual	38.4a (1)
Cities, 50,000–100,000 population		46.0 (1)
Cities, 30,000– 10,000 population		45.9 (1)
England, Wales and Scotland (local)	1929–30 budget	22.2 (2)
Japan (all local including second level of government)	1930, actual	28.1 (3)
China (57 counties of Hupeh Province)	1932–33 budget	18.26 (4)

(1) *Recent Social Trends in the United States.* Calculated from Tables on pages 1324 and 1326; also National Education Association, Department of Supervision and Research Service, Circular No. 9, September, 1933, Table on page 1.
(2) *Statesman's Yearbook*, 1933.
(3) See Table 36.
(4) Writer's own calculation; see Diagram 5.
a. $1,306,000,000 divided by $3,410,800,000.

The Combined Budget of All Government Levels

In the United States, 26.8 per cent of the combined expenditures of the federal, state, and local governments was devoted to education in 1929.[10] Since the accounting system in China is imperfect and the budget system has just begun, it is impossible to find comparable data. However, the League of Nations' Mission of Educational Experts estimated an average of "about 25–30 cents per head annually with a general sum of three Mexican dollars of yearly taxes paid on an average by each inhabitant to central and local state funds." "This means that at present Chinese education expenses constitute about 9–10 per cent of budget expenses and in

[10] *Recent Social Trends*, p. 1326.

csae of further demands by the central national budget for debts and administrative tariffs, about 11–12 per cent."[11] It is not exorbitant at present to recommend that China spend at least 25 per cent of the combined budgets of all levels of government for education.

THE COST OF EDUCATION AND MILITARY EXPENDITURES COMPARED

A study of the expenditures of all the different functions of the government involves considerable time and labor and lies outside the scope of the present study. Tables 34 and 39 serve to show that expenditures for national economy, productive enterprises or social welfare other than education are not significant, since military expenditure consumes one half of the Central budget, and debt service and indemnity almost a third, leaving approximately one sixth to one fifth for all other purposes.

TABLE 39

SUMMARY OF THE CENTRAL EXPENDITURE BUDGET CHINA

YEAR	PER CENT FOR DEBT SERVICE AND INDEMNITY	PER CENT FOR MILITARY PURPOSES	PER CENT FOR CIVIL ADMINISTRATION
1928–29	36.82	48.23	14.95
1929–30	37.13	45.5	17.37
1930–31	40.52	43.62	15.86
1931–32	39.5	44.4	16.1
1932–33	25.48	48.44	26.08
1933–34	29.1	50.14	20.76
1934–35*	33.1	38.80	28.10

Source: Reports of Finance Ministry and Directorate of Budget Statistics.

*Shun Pao, July, 1934, p. 3. Official announcement by the Central Political Council.

[11] *The Reorganization of Education in China*, p. 50.

Military expenditure is the biggest burden and obstacle in Chinese public finance; hence, this item is chosen for emphasis to show why education has been neglected. One must be reminded that the period of military dictatorship in China's revolutionary program has been prolonged, due to further uprisings of reactionary forces. The history of revolution and civil wars in other countries shows that this state of affairs is necessary for the unification of the country and the final triumph of peace and prosperity. Nevertheless, the prolonged internecine warfare, banditry, communism, and foreign aggression would be more and more ameliorated if fifteen or twenty years ago statesmen had been farther-sighted and had given more attention to the enlightenment of the people and to economic reconstruction. China has the largest standing army in the world. The grand total for army, air, and navy is 1,743,831 as reported in the *Armament Yearbook* of the League of Nations for 1933. The actual figure has been believed to be more than 2,000,000. Yet these forces have failed to defend China against Japanese invasion. Evidently it is quality and not quantity that counts in modern warfare. It is imperative that China should disband part of the army in order to relieve the burden of expenditure for educational and economic reconstruction.

An inquiry into the military budgets of other countries shows that no country spends more than China, as measured by the percentage of the National budget (see Table 40). It is reasonable to propose that in normal years China should spend not more than the median percentage, i. e., 16.6 per cent, and in times of military campaign as at the present not more than the third quartile, i. e., 22.88 per cent or thereabouts.

In China, not only the Central Government bears the burden of military expenditure; the local governments

Education and Government Costs Compared

TABLE 40

PERCENTAGE THAT MILITARY BUDGET IS OF TOTAL NATIONAL BUDGET, CHINA COMPARED WITH OTHER COUNTRIES

PERCENTAGE	NUMBER OF COUNTRIES	BUDGET YEARS	
50–55	1 (China)	1933–34	11
45–50	1 (Albania)	1932–33	33
35–40	1 (India)	1931–32	9
30–35	3 (Japan)	1930–31	5
25–30	5 (Mexico)	1929–30	2
20–25	10 (France)	1925–27	1
15–20	14 (U. S. A.)		
10–15	13 (U. K. & N. Ireland)		
5–10	7 (U. S. S. R.)		
1– 5	6 (N. Zealand)		
Total=61		Total=61	

Median   16.6 per cent
Third Quartile   22.88 per cent

Calculated from original sources in League of Nations, *Armament Yearbook*, 1933. Figures for China from Table 32, 1933–34 and see Unpublished Document No. 12, A, on opposite page.

also bear an abnormal burden. Figures in Table 34 tell the story. The provincial governments reporting spent on the average 61.6 per cent, 61 per cent, 54 per cent, 55 per cent, 20.34 per cent of the budgets of 1913–14, 1914–15, 1916–17, 1919–20, and 1929–30 respectively. Of the available budgets for 1932–33 of four provinces, an average of 17.8 per cent was given to military purposes. In budget, the figure for Hupeh was 17.4 per cent, but in actual expenditure it was 26.6 per cent. Although the situation has improved in recent years, the military burden is still abnormal. The counties of Hupeh assigned an average of 54.73 per cent of the budgets in 1932–33 for self-defense against banditry and communism. No doubt this is a temporary measure.

CHAPTER VI

HOW THE PRESENT EDUCATIONAL PROGRAM IS SUPPORTED

FISCAL CONTROL

The Legislative Basis of Educational Fiscal Control

The fundamental educational fiscal policies originate from the platform of the Kuomintang,[1] the Provisional Constitution,[2] and the resolutions of the plenary sessions of the Central Executive Committee[3] and the National Party Congress.[4] The Central Political Council, in collaboration with the Legislative Yuan, is the highest legislative body which enacts basic educational laws and decides upon government budget and fiscal programs.[5]

Article XIV of the Internal Policies of the Kuomintang Platform reads as follows:

"Universal education will be effectively carried out. Education for the development of children's individuality will be specially attended to, school systems will be revised, educational

---

[1]Tyau, M. T. Z., *Two Years of Nationalist China*, 1930, p. 33, "Relations (of the Kuomintang) to the National Government."
[2]Hunan Department of Education, *Hunan Educational Administration Documentary Bulletin*, No. 8, April–June, 1931, Section on Central Laws, pp. 1–8, "The Provisional Constitution of the Republic of China." See preamble of the complete text. (Promulgated June 1, 1931.)
[3]Publicity Department of the Central Executive Committee of the Kuomintang, Compiler, *The Manifesto and the Resolutions of the Third National Congress of the Kuomintang*, March, 1929, pp. 43–44, Article 5.
[4]*Ibid.*, Article 1, on powers of the National Party Congress.
[5]Tyau, M. T. Z., *Op. cit.*, p. 36. "Regulations Governing the Power of Formulating Governmental Policies Delegated to the Central Political Council." See Article 4.

budgets will be increased, and the independence of educational funds will be guaranteed."[6]

Article 6, Chapter V, of the Provisional Constitution reads as follows:

"The central and local governments should [amply] raise [the necessary funds] for education and make provision for safeguarding those funds of which the independence is secured according to law."[7]

The Draft Constitution to be adopted by the National People's Congress in March, 1935, makes the following provision:

"Part IV, Article 37. All children of school age shall receive free education. Those who have not had free education shall receive special adult education.

"Part IV, Article 40. The expenditure on education shall not be less than 15 per cent of the budget of the entire administrative expenditure for the central government and not less than 30 per cent for the local government. The security of funds which are, by law, specially set apart for educational purpose shall be guaranteed."[8]

The provincial government council holds the power to pass on the budgets of the entire province and hence controls the fundamental educational fiscal policies of the province.[9] For example, certain special appropriations for education, such as capital outlays, increase of teachers' salaries, and aid to rural schools, must be decided upon in a meeting of the provincial government

[6]Hsu, Leonard S., *Sun Yat-sen, His Political and Social Ideals*, A Source Book. 1933, p. 138.
[7]*The First Education Year Book of China*, 1934, Section B, p. 1, "Central Educational Laws." Translated by writer.
[8]*Chinese Affairs* (published fortnightly), Volume V, No. 19, March 15, 1934, pp. 297 sqq. The document is translated into English.
[9]Kwo-wei, Editor, *A Complete Collection of Administrative Laws of China*, 1933, pp. 96–101, "Revised Organic Law of the Provincial Government," Article V, No. 4.

council, in which the provincial Commissioner of Education takes part.[10] In actual practice the degree of legislative control of educational expenditures by the provincial government council varies inversely with the degree of fiscal independence of the provincial department of education.[11] The degree of fiscal independence in those provinces having it is never 100 per cent.[12]

The county educational budget, which is included in the general budget of the county government, is legally under the supervision of the provincial government.[13] In the provinces where the county bureau of education is fiscally independent, the sources of school revenue are sometimes collected directly by the bureau itself, but the fundamental policies of spending the money are regulated by rules set up by superior authorities.[14]

In the local school districts, the local gentry generally raise their own money for the district or rural schools.[15]

Both the central and the provincial educational executive have some legislative powers concerning fiscal matters, provided there is no deviation from fundamental policies and no conflict with laws and statutes of their respective superior authorities.[16] The University

---

[10]Secretariat of the Hupeh Provincial Government, *Administrative Report of the Provincial Government of Hupeh*, Jan.–Aug., 1932. See Minutes of the meetings of the Provincial Government Council.

[11]Honan Department of Education, *Honan Educational Year Book*, 1930, pp. 290 *sqq*. "The Honan Education Finance and Property Administration."

[12]Honan Department of Education, *Special Bulletin on the Educational Funds and Property of Honan Province*, Kaifeng, 1930. Chapter 22, "A Retrospect of Honan's Struggle for Fiscal Independence," pp. 93–96.

[13]Hupeh Department of Finance, *The Revenue and Expenditure Budgets of the County Local Governments* for the Fiscal Year 1932–33. Introduction, quoting, "the tentative Laws Governing the Supervision of Local Finance," promulgated by the National Government in 1930.

[14]See Table 41, Sources of Data.

[15]*The First Education Year Book of China*, 1934. See section on fiscal control in each province, *passim*.

[16]*Ibid.*, Section A, p. 51, "Statute of the Organization of the Provincial Department of Education" (Hupeh cited as typical), Article 3.

Committee in the Ministry of Education has a theoretical legislative function respecting financial policies and budgets, but since the Minister acts as its chairman, it becomes an advisory body in fact.[17] The provincial city or county educational associations, composed of laymen and professional leaders, can only propose fiscal matters; hence this body also exists only in an advisory capacity.[18] In many provinces, munipalities, and counties there exists an educational finance committee composed of the *ex-officio* members of the government and of professional men.[19] Where educational finance is independent, this committee has large legislative powers. Where educational finance is dependent, such committees are only advisory in function.[20] The educational finance supervisory or audit committees which operate under various titles also exist in many provinces and counties.[21]

It can be seen that with the exception of those provinces in which educational finance is conducted independently (though often not completely so), and in which there is greater legislative power and control on the part of the local educational authority, educational finance in China is, in general, very much dependent upon the general government authorities. Both legislative and executive control of finance must follow a roundabout route and, hence, educational reforms have been unnecessarily slow and inefficient. Such an administrative set-up does not in reality carry out the provisions of the Provisional Constitution and the party platform, which expressly guarantee educational fiscal independence. The realization of this constitutional and party objective has been only partly effected

[17]*The First Education Year Book of China*, 1934, Section B, p. 2, "Revised Organization Law of the Ministry of Education," Article 13.

[18]*Ibid.*, Section B, p. 120, "Law of Educational Associations," promulgated January 27, 1931, Article 3.

[19-21]*Ibid.*, Section C. See section on fiscal control in each province, *passim*.

through a long period of struggle under professional leadership.[22]

The Degrees of Educational Fiscal Control

There are varying degrees of fiscal control according to where the powers of various aspects of control are located. For the purpose of convenience, educational fiscal control may be classified into three types: (1) Control under the "appropriation" policy; (2) control under the "allocation" policy; and (3) control under the "independence" policy.

"Under the 'appropriation' policy, state receipts are paid into a general fund, or general treasury, from which expenditures are made pursuant to legislative appropriations."[23]

Under the "allocation" policy, "receipts from certain taxes or other sources of revenue are set aside at the time they are collected, usually in expendable funds, and may be used only for[24] educational purposes. But the budgetary control is centralized in the general government authority.

Under the "independence" policy, as that term is used in this study, there is a complete control of budgetary procedure, the collection, custody, and expenditure of educational revenues, by an independent organization with spearate legislative, executive, and supervisory set-ups which are directly responsible to the educational authority. Tai Shuang-chiu, an authority in educational administration in China, defined eight essentials or factors of educational fiscal independence in his proposal for a unified educational fiscal administration in China.[25] These are:

[22]Unpublished Document, No. 17. See all sources listed in footnotes.
[23]Pearman, W. I., *Support of State Educational Programs*, 1933, p. 7.
[24]*Ibid.*
[25]*Proceedings of the First National Conference on Education*, 1928. Nanking: The University Yuan, p. 240, "Tai Shuang-chiu, A Proposal for the Unification of Educational Fiscal Administration in China."

(1) Definite establishment of educational endowment.
(2) Allocation of sources of educational revenue.
(3) Independence of the budgetary system.
(4) Independence of the power to increase taxes or tax rates.
(5) Independence of the collection agency.
(6) Independence of the money-keeping agency.
(7) Independence of the disbursing agency.
(8) Independence of the audit agency or machinery.

As indicated by the above list, there are varying degrees of fiscal independence in China. Many provincial and local educational authorities who call themselves independent are only partially independent, because they have realized only part of the essentials of independence listed above. For the sake of convenience, all degrees of independence that have fulfilled at least Factor 2 and any of the Factors 3 to 8 (as listed in Tai Shuang-chiu's eight essentials) are classified under the category of "Independence Policy."

The Status of Educational Fiscal Control

Except the income from property and some administrative receipts, all phases of the central educational program are financed under the "appropriation" policy. When the new minister, Dr. S. C. Wang, came into office in 1933, he made it one of the objectives of his administrative program to put into practice central educational fiscal independence and, within possibilities, to promote the same in the provinces. It was announced that the inheritance tax should be levied for education and that an educational finance committee should be organized.[26] The actual practices resulting from this policy remain to be seen.

The present status of educational fiscal control in the various provinces and special municipalities and counties of China is kaleidoscopic. A narrative of each of

[26] *Shun Pao*, June 2, 1933.

these different educational administrative units with varying degrees of fiscal independence or dependence and complicated by numerous qualifying factors and exceptions, would be rather cumbersome. Instead of a complete narrative, Table 41 has been prepared.

In this table, fiscal control is analyzed according to the eight factors or criteria of fiscal independence listed above. The actual conditions under each factor of each administrative unit—provincial, county, or special municipal—are summarized briefly in a separate column.

In the above table, summary statements have been made at the end of each column and row, followed by supporting data notes.

The Status in the Provinces and Special Municipalities:
The status of fiscal control of all provincial and municipal educational authorities is shown in Table 42. This table is designed to generalize the situation from another angle.

TABLE 42

ADMINISTRATIVE UNITS CLASSIFIED ACCORDING TO POLICIES OF FISCAL CONTROL, 1934

Policy of Fiscal Independence	Policy of Allocation	Policy of Appropriation
Very highly: Yunnan Honan	Anhwei Sikang Szechwan?*	Hupeh Kwangtung Kwangsi Kweichow
Highly: Kiangsu Fukien Chekiang	Proposed: Ninghsia	Shantung Hopei Shansi Kansu** Chahar
Slightly: Hunan Shensi		Sinkiang Ninghsia Chinhai Szechwan
Proposed: Hupeh Anhwei Nanking Shanghai		Nanking Shanghai Peiping Tsingtao Weihaiwei

Sources: See all sources listed in Table 41, and notes.

*Szechwan has the meat tax earmarked for education, and had once an Educational Funds Receiving and Disbursing Bureau, but since she is so much dependent upon the military authority that collects the tax, it is better to put this province in the appropriation category.

**In 1928–29 Kansu had the livestock tax and special levy on rolled tobacco earmarked for education, plus appropriation from the provincial treasury (see Table 50, Source 6). *The First Education Year Book of China*, 1934, mentions that Kansu is actually dependent upon appropriations from the provincial treasury in 1931 (see Section C, p. 283). This latest information is used in the table above.

Table 42 shows that six provincial departments of education are fiscally independent. Yunnan and Honan are very highly independent; Kiangsu, Fukien, and Chekiang are highly independent; Hunan and Shensi are only slightly independent. Hunan is struggling for further independence by securing an increase in the rate of the earmarked salt surtax.[27] Anhwei has proposed to have more independence since 1930.[28] Hupeh is petitioning the central government to earmark the salt tax or tobacco and wine tax for education.[29] Professional organizations of Shanghai and Nanking Special Municipalities have also started similar movements.[30] Only Anhwei and perhaps Sikang may be said to be under the allocation policy. Szechwan has been under the allocation policy, but now she may be put under the category of appropriation policy along with 12 other provinces and 5 municipalities. It is safe to say that, in China, the provincial and special municipal authorities are predominantly dependent with regard to the eight criteria of educational fiscal independence.

The Status in the Counties:

The status of educational fiscal independence of the county bureaus of education is shown in Table 41. In

[27] *Shih Sze Hsing Pao* (Daily News of Current Events), June 21, 1931.
[28] Anhwei Department of Education, *One Year of Education in Anhwei Province*, 1930, pp. 1–4, Section III.
[29] *Shun Pao*, May 20, 1934.
[30] *Shun Pao*, June, 1933.

six provinces, Chekiang, Kiangsi, Fukien, Yunnan, Honan, and perhaps Shantung, the county bureaus of education are highly independent, with the exception of many backward counties.

In seven provinces, Kiangsu, Anhwei, Hunan, Kweichow, Kwangtung, Kwangsi, and Shensi, the county bureaus of education are independent to a slight degree. In other words, in two provinces, Shansi and Chinhai, the county bureaus of education are under the appropriation policy, and in eight provinces the county bureaus of education are under the allocation policy. In twenty provinces the county schools have some endowments in land and other property, but little invested funds as a whole. In twenty provinces, the county schools are supported by earmarked sources of tax revenue. All county educational budgets must be approved by the provincial department of education, under the general supervision of the provincial fiscal authorities, while directly under the supervision of the county government. In only five provinces, Honan, Shantung, Yunnan, Kweichow, and Chekiang, the county bureaus of education collect their school taxes directly by thmselves (with exceptions, of course). In twenty provinces, the counties have their own treasuries or depositories, either in the bureaus of education or in agencies directly under the control of these bureaus. No county bureau of education has the power to raise school taxes or tax rates independently. In only twelve provinces the county bureaus of education have fulfilled four or less factors or essentials of fiscal independence.

Does the Present Status of Educational Fiscal Independence Guarantee Adequacy and Stability of Support?

Since no educational authority in China enjoys complete fiscal independence with regard to the eight criteria listed above, partial independence does not necessarily guarantee fiscal adequacy and stability in many cases. The chief difficulty lies in the lack of complete independence in budgetary control and of the power to raise taxes and tax rates.

Some instances where the present degree of fiscal independence does not guarantee fiscal adequacy and stability may be cited as follows:

A. In 1931–32, the provincial department of education in Kiangsu found a sharp decrease in the tax collections earmarked for education. There was an arrear of three months on the pay roll. The Educational Finance Administration Bureau had to borrow large sums from the Shanghai county and the Central Bank of China to meet the deficit.[31]

B. In 1931, six counties of Kiangsu had deficits in their educational budgets, and their salary arrears and cuts were violently protested by the teachers.[32]

C. In 1931, the Commissioner of Education of Hunan Province tendered his resignation to the Ministry of Education, owing to the failure of the Central Government to take action on its promise to raise the salt tax rate earmarked for education in Hunan and guarantee its independence.[33]

D. Thirteen counties of Shantung, where educational finance is independent to the degree indicated above, often face shortage of funds. The current income of the county schools is generally unstable.[34]

However, the lack of complete independence is not necessarily the only factor that affects the stability of support. The general economic depression and some other extraneous factors must also be considered.

---

[31]*The Chung Hua Educational Review.* All numbers for the year 1931–32, the Educational News Section.
[32]*Ibid.*
[33]*Ibid.*
[34]*The First Education Year Book of China,* 1934, Section C, p. 465.

CHAPTER VII

HOW THE PRESENT EDUCATIONAL PROGRAM IS SUPPORTED (*Continued*)

THE SOURCES OF EDUCATIONAL REVENUE

The Meaning of Sources

In the last analysis, educational revenue like all other revenue comes from the pockets of the people. There is but one source, i. e., the income of the people. Behind the income there are two major factors that operate to influence its possessor in determining the proportion to be paid to education, namely, (1) the psychological factor, the willingness to pay and the faith in or the desire to buy education, and (2) the economic factor, the ability to pay for education in addition to other necessary wants and obligations. The first factor is probably affected, in turn, by the extent to which the people recognize the value of education. When the element of compulsion enters in, or when popular control of education is only in the preparation stage, as is the case in China to-day, the proportion of the people's income that finally reaches the schools is determined by a third factor, the mechanism by which the government taps and spends this income, or the government's willingness and ability to pay for education.

The amounts paid for education from the income of the people are collected through various channels, by various mechanisms, and in various forms. Thus, one single source turns into diversified sources which refer to the places or channels or authorities from which they come from the original source—the pockets of the people—, and to the form in which they come until they finally reach the schools in expendable sums.

Channels from which the Revenue for the Total Current Cost of the Entire Educational Program of China Comes

As revealed by the writer's estimate of current expenditure in Table 15, about 29 per cent of the entire revenue of the educational program of China to-day is paid from sources which are privately controlled, and 71 per cent from sources which are publicly controlled. The writer's estimate of the total current cost of the public educational program reveals that about 10 per cent of the total revenue for the public educational program of China to-day may come from sources controlled by the National or Central Government, 27 per cent from sources controlled by provincial and municipal government, and 63 per cent from sources under the control of local governments.[1] It is impossible at present to ascertain the exact proportions that the national, provincial, local, and private sources constitute of the total educational revenue of China, because of inadequate facts concerning the elements of students' fees, private contributions to public schools, government aid to private schools, and subventions and contributions on the different government levels. Furthermore, to estimate revenue from expenditure is not very accurate, because educational revenues in China generally lag behind expenditures.

Educational Revenues and Expenditures Compared

Educational revenue reports in educational statistics in China are also expressed in totals classified only under school organizations and by geographical divisions. Table 19 compares the total elementary and secondary educational revenues and expenditures in the various provinces and municipalities for the year 1929–30.[2] There are deficits in half of the 36 adminis-

[1] See page 47.
[2] See page 57.

106 *The Financing of Public Education in China*

trative units reporting, and surpluses in only 13 of them. The combined revenue was $107,117,269, and the combined expenditure, $109,218,507. There was a combined deficit of $2,101,238.

The Classification of Educational Revenues of China

"For convenience in accounting and in considering the many problems relating to income, the most desirable classification is by source. . . . Grouping in this manner facilitates an analysis of the amounts received from various sources each year and provides a convenient basis for comparing receipts over a period of years and with those of other school systems."[3]

Classified data concerning educational revenue or receipts are rare in China. However, all available revenue reports are classified by source, though the classification falls short of scientific procedure. In the statistics of 1907–09, China's sources of educational revenue, both public and private, for 23 provinces reporting, were classified as follows:

TABLE 43

PROPORTION OF VARIOUS SOURCES OF EDUCATION REVENUE, 1907–09

Source	Per Cent Each Item Is of Total Revenue			
	China			U.S.
	1907	1908	1909	1930
1. Income from school land and property	6.92	5.15	7.17	Public treasury 78.60
2. Interest of invested funds	7.27	4.21	4.51	
3. Official appropriations and public moneys	56.87	65.78	54.97	
4. Tuition or students' fees	8.79	7.47	10.01	Fees 6.25
5. Compulsory or allocated contributions	8.01	7.60	11.45	

[3] Engelhardt, N. L., and Engelhardt, Fred, *Public School Business Administration*, 1927, p. 242.

TABLE 43 (*Continued*)

SOURCE	PER CENT EACH ITEM IS OF TOTAL REVENUE			
	CHINA			U.S.
	1907	1908	1909	1930
6. Voluntary contributions	8.93	4.49	6.83	Gifts 4.10
7. Miscellaneous income	3.21	5.39	5.06	Other local sources 11.05
Total per cent	100.00	100.00	100.00	100.00
Amount in Millions	$15.30	$27.70	$23.30	G$3,459.4

Figures for China freshly calculated from original tables on revenues in Sources A, B, C (see Bibliography).
Figures for U. S. A. from U. S. Office of Education, *Biennial Survey of Education*, 1928–30, p. 10.
All figures are read from the slide rule and therefore not very exact.

Later reports on total educational revenues of the school organizations are not so classified except those dealing with higher education since 1928. Higher education revenues of all China are classified as in Table 44, where the proportion of each source is also shown.

The Revenue Budgets of the Government Educational Authority

Very few educational revenue budgets have been prepared by the governments, especially by the provincial governments,[4] owing to the fact that the income of the latter educational authority is mainly derived from appropriations and the income from sources other than appropriations is so insignificant as to require no separate report. Two educational revenue budgets of provinces in which educational finance is independent are shown in Tables 45 and 46. The variation of sources and the manner of classification offer an interesting study.

[4]See all educational budgets of the provinces in the educational reports listed in the Bibliography.

108   *The Financing of Public Education in China*

TABLE 44

THE PROPORTIONS OF VARIOUS SOURCES OF HIGHER EDUCATION REVENUE IN ALL CHINA, 1931-32

Source Classification	Per Cent Each Source Is of Total Revenue in All Public and Private Institutions
1. Government appropriations	52.25
a. National . . . 31.45%	
b. Provincial . . 20.80%	
2. Income from property, etc.	5.28
3. Contributions	26.30
4. Students' fees	10.42
5. Miscellaneous	5.75
Total percentage	100.00
Total amount	$33,619,237

Adapted from Table , *Higher Education Statistics in All China, 1931-32,* July, 1933, Section 1, p. 15.

TABLE 45

CLASSIFICATION OF EDUCATIONAL REVENUE BUDGET OF KIANGSU PROVINCE, 1929-30

(For provincial government education only)

Sources	Per Cent of Total
1. Earmarked income from land tax	30.00
2. Provincial grain-tribute	25.00
3. Business brokerage tax	14.90
4. Butchery business tax	14.90
5. Delinquency levy	7.50
6. Administrative receipts	3.70
7. Other receipts	4.00
a. Arrears of provincial aid	
b. Tax increase as result of efficient management	
Total percentage	100.00
Total amount	$4,017,552

Kiangsu Department of Education, *Recent Educational Conditions in Kiangsu Province,* 1930, p. 2 of appendix. %'s freshly calculated.

TABLE 46

CLASSIFICATION OF REVENUE BUDGET OF HONAN PROVINCIAL EDUCATIONAL PROGRAM, PREPARED BY THE HONAN EDUCATIONAL FUNDS AND PROPERTY ADMINISTRATION BUREAU, 1929–30

Sources	Per Cent of Total Revenue
1. Sales title deeds regular tax	68.90
2. Mortgage title deeds regular tax	7.82
3. Water benefit levy	1.96
4. Price of title deeds blanks	8.72
5. Miscellaneous administrative fees respecting title deeds tax	9.26
6. Income from invested funds	0.70
7. Income from lease of land and houses	0.64
8. Tuition	1.95
9. Others	0.05
Total percentage	100.00
Total amount	$1,801,614.67

Honan Department of Education, *Special Bulletin on the Educational Funds and Property of Honan Province*, 1930, pp. 3–4.

Notes: (1) Original budget gives 17 items. These are combined and reclassified into 9 items. %'s are freshly calculated.

(2) a, refers to water conservancy, irrigation and communication, etc.

A Better Classification of Educational Income or Receipts Needed

Some samples of local educational revenue budgets are presented under the heading, "Sources of County Educational Revenue." These samples show interesting variations, owing to the diversification of sources. On the whole, there is no uniform classification in China and various classifications are not well planned for purposes of comparison. Engelhardt recommends to the American school systems the classification of receipts recommended by the National Association of Public School Business Officials (of the United States).[5] All receipts are first classified into two general groups,

[5] Engelhardt, N. L., and Engelhardt, Fred, *Op. cit.*, p. 243.

(1) revenue receipts "which are applicable to the current period, which increase assets or decrease reserves without increasing liabilities or reserves which do not represent the recovery of particular expenditure and the sources of which are known or ascertainable,"[6] for example, taxes and state appropriations, and (2) non-revenue receipts which "either incur indebtedness or result in decreasing the amount or value of school property,"[7] for example, receipts from book sales and short-term loans. The general pattern of this classification[8] can be adapted to Chinese use without very much change.

However, for the sake of a more rational classification of the available sources of school revenue in China, a tentative one has been suggested by the writer:[9] All sources of educational revenue are classified into two major groups: (1) non-tax sources, such as rent of school land and other property, interest on school funds, tuition, grants-in-aid, private contributions, sales proceeds, loans, balance from previous year, fines, diverted funds, and so forth; and (2) tax sources, such as land surtax, direct tax other than lands, contract tax or title deeds surtax, business and sales taxes and surtaxes, consumption and commodity taxes, and the like.

The above Chinese tax terms and some others used elsewhere need to be explained for the convenience of the readers. They are as follows:[10]

1. Surtax. A surtax is that part of the regular tax of a higher level of government allocated to a lower level of government for all purposes according to a legal ratio or tax rate. It is collected by the same tax collector, in theory.

---

[6]Engelhardt, N. L., and Engelhardt, Fred, *Op. cit.*, p. 242.
[7]*Ibid.*, p. 245.
[8]*Ibid.*, pp. 243–45.
[9]See Table 54.
[10]Chia, Sze-yi, *Financial History of the Republic of China*, 1917, *passim*.

2. Land tax. A land tax is tax on farm land and has a history of forty centuries. There are the following major types of land tax:
> (a) Land-capitation tax is the land tax which was amalgamated with the poll tax during the Manchu Dynasty.
> (b) Grain Tribute is land tax paid originally in produce.
> (c) Mow Tax is a land tax levied according to a rate per mow of land (approximately one sixth of an acre).
> (d) Military colonial land tax is the tax on land that was originally used by military settlements and has long been turned to the people for cultivation.
> (e) Rent grain, or rent, is the rent on the lease of government land which has been collected at the same time as the regular land tax. Its yield has always been classified with the land tax. All land taxes have been paid in terms of the silver tael until its recent abolishment; hence, land-capitation tax is also called capitation-silver or poll-silver.

3. Contract tax is the tax on title deeds during the selling and mortgaging of real estate. There are various surcharges in connection with this tax, such as the price on the title-deeds blanks issued by the government, and administrative fees.

4. Ya-Hsui or Brokerage tax, Ya-Tieh, or Brokerage license. A brokerage tax is a tax on the agent doing business or a tax on its license or license fee.

5. Likin is the tax on commodities transported from one place to another through any official pass. It is similar to the French octroi.

6. Butchery tax is a tax on the slaughtering of domestic animals. The tax on the buying and selling

112 The Financing of Public Education in China

of cattle and sheep, and so forth, is called the livestock tax. A meat tax is a tax on pork or beef, and the like

7. Miscellaneous taxes on commodities. There are hundreds of names of taxes on commodities. They are described under the topic, "County Sources of Educational Revenue."

THE NONTAX SOURCES OF EDUCATIONAL REVENUE IN CHINA AS A WHOLE

It is not possible to determine just how much the income from school lands and funds and tuition contributed to the total revenues listed in the table. Only sample data are available.

Permanent School Funds

In the early history of the United States, permanent school funds were "wheel, ballast, and lever of the states' system of free schools."[11] Although these funds have dwindled into an insignificant part of the total school revenue, "they still exert, when properly and scientifically managed, a powerful influence for scientific organization and for the improvement of the educational standards."[12] In 1930 permanent school funds in the United States contributed only 1.1 per cent, the lease of school lands .2 per cent, and Federal aid .4 per cent of the total revenue of the public school system, while 94.5 per cent was derived from appropriations and taxation.[13] Forty-six states have permanent school funds totaling G$409,000,000, and 22 states have school lands (unsold) totaling 41,000,000 acres (or 272,000,000 Chinese mow) valued at G$446,700,000. It is primarily due to the development of industry and

---

[11] Swift, F. H., *Federal and State Policies in Public School Finance in the United States*, p. 68.
[12] *Ibid.*
[13] *Biennial Survey of Education*, 1928–30, p. 26 (published by the U. S. Office of Education).

How the Present Program Is Supported

commerce that intangible wealth has become increasingly important. Due to the growth of governmental functions, resulting in swollen tax receipts, the permanent school funds and lands in the United States have become more and more insignificant factors in school support in comparison with tax revenues.

School Lands

In 1644 China had 10,581 mow of government-owned school land. It increased to 388,678 mow in 1724, and to 1,158,615 mow in 1753, the last known figure on record. The distribution of government-owned school land is shown in Table 47.

TABLE 47

DISTRIBUTION OF GOVERNMENT-OWNED SCHOOL LAND, 1753

Province	Estimate* in Mow	Estimate** in Mow
Chihli (Hopei)	142,988	249,088
Kiangsu	41,858	4,858
Anhwei	22,018	18,387
Chekiang	30,017	
Kiangsi	6,800	6,735
Fukien	9,070	
Shantung	41,772	41,742
Shansi	27,798	
Honan	21,071	199,904
Shensi	5,220	5,520
Szechwan	2,300	22,300
Hupeh	1,257	12,057
Hunan	730,080	7,380
Kwangtung	15,116	15,117
Kwangsi	13,407	3,407
Yunnan	1,488	1,490
Kweichow	4,418	4,442
Kansu	31,125	25,524
Total	1,158,600?	?

*Chang, Hsiao Mien, *The Problem of Chinese Farm Land in the Different Dynasties*, pp. 303–04.
**Different figures given for the same year, as found in: Hsiao, Yi-shan, *General History of Manchu Dynasty*, Volume II, pp. 440–41; and in Chia, Sze-yi, *Financial History of Republican China*, Volume II, p. 226.

Discrepancies in data presented in Table 47 bear out the writer's statement at the beginning of this study regarding the neglect of accurate records on the part of writers in the past.

Up to the present, so far as can be determined, only Shantung Province has made a survey of school lands and funds.[14] In 1931, Shantung had 625,323 mow of school land and $1,457,298 invested in school funds. If the figure for 1753 (41,772 mow) is accurate, it means an increase of fifteen-fold in 179 years. For all China, school land has probably increased to at least 10,000,000 mow. According to Chen,[15] school land comprises 1.21 per cent of the total cultivated land of Kwanyun County, Kiangsu, and 3.78 per cent of the total cultivated land in Tsinan County, Shantung. In Yunnan Province, the income from school land constitutes 55 per cent of the total education fund.[16]

The importance of school land in agricultural China makes it imperative that all provincial and local governments make statistical surveys of the situation as soon as possible. These surveys should include a study of school funds as a lever to set the school system in motion.

In the United States, the total area of land made available for public schools from Federal land grants since 1785 is 154,314,185 acres (or 1,016,930,479 mow), of which about 42 per cent are swamp lands. Of this total, 77,510,737 acres (or 500,930,479 mow) of land other than swamp lands were specifically granted for the common schools.[17] To-day 41,000,000 acres remain unsold.

[14]The Shantung Department of Education, *A Survey of the Educational Funds and Property of the Counties of Shantung*, 1932. Table following p. 4479, Volume 4.
[15]Chen, Han-seng, *The Present Agrarian Problems of China*, p. 12.
[16]*The Nationalist Daily of Yunnan*, April 4, 1932.
[17]Swift, F. H., *Op. cit.*, pp. 20, 25, and 26.

How the Present Program Is Supported

The land situation in China is critical. The entire cultivated land area in China to-day, 1,248,781,000 mow, comprises only 10.3 per cent of the total land area.[18] The per capita area of cultivated land in China is only 3.65 mow, while in the United States it is 19.3 mow.[19] In view of the shortage of land, even after making allowance for maldistribution, it is evidently impossible for China to emulate the United States in the allocation of lands to schools. Nevertheless, according to the Ninth Report of the Ministry of Agriculture and Commerce,[20] China had 848,935,748 mow of waste land in 1918. This number increased to 1,177,340,261 mow for only 567 counties in 21 provinces reporting, August, 1929, to October, 1930.[21] If all the 1,770 counties had reported, the figure might not be far from 3,000,000,000 mow.

Can this waste land be turned into productive areas, and can at least one fourth to one third of it be granted to schools? This is a problem for the economist as well as for the educational statesman. In 1922, the government reported that there were 80,411,813 mow of forest land, of which 49,672,221 mow were owned by the government.[22] Since there are approximately 52,000,000 mow in the four lost provinces, there remain at least 30,000,000 mow available. Can part of this land be used in the establishment of schools of forestry? A careful study of the forest areas in Manchuria, made by Japan in 1930, revealed a total of 361,680,000 mow, or approximately seven times that of the Chinese report.[23] It

---

[18]Chang, C. C., *An Estimate of China's Farms and Crops*, Table 1, p. 11.
[19]According to D. K. Lieu, citing from *International Agricultural Statistics* for 1926. Cf. Table IX, p. 54, in *Chinese Economic Problems*.
[20]*Ninth Report of the Ministry of Agriculture and Commerce*, 1924.
[21]Ministry of Industry, *The Industrial Statistics*. Volume I, No. 1, Table on Waste Land, p. 12.
[22]*Seventh Report of the Ministry of Agriculture and Commerce.*
[23]*Shun Pao Year Book*, 1933, p. M262.

would seem, therefore, that a more accurate report would reveal the fact that there is more forest land in China to-day than has been reported. China can afford to use part of this area for schools. There have been precedents for such uses, as, for example, in the province of Kiangsu. It certainly challenges the talents of any Chinese Morrill to urge the government to make such grants for productive education, the dire need of China to-day.

The possibility of turning temple land into educational use will be discussed later.

Tuition Fees

In the United States in 1930, students' fees comprised 6.25 per cent[24] of the grand total income of both public and private education. In China, in 1909, students' fees comprised 10.01 per cent of the total educational revenue (see Table 43). Hsu Hsing-chen estimated the proportion of tuition paid by Chinese pupils and students, as shown in Table 48.

Hsu's proposal for the abolishment of student fees as a source of revenue was passed by the First National Conference on Education.[25] Kiangsu has taken the initiative in abolishing tuition charges in the secondary schools this year. In the financial plan for China's new educational program, this source of revenue should be eliminated and new sources, such as those suggested by Hsu, should be tapped to make up the loss. The reasons for this proposal are plain in a democratic country.

---

[24] U. S. Office of Education, *Biennial Survey of Education*, 1928–30, p. 10:

Note: Students' fees in the public school system constituted only 2.02 per cent of the total income of the public school system; see Table 6, Column 6, Row 6, and Column 9, Row 6.

[25] *Proceedings of the First National Conference on Education*, 1928, pp. 195–96.

TABLE 48

TUITION FEES PAID BY CHINESE STUDENTS, 1922-23, 1925-26

School Level	Enrollment 1922-23, 1925-26	Annual Tuition per Pupil	Total Tuition Paid	Total Expenditure
		$	$	$
1. Higher education	22,113	25	552,825	11,085,256
2. Secondary education	78,097	10	786,930	5,310,789
3. Higher elementary	582,479	3	1,747,337	10,089,731
4. Lower elementary	5,814,789	1	5,814,375	20,759,762
5. Industrial and vocational education	12,765	8	162,212	1,448,267
Total			$9,003,679	$48,643,805
Per cent that tuition is of total expenditure— 18.5 per cent				

From *Proceedings of the First National Conference on Education*, pp. 195-96.

Notes: 1. "Tuition rates from actual reports, personal investigation, and educational laws."

2. Enrollment on higher, secondary, and vocational level from 1925-26 excluding private school enrollment. The writer's figure for total educational expenditure, 1922-23, is $59,424,541.

Tax Sources of Educational Revenue of the Central and Provincial Governments

The Central Government

The Central Government in 1933-34 derived 42.8 per cent of its revenue from customs duty, 17.7 per cent from salt tax, 11.7 per cent from the consolidated taxes on rolled tobacco, flour, matches, cotton yarn, and cement, 4.4 per cent from tobacco and wine and stamp taxes, 3 per cent from miscellaneous revenues, 2 per cent from administrative fees and income from public property and public enterprises, and only .5 per cent from taxes on banks, stock exchange, and mines. There is a deficit of 17.9 per cent which usually has been met by borrowing. Thus, 93 per cent of the revenue budget, excluding the deficit, is dependent upon indirect taxation and less than 1 per cent on direct taxation (see Diagram 4).[26]

In the United States in 1930 the combined revenues of the federal, state, and local governments were derived from the following sources:[27]

General property tax	48.3 per cent	
Income tax	25.8 ,, ,,	
Inheritance and estate	2.5 ,, ,,	
Total Direct Taxation		76.6 per cent
Liquor and tobacco	4.5 per cent	
Customs duty	5.4 ,, ,,	
Motor vehicles, etc.	8.0 ,, ,,	
Total Indirect Taxation		17.9 per cent
Other Taxes	5.5 per cent	5.5 per cent
TOTAL	100.0 per cent	100.0 per cent

It is evident that direct taxation produces more than three fourths of the combined revenues in the United States. It is usual in China to criticize the injustice of the American economic system; yet America's tax system is far superior to that of China in the application of the principle of ability to pay.

In 1931–32, 85.9 per cent of the central educational budget[28] was provided by appropriation or tax resources. It follows that the money paid to education under the central government comes almost entirely from the

---

[26]Chang Jo-jen, "Chinese Public Finance in 1933." *Chinese Economy* (monthly), Volume II, No. 1, p. 4. See Central budget for 1933–34 and Unpublished Document No. 16.

[27]*Recent Social Trends in the United States.* Report of the President's Committee on Social Trends, 1933. Volume II, p. 1365.

[28]Unpublished Document No. 15 and Directorate of Budget and Statistics, *The Revenue and Expenditure Budget of the National Government of the Republic of China,* 1931–32, pp. 9–11, "The Revenues of the Ministry of Education." *Note:* $3,396,193, or 14.1 per cent, of its budget was provided by the proceeds from property, tuition, etc.

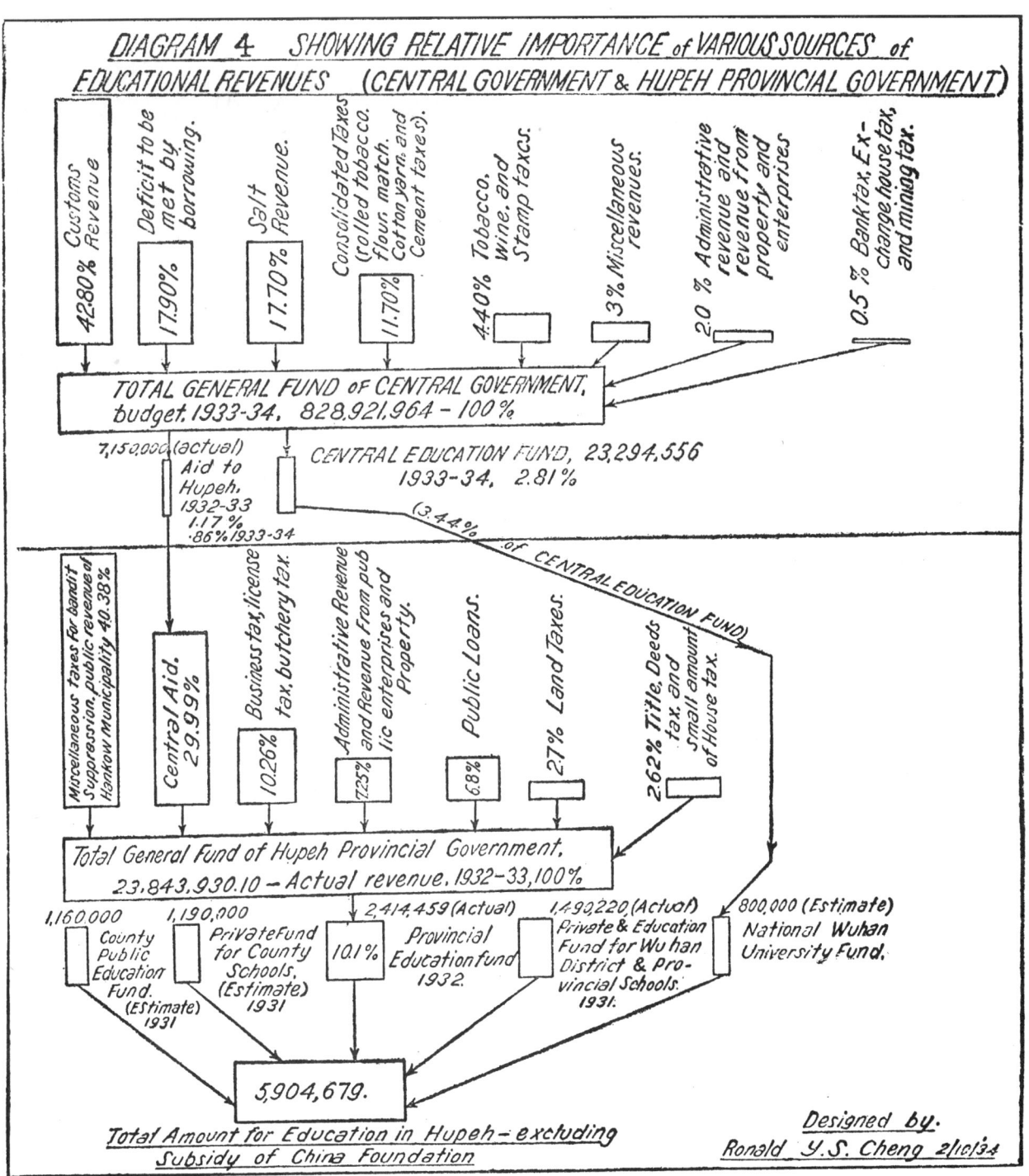

Sources of Data: 1. Central budget, see "Chinese Public Finance in 1933." *Chinese Economy* (monthly), Volume 2, No. 1, p. 4. Central Budget for the fiscal year, 1933–34.
2. Hupeh Provincial Budget, See Hupeh Department of Finance, *Financial Report*, March to June, 1933, Appendix.

pockets of the poor classes of the population. This fact has been indicated in an address of Dr. Ma Yin-chu, on "The Relationship of Economics and Education," delivered at Wuchang Normal University on August 23, 1924. He says:

"We therefore know that all the money is in the hands of the wealthy. In foreign countries, the wealthy people pay money to [educate] the poor. Only in China, the poor people pay money to [educate] the wealthy...."[29]

To remedy the situation is the task not only of educators. The National Finance Conference in 1928 proposed the levying of income taxes, inheritance taxes, corporation taxes, and the like, for central governmental revenue. In June, 1933, the Minister of Education proposed the use of the inheritance tax to provide fiscal independence in central education. When will these proposals be put into practice?

The Provincial Governments

There are two types of sources of educational revenue on the provincial level: (*a*) provincial tax and non-tax sources that yield enough income to make possible significant educational appropriations out of the provincial government general funds; and (*b*) provincial and national taxes, the proceeds of which are definitely earmarked or allocated in whole or in part to public education under the control of the provincial government. Time does not permit the writer to calculate the amount and the proportion of each type of revenue or tax for each province and for all provinces so as to determine exactly which contributes most to the indirect support of education. With some actual data and budgets available, he has ranked the types of revenue in

---

[29] Ma Yin-chu's *Lectures*, 1928 edition, Volume II, p. 193.

each province or municipality in order of their importance in amount of yield, in Table 49.

TABLE 49

SOURCES OF REVENUE SUPPORTING EDUCATION INDIRECTLY UNDER THE APPROPRIATION POLICY, IN ORDER OF THEIR IMPORTANCE IN THE PROVINCES AND SPECIAL MUNICIPALITIES, 1931–32

Provinces and Special Municipalities Collecting the Revenue	Tax Sources									Non-Tax Sources						
	Land Tax	Title Deeds Tax	Business or Sales Tax	Business Brokerage Tax	Butchery Tax	Pawnshop Tax	Interior Fishery Tax	House Tax	Ship Tax	Government Enterprises	Government Property	Administrative Receipts	Government Institution Receipts	Central Aid	Public Loans	Miscellaneous & Unclassified Tax Revenues
A																
Kiangsu	1	10	5					7		8	11	6	9	4	2	3
Chekiang	3	5	4							8	10	7	9	6	1	2
Anhwei	1	8	4							5	6	7	9		3	2
Hopei	1	4	2						7		6			5	8	3
Honan	1		4							6	7		8	5	3	2
Shantung	1	2	3							6	7	5	8			4
Hupeh	5	6	4					8		7	9	10		2	1	3
Hunan	2	3	5					6	8	10	9	7	11	4		1
Ninghsia	1		3													2
B																
Shensi	2	5	4							6	7	8	9		1	3
Yunnan	2	7			3	7				5	6	8		1		4
Kweichow	2	3		6	4									1		5
Shansi	1	3		4	5	8				7	9					2
Kwangtung	2	3	5		4	7				6						1
Kwangsi	2	4			3	5										1
Fukien	2	4		5	3	6										1
Sinkiang	1									4		3				2
Szechwan	1	2		4		5										3
Chahar	1	6	5	2	3	9				8	7					4
Shanghai	5	4	9			10			1	7	6	2	8			3
Nanking		6	4	11	9	12	10		5	13		1	7	8	3	3	2
Peiping	5											3	2		4		1
Tsingtao											1				3		2

Sources: A, Actual reports. *Statistical Monthly,* March and April, 1933, No. 10, Table on Revenues and Expenditures of the Provincial Treasuries, 1931–32.

B. *Budgets of the Provinces and Special Municipalities for the Fiscal Year 1931-32.* Published by the Directorate of Budget and Statistics, Nanking, 1932.

The rolled tobacco surtax and salt surtax of Yunnan and the salt merchant tax of Kweichow are classified under central aid. The revenue from cart tax of Shansi ranks No. 6. Those provinces and municipalities without comparable classification of revenues are omitted.

Table 49 shows that the provinces are largely supported by the land tax, miscellaneous and unclassified tax revenues, public loans, central aid, title deeds tax, and business taxes. Besides the insignificant amounts of house tax, land tax is the only direct tax. Although land tax ranks first or second among the different types of revenue in nearly all the provinces, it is but a small percentage of the total revenue in many. It carries with it multifarious surtaxes in the local districts, and burdens the poor farmers beyond endurance. The landlords can shift much of the burden to the tenants through high rents. Central aid is given to 11 provinces and municipalities, not because of any progressive step taken by the national government but to make up the losses incurred due to the abolishing of likin or octroi and the taking over of certain taxes by the national government. The increasing use of public loans indicates that the provincial governments are facing large deficits. Other nontax sources do not yield significant amounts except in one or two cases. Thus it is seen that education is financed largely by indirect taxation, the burden of which falls heavily and almost entirely upon the poor classes of the population. Such an antiquated and unjust tax system should be reformed at once.

Under the allocation or independence policies, there are ten taxes definitely earmarked in whole or in part for education. These are in effect severally in 10 provinces and in proposal in 2 provinces. Another tax, the house tax, has been proposed recently to provide fiscal independence in Nanking and Hankow. Of these taxes, three are national taxes, namely, rolled tobacco tax, wine and tobacco tax, and salt tax, and are collected by the central tax agencies within the provinces concerned and the allocated proceeds are paid directly to the educational finance administration. The allocation policy under the provincial government has a history of not more than ten years. The amount of yield of each earmarked tax ranges from $200,000 to $2,400,000, but ten of them each reaches more than $1,000,000. It is evident that the yield can barely support the present educational program in some provinces, and is insufficient in many, needing to be supplemented by appropriation from the provincial treasury. Any expansion of the program requires additional earmarked sources, an increasing proportion of the allocated proceeds of the present tax, or an increase in the tax rate. All these measures involve direct conflict with the legislative and fiscal authorities of the provincial and the national governments. Tax rates are already very high, and the raising of the rate of educational tax alone cannot be secured separately.

TAX AND NONTAX REVENUE

Sources of County Education Revenue

All of the 1,770 counties are required to maintain public schools. Usually each county is divided into several school districts, which in turn support their own local schools. As these local units bear an increasing share of the total burden of school support in China, it is imperative that school administrators know where the school moneys come from, how they are collected, and the extent and distribution of the burden upon the different classes of the population as well as upon the different administrative units. This information is necessary in order that inequalities may be discovered

TABLE 50

EARMARKED TAX SOURCES OF EDUCATIONAL REVENUE UNDER THE ALLOCATION AND INDEPENDENCE POLICIES

Name of Tax	Province or Municipality Levying (1)	Beginning Year (2)	Partly or Completely Earmarked (3)	Estimated Annual Yield (4)	Remarks (5)
A. Provincial Taxes					
1. Grain tribute surtax	Kiangsu	1925	C	$1,470,000	$1 per tan
	Kiangsu	1933	Additional		$0.20 per tan
2. Land tax	Kiangsu	1927	P	1,800,000	
	Anhwei	1931	P		
3. Butchery tax	Kiangsu	1925	C	600,000	$.30 and .40 per head
	Chekiang	1933	C	600,000	
4. Business brokerage tax	Kiangsu	1925	C	600,000	
5. Title deeds tax	Honan	1923	C	1,493,060	(1928) Actual amount
6. Sacrificial metallic paper sales tax	Chekiang	1933	C	1,200,000	
7. Livestock tax	Kansu	? 1928			Status unknown to writer
8. House tax	Nanking	Proposed			
	Hankow	Proposed			
B. National Taxes					
9. Rolled tobacco	Yunnan	1928–29		800,000?	⎧ Present status
a. Special tax	Kansu	? 1928			⎨ unknown to
b. Business license	Anhwei	1928		1,200,000	⎩ writer Central aid
10. Wine and tobacco surtax	Chekiang	1933	C	200,000	
11. Salt surtax	Fukien	1928	P	1,750,000	
	Kiangsi	1927	P	2,140,000	
	Hunan	1928	P	1,100,000	$.80 per bale
	Hunan	Proposed	P	2,316,000	$2.30 per bale
	Hupeh	Proposed	P	2,400,000	
	Shensi	1931	P	600,000?	

Sources: 1. Kiangsu Provincial Department of Education, *Recent Educational Conditions in Kiangsu Province*, 1930, Appendix, p. 1.
2. *Education Weekly* of the Fukien Department of Education, No. 10, December 11, 1928. Special Issue on Educational Fiscal Independence.
3. *Special Bulletin on Education Funds and Property in Honan.* Office of Education Funds and Property Administration in Honan, 1930.
4. *One Year of Education in Anhwei Province.* The Anhwei Provincial Department of Education, 1930, pp. 3–4.
5. *The Political Year Book of Hunan Province*, 1930.
6. *Statistical Monthly*, Volume I, No. 10, December, 1929. Table on Educational Finance in 12 Provinces.
7. Liu, Nai Chien, "Educational Fiscal Independence in the Provinces and Municipalities." *Current Events Monthly*, Volume X, No. 2, February, 1934, pp. 64–65.
8. News in *Shun Pao*, December 29, 1933.
9. Correspondence with the Shensi Department of Education.

and the possibility of raising more money for the expansion of the educational program may be investigated.

Complete data concerning county sources of education revenue are not available. Data concerning the local school districts are rarely available. The best that can be done is to make a sampling study of the counties in five selected provinces: Hupeh, with 68 counties; Hunan, with 76 counties; Shantung, with 108 counties; Honan, with 110 counties; and Kiangsu, with 61 counties—a total of 423 counties in all. The data for Hupeh and Hunan are derived from the items given in the county government budgets.[30] The data for Kiangsu are found in direct narrative in the Commissioner's report and in a pamphlet.[31] The data for Shantung and Honan are found in the county education budgets.[32]

Only Shantung Province has some sort of a uniform classification of revenues, as follows:

[30]Hupeh Department of Finance, *The Revenue and Expenditure Budgets of the County Local Governments of Hupeh Province for the Fiscal Year, 1932–33;* Secretariat, Hunan Provincial Government, *The Political Year Book of Hunan Province*, 1930.

[31]See Table 50, Source No. 1, and Kan, Yu Yuan, *County Education Finance in Kiangsu.*

[32]County Local Education Budgets in Shantung for the Fiscal Year, 1932–33; Honan Department of Education, *Honan Educational Year Book*, 1930, Section B, pp. 1–510.

How the Present Program Is Supported

1. Ordinary Revenue.
    a. Surtaxes (of provincial land taxes).
        (1) Capitation-silver surtax.
        (2) Tribute-rice surtax.
    b. Rent.
        (1) School land annual rent.
        (2) Building and site annual rent.
    c. Interest (all types of school funds).
    d. Miscellaneous items of revenue (including sales taxes, commodity taxes, fees, etc.).
2. Extraordinary revenue (including, sometimes, appropriations, subsidy, loans, balance from previous year, etc.).

The proportion of each source of revenue in all counties of Shantung for the year 1932–33 is shown in Table 51.

TABLE 51

SOURCES OF COUNTY EDUCATION REVENUE IN SHANTUNG PROVINCE, 1932–33

Source	Proportion		Tax Burden	
	Amount	Per Cent	Amount	Per Cent
Surtaxes	$3,335,226	75.2	$3,335,226	88.67
Rent	461,036	10.8		
Interest	186,974	4.4		
Miscellaneous items	374,232	8.7	374,232	10.29
Balance	16,449	.4	16,449	.45
Grants-in-aid	16,942	.4	16,942	.47
Other revenue	4,466	.1	4,466	.12
Total	$4,285,325	100.0	$3,637,315	100.00

Adapted from Table opposite page 1128 of the budgets.
Source No. 14 of this chapter, p. 114.

The proportion of each source of revenue in all counties of Kiangsu for the year 1927–28 (actual) is shown in Table 52.

TABLE 52

SOURCES OF COUNTY EDUCATION REVENUE IN KIANGSU PROVINCE, 1927-28

Source	Proportion		Tax Burden	
	Amount	Per Cent	Amount	Per Cent
Land surtaxes	$ 3,401,494	59.6	$ 3,401,494	75.5
Rent and interest	727,037	12.7		
Tuition	465,672	8.2		
Title deeds surtax	352,367	6.2	352,367	7.8
Sales and commodity taxes	429,901	7.5	429,901	9.5
Petty taxes and miscellaneous	326,420	5.8	326,420	7.2
Total	$5,702,891	100.0	$4,510,182	100.0

Adapted; see Table 50, Source (1).

The writer has calculated similar data for 58 counties of Hupeh on the basis of the 1932-33 budget, as shown in the Table 53.

From Tables 51, 52, and 53 it is evident that the land tax is the most important single source of county school revenue. The next sources in order of importance are (1) school property and funds, which contribute about 13 to 19 per cent of the total education revenue, and (2) title deeds in Hupeh Province and tuition in Kiangsu. Kiangsu has abolished tuition in the secondary schools. Recently the sales and commodity taxes have supplied 7.5, 8.7, and 15.4 per cent of the total revenue in Kiangsu, Shantung, and Hupeh, respectively; of the total tax revenue, these taxes bear 10 to 20 per cent of the burden. The land tax supplies, on the average, more than 50 per cent of the total revenue, reaching 75.2 per cent in the case of Shantung. Of the total tax revenue, however, the land tax bears 56.9, 75.5, and 88.67, respectively,

TABLE 53

SOURCES OF EDUCATIONAL REVENUE IN 58 COUNTIES OF HUPEH PROVINCE, 1932–33

Source	Proportion		Tax Burden
	Amount	Per Cent	Per Cent
Land surtax	$ 531,800	45.0	56.9
Land-capitation.	386,360		
Grain-tribute	112,010		
Land tax certificate	20,209		
Military settlement	12,486		
Land rent	735		
School lands and funds	225,139	18.9	
Title deeds surtax	220,096	18.5	23.5
Business and sales taxes	183,288	15.4	19.6
Butchery surtax	96,056		
Short-term brokerage license. . . .	13,033.3		
Miscellaneous petty commodity taxes.	74,199		
Unaccounted for (appropriation?) . .	32,570.74	2.7	
Total	$1,192,894	100.0	100.0 ($935,184)

Cf. Table 57 and Diagram 5. See sources listed therein.

of the burden in the three provinces. Obviously, the farmers bear this proportion of the burden. Since the introduction of the eight-cent mow tax on lnad for obligatory education in Kiangsu, the farmers of that province must have berne at least 80 per cent of the tax burden for education. Since nearly all sales and commodity taxes are levied upon necessities, and their burden rests upon the consumers in the long run, it follows that at least 80 to 85 per cent of the total county public education burden is borne by the laboring population, and especially by the poorer classes of the farmers and workers.

Detailed Analysis of County Sources of Education Revenue

For convenience in this study, an attempt has been made to classify a little more rationally the various types of sources of school revenue and the numerous petty school taxes in the counties of the five provinces mentioned and in certain local school districts of Honan and Hunan. Data concerning 670 sources and taxes were collected and sorted. It was found that for each type of tax there were sometimes more than ten names actually in use, varying according to time of collection, kind of levy, nature of base, origin, purpose and proportion of levy, and so forth. The major or significant types of sources mentioned previously in this study appear in almost every county. Petty taxes are levied severally; each county levies one or more of these petty taxes, which often differ from those levied in other counties. Each petty tax name occurs infrequently, and, since space does not allow a tabulation of all of them, they are presented briefly in the Tables 54, 55, and 56.

A CASE STUDY OF THE COUNTY SOURCES OF EDUCATIONAL REVENUE IN HUPEH PROVINCE

County education in Hupeh Province is financed by partly allocated local taxes with specified tax rates. A detailed analysis of the sources of school revenue of each county, the tax rates and school tax rates, the ratio of the two, the amount of yield, and the proportion of yield for education, is presented in Table 57, and is graphically presented in the accompanying Diagram 5.

TABLE 54
A GENERAL CALSSIFICATION OF SOURCES OF COUNTY AND LOCAL EDUCATIONAL REVENUE IN HUPEH, HUNAN, HONAN, SHANTUNG, AND KIANGSU PROVINCES

Sources	Brief Description		
	Importance of Yield	Characteristics	Trend
I. Nontax Sources			
1. Rent of school land and property	Second and third in importance. Appears in almost all counties.	Stable but liable to mismanagement.	Decreasing importance as school costs rise, as in U. S.
2. Interest on school funds	Far lower yield than school property rent.	Very stable income but liable to loss.	As above. Will be specific in purpose.
3. Tuition	Yield significant. 5–10 per cent of total revenue.	Indefensible in principle.	Tends to be abolished or decreased.
4. Grant-in-aid	Insignificant, piecemeal and intermittent.	Very defensible for equalization. Actually much used for reward.	Tends to increase.
5. **Private** contributions	Very insignificant and rare for public schools. Frequent for private schools.	Both in property and funds. Needs constant encouragement and solicitation.	Gifts to private rather than public schools.
6. Sales proceeds	Very insignificant and rare.	Only the sale of property or products directly owned by students.	Tends to emphasize products made by students.
7. Loans	Only 4 cases. Amount very small.	Borrowing for current expenses not a good policy.	Some outlook in bonding for buildings.
8. Other nontax revenues (balance, fine, diversion)	All very rare.	Unpredictable and unreliable as sources.	Tends to stress reserve rather than balance.

TABLE 54 (*Continued*)

Sources	Brief Description		
	Subject of Tax	Object or Base of Tax	Burden or Incidence of Tax
II. *Tax Sources*			
1. Land surtax	Landowners or farmers.	Original quota in taels based upon size of farm land or amount of product.	All farmers, but largely small owners and tenants.
2. Direct taxes other than land	Wealthier classes of population, urban rather than rural.	Value of property, total wealth, etc.	Probably the wealthier classes of the population.
3. Contract surtax (transfer of realty through sale and mortgage) or Title Deeds Surtax	Buyers of realty or mortgagees. Propertied class in general.	Value of realty, mostly land, bought or acquired by mortgage.	Largely sellers or mortgagors, according to Seligman.
4. Business and sales tax and surtaxes	Business men— dealer, agent, or broker.	Value of sales of goods and services.	Partly business men and partly consumers (see Buehler, p. 17).*
5. Consumption and commodity taxes a. Taxes on necessities	Sellers of commodities and merchants.	Weight, quantity, or volume and sometimes value of commodities or necessities sold.	General consumers largely on the low income level.
6. b. Superstition taxes	Sellers or merchants.	Commodities and services of superstitious nature.	All superstitious people buying them.
7. c. Luxury taxes (applies to rural China mostly)	Sellers or merchants.	Commodities and services of luxury.	People who pay the price, mostly the wealthy but sometimes the less well-to-do.

*See Secondary Source No. 10, in Bibliography on p. 273.

TABLE 55

FREQUENCY OF EACH TYPE OF REVENUE IN COUNTIES OF HUPEH, HUNAN, HONAN, SHANTUNG, AND KIANGSU, AND IN CERTAIN LOCAL SCHOOL DISTRICTS OF HONAN AND HUNAN

Sources	Frequency of Occurrence				
	Hupeh 1932–33 (1)	Hunan 1930 (2)	Honan 1930 (3)	Shantung 1932–33 (4)	Kiangsu 1928 (5)
I. Nontax sources					
1. Rent of school land and property	49	78	156	108	110
2. Interest on school funds	6	5	62	101	17
3. Other non-tax sources	?	8?	63	99	34*
II. Tax sources					
1. Land surtax	56	132	110	124	179
2. Direct taxes other than land tax	?	11	11	4	3
3. Contract surtax or title deeds surtax	52	37	110	102	129
4. Business and sales taxes:					
a. General	55	2?	14	43	55
b. Food and related taxes	?	42	29	104	50
c. Clothing, housing, etc.	?	1	5	12	2
d. Other commodities and services	?	3	9	16	3
5. Consumption-commodity taxes:					
a. General	?	4	1	?	1
b. Food and related commodities	?	37	29	27	14
c. Clothing, etc.	?	4	16	20	4
d. Housing, etc.	?	12	19	14	4
e. Communication, etc.	?		12	10	10
f. Other commodities and services	?	4	7	44	2
g. Superstition taxes	?	6	13	15	2
h. Luxury taxes	?	2	33	27	4
General inclusive names with subject and object of tax not specified	?	4	20	19	1

*Tuition.

(1) Refers to numbers of counties only; there are little or no data on petty commodity taxes.

(5) Concerning commodity taxes, the numbers refer to numbers of the kinds of taxes, and not to the number of cases nor the number of counties.

TABLE 56
TYPES AND NAMES OF SOURCES OF REVENUE FURTHER CLASSIFIED

Sources and Types of Derivation	Examples of Names in Actual Use	No. of Names Actually Given to One Type
I. Nontax Sources		
1. Rent from school land and property:		
a. General	Revenue from educational property	5
b. Farm land	School grain rent	20
c. Swamp and waste	Swamp land rent; waste land rent	6
d. Auxiliary land	Pond rent; dike rent	6
e. Origin, donation, confiscation, etc	Temple land rent; Confucian memorial land; rebel property rent	22
f. Produce	Reed rent; hemp rent	7
g. Location	Lakeside farm land rent	6
h. Ownership	Local district school land rent	6
i. Building and site	House rent; site rent	7
2. Interest on school funds		
a. General	School fund interest	14
b. Purpose	Obligatory education foundation interest	12
c. Kind of investment	Government bonds	7
d. Depository	Pawnshop interest	3
e. Origin of fund	Old-style college foundation interest	19
3. Tuition		
a. School organization	High school tuition	3
4. Grant-in-aid		
a. Source of aid	Appropriation by finance bureau	9
5. Private contribution		
a. Kind of contributors	Private individual voluntary contribution	8
6. Proceeds from sales		
a. Kinds of property sold	Sale of sacrificial offerings	12
7. Loans	Loan from permanent fund	4
8. Other non-tax sources		
a. Fine	Fine upon old-style tutorial school	4
b. Balance	Surplus from previous year	3
c. Diversion	35 per cent self-government corps tax diverted to education	2

TABLE 56 (*Continued*)

Sources and Types of Derivation	Examples of Names in Actual Use	No. of Names Actually Given to One Type
II. Tax Sources		
1. Land surtax		
a. General	Capitation and grain tribute surtax; mow tax	12
b. Capitation or poll	Land capitation surtax	6
c. Grain tribute	Tribute rice surtax; Tsao rice surtax	10
d. Specific purposes	Obligatory education mow tax	15
e. Specified rates	Thirty-cent capitation land surtax	3
f. Military land	Military land surtax	4
g. Government land	Land rent	5
h. Waste and swamp land	Waste land surtax	7
i. Tax certificate	Land tax certificate fee	4
j. Delinquency	Land tax delinquency fine	6
2. Direct taxes other than land tax		
a. Wealthy people	Gentry and wealthy people tax	4
b. Realty	House tax (urban)	7
c. Poll	Buddhist monk tax; Japs tax	2
3. Contract surtax (on transfer of property through sale and mortgage)		
a. General	Title deeds surtax	9
b. Specified purpose	Title deeds education tax; one-cent title deeds tax	11
c. Title deeds paper	Title deeds paper tax	4
d. Middleman	Middleman fee	3
e. Other fees	Title deeds inspection levy	2
4. Business and sales tax (general and selective)		
a. General	Brokerage license tax; agent tax; shop tax; guild tax	30
b. Food and related commodity sales	Butchery surtax; poultry agent tax; fish dealer tax; grain dealer tax; fruit market tax; brewery tax; oil dealer tax, etc.	74
c. Clothing, housing, and related commodities	Silk brokerage tax; cotton agent tax; coal firm tax; etc.	14
d. Other commodities and services	Pawnshop tax; hotel tax; ship agent tax	16

TABLE 56 (*Continued*)

Sources and Types of Derivation	Examples of Names in Actual Use	No. of Names Actually Given to One Type
5. Consumption or commodity taxes		
a. General	All commodities tax (Pei ho chuan); production tax	3
b. Food and related taxes	Taxes on swine, pork, beef and mutton, poultry and duck, fish, eggs, grain, rice, beans, bushel, sesamum, flour, cabbage, onion, dried lily-flour, peanuts, dates, persimmons, betel nuts, melon seeds, tobacco, wine, tea, herbs, sugar, salt, oil, etc.	61
6. Other commodities and services	Confucian memorial service charge; foreign goods tax; oil cake tax; pond tax; saltpeter tax; forestry public benefit tax; mountain products school tax; also taxes on cotton gin, hoof and horn, intestines, rope for cows, etc.	17
7. Superstition taxes	Temple ceremony tax; ancestral shrine society tax; religious festival tax; All Souls Day festival tax; paper horse tax; sacrificial tin-paper tax, etc.	13
8. Luxury taxes (relative in China only)	Feast; theatrical play tax; silk fabrics tax; "happiness" tax; marriage permit tax; petition tax; electric light tax, etc.	10
A. General inclusive names with subject and base not specified	Special tax; public benefit tax, etc.	16
B. Tax names unknown to writer		54
Total number of names		670

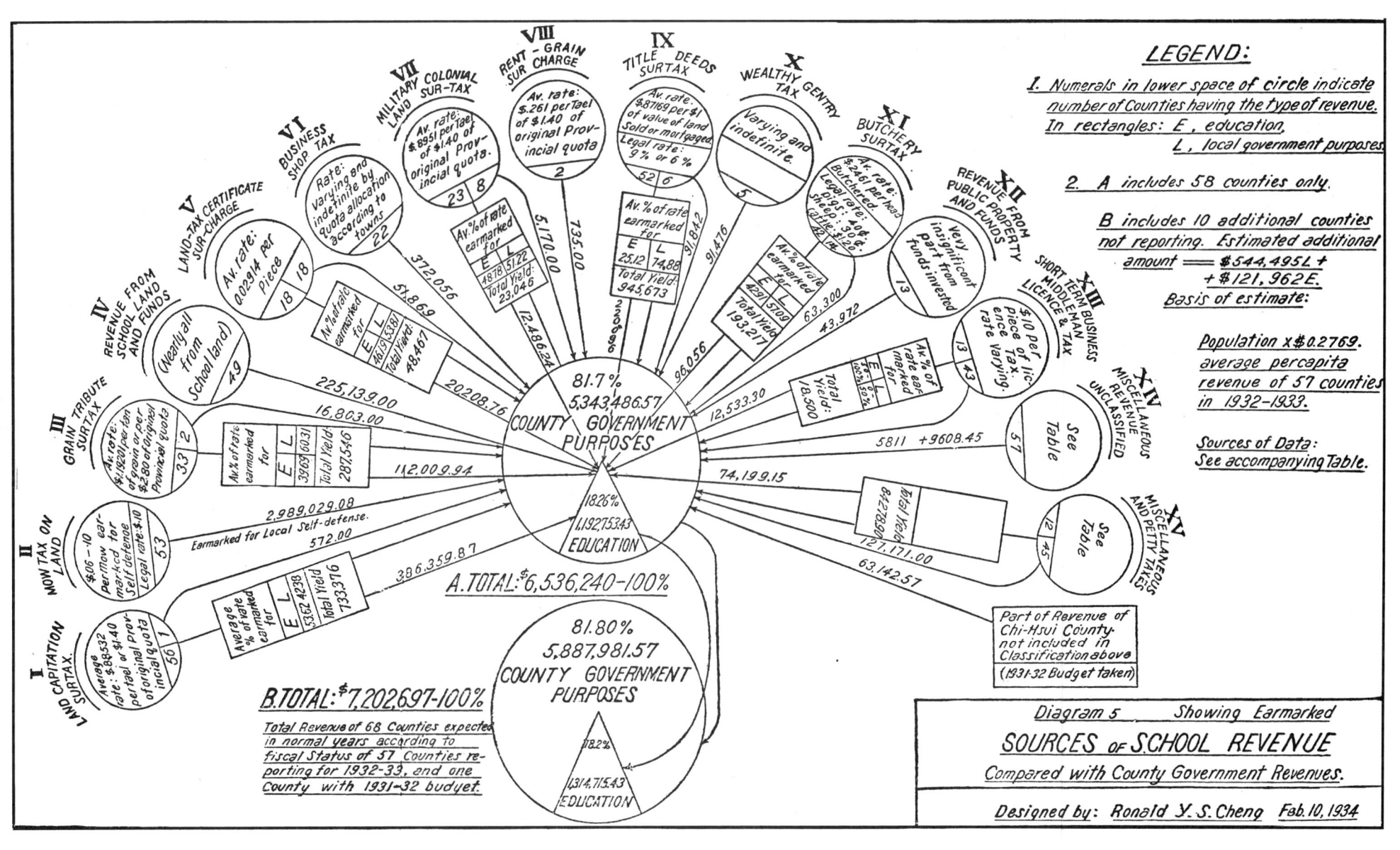

How the Present Program Is Supported 135

Important Observations from Table 57 and Diagram 5:

1. The proportion of different sources of school revenue, only 18.9 per cent of which is from school lands and funds (see Table 53).

2. *School tax burden.* The farmers bear 56.9 per cent of the burden through land tax, while the owners of land and property at the time of sale and mortgage bear 23.9 per cent. In other words, 80.4 per cent of the burden is borne by the farmers directly. Only 15.4 per cent is borne by business, the burden of which in the long run falls on the consumer.

3. Out of 58 counties, 49 have income from school lands, a few of which derive an income from school funds. Fifty-six of the counties allocate the land surtax partially for education; 52 allocate the contract tax or title deeds tax; 42, the butchery tax; 13, the short-term business license tax. The mow tax on land earmarked for local self-defense yields the largest amount and may be devoted to school uses when peace and order are restored. Only 22 counties levy business shop taxes and 5 wealthy gentry taxes, and these not for education.

The miscellaneous petty taxes for education not specified in the table or diagram include fish tax, ship tax, steamship ticket tax, coal tax, paper mill tax, tea tax, hemp tax, cotton tax, lime tax, cement tax, cart tax, native sugar mill tax, peanut tax, oil tax, theater tax, broker tax, mountain products tax, fungus tax, peach seed tax, wine and tobacco tax, imported yarn tax, white cloth tax, kiln tax, bean flour mill tax, cotton gin tax, tobacco leaf tax, brewery tax, temple offerings tax, house tax, fuel tax, salt tax, ox tax, calendar copyright tax, bamboo and wood tax, cattle and horse stable tax, hides tax, meat tax, lumber tax, export tax, and miscellaneous grain taxes. These are levied severally by 33 counties. The Department of Education classifies all these under the item of "miscellaneous taxes." This item in 1932 yielded from $156 in Yang-hsing County to $13,800 in Chi-chuen County. In 15 counties it yields less than $1,000; in 24 counties the yield is less than $2,000.[33]

4. *The tax rates.* Both the local tax rates and the school tax rates vary widely in the different counties. In the case of the land capitation surtax, although no county levied a total surtax higher than the regular provincial tax quota, which is one tael or $1.40 as specified by law, the diversification of the rates carried over to the absurdity of the fourth decimal point does not necessarily conform to the ability and need of the respective counties. The principle of diversification operates at a too great expense of the principle of economy of operation. These rates probably arise arbitrarily from the rule of thumb. The original land tax rates themselves do not conform to the ability to pay. A careful examination of this table and of Table 90, Column 18, will throw light upon this contention.

The ratio of school tax rate to total local tax rate in the case of land capitation surtax varies from 27.16 per cent to 100 per cent. This variation serves merely to complicate the situation.

All other allocated school surtaxes show the same condition of diversification of rates. Since the yield from many of these surtaxes is not great for education, such complications cause an unnecessarily high cost of collection.

---

[33]Hupeh Department of Education, *Hupeh Education Status and Statistics for the Year 1933*. Wuchang, January, 1934, pp. 5–11.

CHAPTER VIII

THE FINANCIAL IMPLICATIONS OF THE NEW EDUCATIONAL POLICY

"The essentials of governmental function are education and nourishment."[1] This statement constitutes the first point of emphasis in the outline of national reconstruction of Sun Yat-sen, the founder of the Chinese Republic. Since the unification of China under the Nationalist Government, numerous resolutions have been adopted by the Kuomintang concerning the reorganization of the educational system. Two national conferences have been called to redirect the educational program in terms of Chinese social, economic, and culture needs.

The new aim of education was outlined by the First National Conference on Education in 1928, as follows:[2]

"(1) To promote nationalism, education shall seek to instill into the minds of youth a national spirit, to keep alive the old cultural traditions, to raise the general level of moral integrity and physical vigor, to spread modern scientific knowledge, and to cultivate æsthetic tastes.

"(2) To attain democracy, education shall seek to inculcate such civic virtues as law-abidingness and loyalty, to teach organizing ability and a spirit of service and coöperation, to disseminate political knowledge, and to inform the people of the true meaning of liberty and equality; and

"(3) To realize social justice, education shall seek to develop the habits of manual labour and productive skill, to teach the

[1] *Central Party Affairs Monthly*, No. 40, November, 1931, pp. 2479 *sqq.* As quoted from one of Dr. Sun's lectures. See also *The First Education Year Book of China*, 1934, Section A, p. 15, "A Bill Concerning the Ascertaining of the Policy of Execution of the Educational Program According to Provisions of the Provisional Constitution."
[2] Tyau, M. T. Z., *Two Years of Nationalist China*.

application of science to everyday life, and to enlighten the people on the interdependence and harmony of economic interests of various classes."

This aim was restated by the Third National Party Congress in its eleventh session in March, 1929. It reads as follows:

"Based upon the 'Three Principles of the People,' the aim of education of the Republic of China is to enrich the life of the people, implant the existence of society, develop the economic well-being of the citizens, and perpetuate the life of the nation with a persistent end in view in the attainment of national independence, universal democracy, and economic development so as to promote cosmopolitanism."[3]

To realize this aim, a set of principles governing the execution of the entire educational program was formulated by the Third Session of the Central Executive Committee on September 3, 1931.[4] The scope, objectives, content, and method of all types and levels of educational institutions were thus clearly defined.

The Expansion of the Educational Program

From Diagram 2 it may be seen that 38,258,767 more children of school age should be placed in school, and 234,873,517 youths and adults should be taught to read and write. Excluding a population of 29,437,719 with an enrollment of 797,406 in all schools in the four lost provinces pending their restoration, the present task is to provide educational opportunities for 37,762,699 more children of school age and 223,926,758 illiterates.[5] It is the determined policy of the National Government to

[3] *The First Education Year Book of China*, 1934, Section A, p. 8, "The Aim of Education of the Republic of China," promulgated by the National Government on April 26, 1929.
[4] *Ibid.*, Section A, pp. 17–22, "Principles Governing the Execution of the Educational Program According to the Three Principles of the People," passed by the 157th conference of the Central Executive Committee.
[5] Unpublished Document No. 13.

effect these changes. Furthermore, improvement of the content and methods of the present educational program is needed. The Second National Conference on Education in 1930 outlined a comprehensive plan of expansion and improvement.

Summary of the Educational Plans:[6]
(1) A twenty-year plan of obligatory education for 40,000,000 children of school age, giving each four years of schooling. A five-year plan for training 1,400,000 teachers and providing 1,000,000 classrooms.

(2) A six-year plan for adult continuation education for the elimination of the illiteracy of 202,435,277 persons, aged 12 to 50, the training of 135,000 teachers for this purpose, and the provision of 112,447 classrooms.

(3) The reorganization and improvement of elementary education.

(4) The reorganization and improvement of secondary education, and a gradual increase in the number of senior, junior, and vocational high schools.

(5) The reorganization and improvement of higher education.

(6) The reorganization and improvement of social education, including development of libraries, museums, art galleries, playgrounds, mass education centers and schools, vocational continuation schools, special education, reformatories, and popular recreation.

(7) The reorganization and improvement of Overseas Chinese education.

(8) A plan for the education of the Mongolians and Tibetans.

The Financial Implications of the Plan

The proposed program of expansion and improvement entails enormous capital outlay and provision for current expenses. The Second National Conference on Education approved an estimate of these costs.[7] Table 58 gives

[6]*Proceedings of the Second National Conference on Education*, Section III, pp. 1–74.
[7]This estimate was originally made by the Commission on the Construction of Educational Plans and passed by the Central Political Council before it was discussed by the Second National Conference on Education, *Ibid.*, Section II, p. 20.

the total estimated cost for a twenty-year period as approximately $5,660,000,000, or an average of $282,500,000 per year in round numbers. However, the amounts are so graduated that they are small during the initial years of the enterprise, and gradually increase up to the twentieth year. The cost of the twenty-year plan for obligatory education and the five-year plan for teacher training is estimated at $3,986,000,000. The cost of the six-year plan for adult continuation education for the elimination of illiteracy is estimated to be $339,500,000. The total annual salary increases of elementary school teachers for the twenty-year period are $265,000,000. The expansion of secondary schools over a twenty-year period requires an estimated expenditure of $205,494,000. The estimated requirement for higher education is $30,000,000; for social education, $805,984,000; for overseas Chinese education, $13,000,000; for the Mongolian and Tibetan educational programs, $17,695,000.

Table 58 A shows that the Central Government is expected to spend, in round numbers for the twenty-year period, $2,427,991,000; the provincial governments, $630,800,000; and the city and county governments, $2,590,568,000—or 43, 11 and 46 per cent, respectively.

The Defects of These Estimates and Their Financial Implications

There is no doubt that in the minds of those who made them, these estimates merely serve to show the magnitude of the financial demands. In view of the widely varying conditions in different parts of China and the rapid social and economic changes, it would be a mistake to consider the estimates as final. It is necessary that each province or locality make a survey of the unit costs involved, collect other essential facts, and then make its own estimate. The sum of such

TABLE 58

ESTIMATED COST OF THE TWENTY-YEAR PLAN OF EDUCATIONAL EXPANSION AND IMPROVEMENT, ACCORDING TO THE SECOND NATIONAL CONFERENCE ON EDUCATION

A. Types of Education

Types of Education	Total Cost	Division of Burden (Percentages)		
		Central	Provincial	Local
1. Obligatory education and teacher training	$3,986,000,000	100 50 45	0 50 10	0a 0b 45c
2. Audlt continuation education for liquidating illiteracy	339,525,000	45	10	45
3. Annual salary increase for elementary school teachers	265,000,000	20	40	40
4. Expansion of secondary schools	205,494,000	0	—	—
5. Expansion of higher education	30,000,000	100	0	0
6. Social education	805,984,000	45	10	45d
7. Overseas Chinese education	13,000,000	100	0	0d
8. Mongolian and Tibetan education	17,695,000	100	0	0
Total	$5,662,768,000			
Average		43	11	46

(a) First year.
(b) Second year.
(c) Remaining years.
(d) From seventh year.

estimates of all provinces would be more accurate than the present estimates.

Certain important considerations have been neglected in the making of the present estimates. They are:

1. *The Increase in Population.* The rate of population increase per 1,000 a year in China has been

TABLE 58 (*Continued*)

ESTIMATED COST OF THE TWENTY-YEAR PLAN OF
EDUCATIONAL EXPANSION AND IMPROVEMENT BY
THE SECOND NATIONAL CONFERENCE ON
EDUCATION

B. Order of Years

Order of Years	Central Burden	Provincial Burden	Local Burden	Total Cost
	$	$	$	$
1st	30,041,000	5,825,000	26,004,000	61,871,000
2d	36,243,000	17,015,000	31,964,000	80,222,000
3d	51,260,000	15,968,000	53,730,000	120,958,000
4th	57,910,000	17,478,000	61,200,000	136,588,000
5th	64,540,000	18,988,000	68,670,000	152,318,000
6th	78,570,000	22,210,000	83,520,000	184,430,000
7th	88,197,000	24,184,000	93,960,000	206,340,000
8th	97,687,000	26,324,000	104,400,000	228,410,000
9th	107,677,000	28,464,000	114,840,000	250,980,000
10th	116,767,000	30,604,000	125,280,000	272,650,000
11th	139,726,000	32,744,000	135,720,000	308,189,000
12th	135,747,000	34,884,000	146,160,000	316,790,000
13th	145,987,000	37,024,000	156,600,000	339,610,000
14th	155,877,000	39,164,000	167,040,000	362,080,000
15th	165,367,000	41,304,000	177,480,000	384,150,000
16th	174,851,000	43,444,000	187,920,000	406,220,000
17th	185,027,000	45,584,000	198,360,000	428,970,000
18th	193,877,000	47,724,000	208,800,000	450,400,000
19th	203,327,000	49,864,000	219,240,000	472,430,000
20th	212,777,000	52,004,000	229,680,000	494,460,000
Total	2,441,461,000	630,800,000	2,590,568,000	5,658,066,000*
			Gross Total	5,662,829,000
Error in Original Table, 11th Year	126,256,508	32,744,000	135,720,000	294,720,000
Corrected Total	2,427,991,960	630,800,000	2,590,568,000	5,649,359,960

Adapted from original table, *Bulletin of Ministry of Education*, Vol. II, No. 14, April 5, 1930, p. 46. Totals freshly calculated.

Differences between totals due to other errors in original data which require too much time for detection.

This was originally estimated by the Commission on the Construction of Educational Plans appointed by the Ministry of Education, before it was passed by the Second National Conference on Education. See *Proceedings*, Section II, p. 20.

estimated by various authorities to be 6.6,[8] 7.8,[9] 10,[10] 11.3,[11] and 14.3.[12] Taking the 40,000,000 children of school age as a base, with a rate of increase of 10 per 1,000 per year, in twenty years the number of children of school age would increase to 48,324,357. This increase of 8,000,000 children would require an expenditure of at least $65,000,000, the amount spent in 1929-30 for educating approximately the same number of children, excluding consideration of some of the following factors.

2. The Changing Value of the Dollar.

"A fundamental factor which must not be overlooked and which, in some respects, is the most significant, is the purchasing power of the dollar, a fact which cannot be neglected in forecasting future costs in education."[13]

It has been shown in Table 16 that the silver dollar in 1929 depreciated to only 62 cents as compared with the 1913 dollar;[14] that is, it had depreciated to this extent within a period of sixteen years. As the prices of commodities go higher with the inevitable growth of industry and commerce, the dollar is bound to depreciate to some extent during the next twenty years. This means that the cost of the expansion program for education must be much more in current dollars than the present estimates.

3. The Variation of Per Pupil Expenditure in Different Parts of China and in Different Years.[15] This factor has a close relation with the preceding factor.

---

[8]Codliffe, J. B., *China, Today*. Economic, 1932.
[9]*Ibid.*
[10]*Ibid.*
[11]*Ibid.*
[12]*Ibid.*
[13]Engelhardt, N. L., and Engelhardt, Fred, *Public School Business Administration*, p. 771.
[14]See page 54, and Unpublished Document No. 6.
[15]See Table 27.

The base used was $5.02,[16] the average per pupil expenditure in the lower elementary school in 1924 in 25 provinces and the metropolitan district. The figure varied from $1.38 to $7.16. To allow for its increase up to 1930, $7 was used to estimate the cost of the obligatory education program. This figure is too low, since the actual average per pupil expenditure in the lower elementary school for all China in 1929–30 was $8.15. This figure would increase; in twenty years it might be doubled, owing to the depreciation of the dollar and the rising cost of the present and proposed offerings. It is known that at present teachers are, in general, underpaid and children poorly housed.

4. Provision for the Abolishment of Tuition. If the principle of free obligatory education is applied, then additional funds equivalent to the tuition abolished must be provided. The figures for per pupil expenditure in the past have included receipts from tuition. Therefore, the estimated totals have already taken into consideration the tuition abolished. Yet the Conference[17] allowed exceptions in charging tuition in wealthy districts. This exception constitutes a violation of a fundamental principle of democracy.

5. The Expenses of Attendance Service, Supervision, and the Training of Teachers in Service. Such a stupendous program must require a large supervisory staff and many administrative officers. Moreover, additional moneys will be required for the training of teachers in service, in summer schools and special courses. These services are not explicitly provided for in the estimates.

---

[16] Hupeh Department of Education, *Hupeh Educational Administration Bulletin*, Nos. 21–22, February 10, 1930, p. 43.

[17] *Porceedings of the Second National Conference on Education*, Section III, p. 22.

6. The Unit Cost Technique Is Not Applied in Estimating Secondary Education Cost.[18] Vocational high schools cost $155.16 per pupil; senior high schools, $110.89; and junior high schools, $77.50, in 1929–30. Such wide differences in cost were not considered in the estimates. For example, in the estimates given, the standards of expenditure and outlay for junior high school and the vocational school are the same, thus making the total estimate much lower than that actually needed.

7. The Cost of the More Expensive Services Are Not Taken into Consideration. The problem of transportation is not considered at all. More adequate provision must be made for health service and instruction, science teaching equipment, and better school libraries.

8. The Cost of Social Education. The estimate for social education does not include provision for more detailed and comprehensive service rendered in the provinces. For example, the cost of motion pictures and radio for the entire period is estimated to be $3,400,-000. These are the most effective modern instruments for instructing the masses. China cannot afford to neglect them. Perhaps the results obtained will be of greater value than those obtained through "book learning," if the above sum of money were provided in each province.

9. Annual Salary Increases Are Not Provided for Secondary School Teachers. If China cannot at present afford to make provision for retirement and pension plans, she must provide funds for annual salary increases for all teachers.

10. School Housing. The problem of housing is no doubt one of the most baffling China has to face. In the

---

[18]See *Proceedings of the Second National Conference on Education,* Section III, p. 28.

estimates, the initial outlays include the cost of school buildings and equipment. The cost was placed at $500 per class, or per 40 pupils, for the obligatory educational program. The initial outlay per school for various types of schools was estimated as follows:[19]

Rural Teachers College	$200,000
Rural Normal School	40,000
Private Tutor Training Institute	2,000
Adult Illiteracy Institute	300
Adult Illiteracy Supervisors' Institute	5,000
Senior High Schools:	
General	40,000
Agricultural	46,000
Industrial	64,000
Junior High Schools:	
General	3,000
Vocational	3,000

The above estimates are low because, as far as possible, existing family shrines, Confucian temples, the old Shu Yuans, public buildings, and Buddhist and Taoist temples are to be used as schoolhouses. For the most part, the initial outlays are intended for remodeling and repairing these buildings. New school buildings must be constructed as economically as possible. Private individuals are encouraged to donate houses or funds for building new ones.

Since no objective data are available regarding the number, condition, and location of existing shrines, houses, and temples, nor are there any unit cost data for estimating the cost of building new schoolhouses, the practice of arbitrarily determining outlays for various types of schools results in only rough guesses. The problem of estimating the cost of a building program is

---

[19] *Ministry of Education Bulletin*, Volume II, Nos. 4–7, Sections on Special Articels; see Explanations on the budget estimate of the Twenty-Year Plan.

a very complicated one. The principles and techniques worked out by Engelhardt,[20] America's outstanding authority on school building plans, can profitably be adapted and applied in China.

11. *The Extent of Utilization of the Present Facilities.* The estimators assumed that the instruction facilities of the present school system have been fully utilized and cannot care for additional enrollment, that is, the $7 used as the basis of estimate is the terminal cost at the saturation point. The facts, however, prove the contrary to be true, despite other influencing factors, as will be seen from the data given in Tables 59, 60, and 61.

Table 59 shows that the average number of lower elementary pupils per teacher is 20.6, and the median, 23.85. Only 12.4 per cent of the teachers have loads of 28.2 to 43.6 pupils, while 68.8 per cent of the teachers have loads of 10.7 to 23.5 pupils. For comparison, Table 61 shows that the median number of pupils per primary teacher in 23 foreign countries is 29.36 pupils. In Soviet Russia, each primary school teacher teaches 41.9 pupils. Numerous experiments have been conducted by experts in the United States to determine the relation of class size to teaching efficiency. The following conclusion has been drawn from all data available in 1930:

"While the traditional position has been to regard class size as of the greatest importance, so far as the objective is achievement many other factors may determine the effectiveness of teaching. The weight of evidence as shown by experiments and questionnaires favors the medium-sized class, a medium-sized class in most studies not varying greatly from the median 38. . . ."[21]

[20]Engelhardt, N. L., *Planning School Building Programs.*
[21]*Annual Report* of the Springfield Public Schools, Springfield, Mass., 1930, p. 59.

TABLE 59

AVERAGE NUMBER OF LOWER ELEMENTARY SCHOOL PUPILS PER TEACHER IN THE PROVINCES AND MUNICIPALITIES, 1929–30

AVERAGE NUMBER OF PUPILS PER TEACHER	NUMBER OF TEACHERS FALLING INTO DIFFERENT CATEGORIES				
	(1) TOTAL	(2) TOTAL TEACHERS	(3) PER CENT	(4) TOTAL 1, 2 & 3	(5) PER CENT
43.6	257				
35.1	15,631				
35.0	678				
32.9	3,522				
32.2	2,080				
29.3	20,379				
28.2 (Q3)	402	42,949	12.4		
27.4	20,293				
26.9	319				
26.4	140				
25.8	3,668				
25.5	637				
24.9	3,932				
24.2	35,926	64,915	18.8	107,864	31.2
23.85 (Med)					
23.5	34,062				
23.1	583				
22.1	8,466				
22.0	407				
19.3	29,816				
17.9	320				
17.8 (Q)	39,994	113,648	35.8		
17.2	1,536				
17.0	9,880				
16.6	9,443				
15.8	25,421				
15.6	37,587				
10.7	36,248	123,802	33.0	237,450	68.8
Number = 28 Averages — 20.6 Totals	345,314	345,314	100.0	345,314	100.0

Adapted from Table (1), in Source J1.

Financial Implications of the New Policy 149

TABLE 60

SIZE OF LOWER ELEMENTARY SCHOOLS IN THE
PROVINCES AND MUNICIPALITIES, 1929–30

Average Number of Pupils per School		Number and Per Cent of Schools Falling into Different Categories				
		(1) Total	(2) Total Schools	(3) Per Cent	(4) Total 1, 2 & 3	(5) Per Cent
208.3		43				
171.8		66				
160.3		84				
153.4		106				
151.3		74				
132.0		180				
116.6	Q3	818	1,371	.8		
72.8		8,214				
70.1		1,656				
63.6		8,627				
53.4		7,521				
51.5		72				
51.5		10,772				
47.2		184	37,046	21.0	38,417	21.8
46.3	M					
45.4		4,111				
44.9		1,494				
44.4		3,774				
41.0		2,333				
39.5		14,599				
39.4		19,863				
38.6	Q1	4,068	50,242	28.6		
37.4		1,699				
36.4		21,962				
36.1		16,298				
34.8		20,498				
34.6		762				
29.1		197				
14.9		25,987	87,403	49.6	137,645	78.2
Number = 28 Average — 40.4 Totals		176,062	176,062	100.0	176,062	100.0

Rearranged and adapted from Table (III) in Source J1; see Bibliography.

TABLE 61

NUMBER OF PUPILS PER TEACHER IN CHINA AND IN OTHER COUNTRIES COMPARED

Number of Pupils per Teacher	Frequency Distribution by Number of Countries		
	In Lower or Primary Schools	In Higher Elementary or Intermediate Schools	In High Schools
51.1–53	2		
49.1–51	1		
47.1–49	1		
45.1–47		1	
43.1–45	2		
41.1–43	1		
39.1–41			
37.1–39			
35.1–37	3		
33.1–35	3		
31.1–33	3		
29.1–31	1	1	
27.1–29	1	2	
25.1–27	2	1	
23.1–25	1		
21.1–23	2	3	3
19.1–21		1	1
17.1–19		1	5
15.1–17		3	2
13.1–15		3	2
11.1–13			2
9.1–11			2
Number	23	16	17
Median	35.6	21.05	18.4
China (Av.)	20.6	13.1	11.93*
U.S.A. (Med.)	29.36**		22.44
Soviet Russia (Av. 1931)	41.9	27.6	21.5

*Junior high schools.
**All elementary schools.

Sources of Data: Percy, Eustace, *The Year Book of Education*, 1933, Table 59, pp. XCIX, C.

Mort, Paul R., *State Support for Public Education*, 1933, p. 435. China: J1, Table 7, and J2, Table 1.

Financial Implications of the New Policy 151

It is true that there are better conditions and aids to teaching in foreign countries than in China, and that these enable teachers to teach a much larger number of pupils without diminishing their efficiency. It is also true that desirable class size in China must be determined by experimentation and research. But China has limited financial resources, and her teachers will have to bear much heavier teaching loads in the future than at present. Probably the 40-pupils-per-teacher basis, as provided in the estimate, is not an excessive demand. Since the present teaching load is only one-half this number, it seems probable that the present number of teachers can take care of approximately 7,000,000 more pupils.

This conclusion might be considered rash if the capacities and sizes of existing schools were not considered. While the actual capacities of the schools are unknown, the number of pupils per school at present is sufficient to show that more pupils can be provided for. The average number of pupils per school in China is only 40.4, and the median, 46.3. Of the lower elementary schools, 78.2 per cent care for only 14.9 to 45.4 pupils per school. Only .8 per cent of them have 116.6 to 208.3 pupils per school. About half of the nation's lower elementary schools have 14.9 to 38.6 pupils per school. With better organization, these schools may be made to care for a doubled enrollment. (See Table 60.)

Allowing for the operation of other factors, the data concerning which are unknown, the capacity of the present school system may be placed at at least an additional one-half or one-third of the present enrollment. This means that approximately 3,000,000 to 4,000,000 additional pupils can be cared for without additional teachers and schoolhouses, and that approximately $20,000,000 to $30,000,000 each year may be saved or excluded from the estimates.

Financial Implications of the Emphasis on Productive Education

For the past few years Chinese educators have seriously evaluated the school system in the light of recent social and economic trends in China. Up to the present, the schools have tended to train more and more youths into the traditional scholar class, with entrance into officialdom or into white-collar positions as the chief aim. For every child educated, society loses a productive citizen. For every child educated away from the rural scene, the farmer loses a helping hand, and the cities and towns receive one more unemployed youth. A flood of literature has appeared to offer remedies for the failure of the schools to meet China's economic needs. Everywhere in China to-day, productive education has become a shibboleth and rural education a widespread movement. To many, productive education carries an emphasis on the element of manual labor, the exploration of natural resources, and the production of abundant goods; while rural education emphasizes agricultural and handicrafts production. But a more careful analysis reveals the fact that mere emphasis upon human muscle and the old pattern of production methods will not go far to make China a wealthy nation. Science and technology must be the prerequisites. Witness the contribution of American vocational education to its advanced material civilization; its foundation lies in the work of the colleges of mechanical arts, of agriculture, and the experiment stations.[22] A glimpse into the pages of Alfred Charles True's *A History of Agricultural Education in the United States* will prove the statement.

[22] True, Charles A., *A History of Agricultural Education in the United States*, 1925, *passim*.

In this sense, productive education requires a very costly program. There is the cost of training special teachers, of equipping the science laboratories, of providing experiment stations, workshops, and plants, to be considered. Twiss[23] has shown clearly how productive education may be achieved through the financing of science teaching in all schools of China. He gave an excellent elucidation of the problem of educational finance, and offered concrete suggestions for the improvement and equipment of teaching science. Following Twiss' suggestions, there has been no attempt to estimate the cost of scientific equipment, and, hence, objective data are lacking.

The policy of productive education, as defined by the laws of the government and the discussions of educators, does not imply the establishment of separate vocational schools only.[24] Productive education is meant to be stressed in all levels and types of schools and institutions. In April, 1931, the Ministry of Education ordered all local educational authorities to restrict the establishment of general high schools and to increase the number of vocational secondary schools as much as possible. A Vocational Education Planning Committee was created,[25] and policies and standards of establishing various types of vocational schools were issued. No less than 35 types of vocational schools are needed. In May, 1931, the People's National Congress further stressed productive education.[26] Elementary and secondary schools should meet the demands of local social needs, and attention should be focussed on training in skills and techniques for making an independent living and increasing productive power. Social education should have productive

[23]Twiss, G. R., *Science and Education in China.*
[24]*Shun Pao Year Book,* 1933, p. Q2, "Trend in Vocational Education."
[25]*The First Education Year Book of China,* 1934, Section B, p. 12.
[26]*Shun Pao Year Book,* 1933, p. Q2, "Educational Plans and Policies Passed by the National People's Convention."

education as its center. As many vocational schools and vocational continuation schools should be established as possible. Special colleges related to the development of industry and national economy should be established. Universities should emphasize natural and applied sciences. The League of Nations' Mission of Educational Experts also recommended the promotion of vocational education to advance the utilization of the abundant natural resources.[27]

Huang Kin-chung, former Commissioner of Education of Hupeh Province, recommended the establishment of the following national special schools by the Central Government located in appropriate regions:

1. National Special School of Forestry.
2. National Special School of Textiles.
3. National Special School of Paper Making.
4. National Special School of Mining.
5. National Special School of Shipbuilding.
6. National Special School of Aëronautics.
7. National Special School of Colonization.
8. National Special School of Animal Husbandry.
9. National Special School of Fishery.
10. National Special School of Technology.

Three years have passed since these proposals and ordinances were presented. As yet there is no concrete plan of financing the program. All the proposals need huge financial outlays. It is imperative that a concrete survey made of cost data be made before a fair estimate of the total cost can be given. The ways and means of financing this program will be discussed later.[28]

---

[27] *Proceedings of the Second National Conference on Education*, Section V, p. 9.
[28] See page 208 *sqq*.

CHAPTER IX

THE ABILITY OF CHINA TO SUPPORT EDUCATION

Can China afford to spend the total of $5,600,000,000 to $6,000,000,000 during the next twenty years, or $280,000,000 to $300,000,000 each year,[1] for the proposed program of expansion and improvement, in addition to the $196,000,000[2] required each year for the present program? If this question cannot be answered in the affirmative, and the mechanism for raising such huge sums of money is not first set up, all plans would be mere "castles in Spain," and vast numbers of the population would be denied their legitimate right to a basic education. China must face realities, discover what she can do, and then do what she can.

The Economic Foundations

There has been much pessimism and a philosophy of defeat connected with the whole question of China's poverty. Dr. Hu Shih wrote that poverty is the first of China's five great enemies.

"... Mr. Yu Tien-shiu said on one occasion that 95 per cent of the population of China was below the poverty line. Mr. Chang Chen-chih has stated that the number of poverty-stricken people in the country runs to over a third of the population. Mr. Chang quotes from Mr. Li Ching-mu of Szechwan: according to investigations made in Kang-Pu-Erh, Ti-Mai-Erh, together with the village of Cheng Fu near Peking and the village of Hu-pien in Anhwei Province, the total of poverty-stricken people in China comes to one half of the population. Mr. Li

[1]See Table 53.
[2]See Table 9.

assumes that the lowest cost of living for one family in a year is $130 to $160, and that every family whose income is less than that is poverty-stricken. Recently the results of social investigations such as Mr. Li Ching-han's report of Peking village families all go to prove that his estimate is roughly correct. There are places where the total is over 73 per cent, or as much as 82 per cent (said the investigations of the International Famine Relief Committee in 1920). This is not very different from Mr. Yu's estimate. This then is our first great enemy."*

Again, he says:

"We must confess that we are terribly poor, and that our people are suffering miseries which horrify the civilized people."†

Economists, sociologists, and educators have repeatedly brought out facts which tend to show that China is menaced by the most trying economic crisis.

CHINA'S PRESENT ECONOMIC CRISIS

China's economic crisis was brought about by a cycle of long-enduring causes and has been exaggerated by the effects of the present world economic depression. Ku Mei listed the causes, from the year 1862 to 1930, as follows:[3]

Causes	Number of Years Affected	Number of Times of Occurrence
Internecine warfare	52	117
Foreign aggression	46	179
Military mutiny	14	125
Notorious banditry	4	13
Foreign loans	43	144
Domestic loans	26	124
Drought	11	26
Flood	34	115
Wind storm	9	15

*Hu Shih, *Which Road Are We Going?* Institute of Pacific Relations, October, 1930.
†Arnold, J., *Some Bigger Issues in China's Problems.* Foreword, p. 1.
[3]Selected from Ku, Mei, "Why the Present Education Is Ill-Adapted to the Social Economic Setting of China." *Chung Hua Educational Review*, Volume XIX, No. 9, March, 1932, p. 19.

Causes	Number of Years Affected	Number of Times of Occurrence
Fire	8	14
Earthquake	2	24
Epidemics	6	9
Insects' plague	3	3
Opium havoc	24	38
Gambling havoc	5	5
Strikes	15	65

The two fundamental causes of China's economic crisis are economic imperialism and internecine warfare. To the school man, the general lack of enlightenment of the population through education is a cause still more fundamental. Below are given some facts regarding the grave situation:

1. Agricultural Decline. Human and natural disasters have caused millions of mow of land to be abandoned, thus constantly decreasing agricultural production. The teeming millions are forced to depend upon foreign foodstuffs. The Chinese Maritime Customs annual report for the year 1932 shows that during that year China imported rice valued at 119,251,125 HK. Tls., wheat valued at 51,863,004 HK. Tls., and flour valued at 36,356,160 HK. Tls. These three items constituted 19.52 per cent of the total value of imports, and had increased 370 per cent, 895 per cent, and 161 per cent, respectively, since 1912. In 1933, the value of rice imports was 150.1 million dollars, of wheat imports 87.9 million dollars, of flour imports 27.8 million dollars, and of cotton imports 98.2 million dollars. In 1932 China imported raw cotton valued at 119,061,471 HK. Tls., and cotton goods, cotton yarn, and threads valued at 84,638,381 HK. Tls. These two items constituted 19.16 of the total value of imports. In 1933 a wheat and cotton loan of G$50,000,000 which has recently been reduced to

G$20,000,000 (or 48,000,000 Chinese dollars) was made from the United States.

2. *The Losses Due to Japanese Invasion and Natural Calamities.* In 1931 China lost to Imperialist Japan a territory of 496,164 square miles with all its mining resources and other treasures. The loss of Manchurian customs revenue, according to 1931 figures, was 26,078,-000 HK. Tls., or $39,117,000. The Shanghai war losses amounted to $194,606,362.81.[4]

"Drought, flood, and famine are recurrent affairs. In the year 1928–29, the total area affected by famine was over 1,093 hsien or counties, comprising a population of 56,622,500 according to the reports of the National Famine Relief Committee."[5]

The flood in 1931 was the most disastrous one in the past century. It directly affected 25,200,000 persons and inundated 87,000,000 mow of farm land with total losses of property and the like amounting to about $200,000,000. The total quantity of food crops destroyed was valued at $475,000,000.

3. *Unfavorable Balance of Trade.* As a result of the world depression China's imports decreased from 1,448,187,154 HK. Tls., to 1,062,630,911 HK. Tls., and her exports decreased from 909,475,525 HK. Tls. in 1931 to 492,988,989 HK. Tls. The total value of foreign trade decreased 31 per cent from 1931 to 1932. It further decreased 12.5 per cent from 1932 to 1933. The total value of foreign trade in 1933 was only 55.1 per cent of that of 1929. From 1864 to 1930, China's unfavorable balance of trade was on the average 150,391,630 HK. Tls., or $225,587,447 per year. e total loss due to the excess of imports over exports for these 66 years was 9,925,847,570 HK. Tls., or $14,898,771,355. The unfavorable balance for the period 1928 to 1933 was as follows:[6]

[4]*China Year Book*, 1933, pp. 504 and 671.
[5]Department of Agricultural Economics of the University of Nanking, *The 1931 Flood in China, An Economic Survey*, p. 10.
[6]Chinese Maritime Customs, *Annual Reports*, 1912–1932.

	HK. Tls.	Silver Dollars
1912	102,577,000	153,865,500
1928	204,614,000	306,921,000
1929	250,092,000	375,138,000
1930	414,912,000	622,368,000
1931	540,125,000	810,187,500
1932	569,642,000	854,463,000
1933	———	733,000,000

In foreign countries an unfavorable balance of trade does not mean national loss because of the compensation in receipts from investments in foreign countries, merchant marine, and the like, in the total balance sheet of the international accounts. In China such compensation is very limited. The annual remittance from overseas Chinese is about $180,000,000, and has recently decreased to only $100,000,000.[7]

4. *Industrial Depression and Economic Imperialism.* According to Fong and Chen,[8] all modern industries with Chinese capital are facing the danger of ruin. Numerous factories have been closed. The causes are political instability, foreign competition under unequal treaties, shortage of capital, lack of purchasing power of the masses, excessive taxation, bad management, and so forth. 1933 was the poorest year for cotton spinning; up to June, eleven mills were closed with 340,000 spindles idle. Of the 180 silk filatures in Kiangsu and Chekiang, about 20 were in operation in 1933.[9]

The severe competition encountered by Chinese industry and commerce may be seen in the amount of foreign investments in China. For the year 1931, the total amount of foreign investments was $3,242,500,000

---

[7] *The Heng Chien Monthly,* Special Number on Planned Economy. Volume II, No. 4, April, 1933, p. 99.

[8] Fong, H. D., and Chen, C. M., "An Analysis of China's Industrial Difficulties," *The Economic Weekly,* Ta Kung Pao, August 23, 1933, p. 3.

[9] Ho Ping-yin, "China's Industry and Commerce During 1933," *Chinese Economic Journal,* XIV, No. 1, January, 1934, p. 19.

in U. S. Gold, of which $2,531,900,000, or 78.1 per cent, was in business investments. Of the total, British investment constituted 36.7 per cent, Japanese 35.1 per cent, and Russian 8.4 per cent. The United States and the other countries each had only 6.1 per cent or less of the total foreign investments in China.[10] Foreign capital constituted one half of the capital invested in electric plants. In 133 cotton mills, 41, or 38.8 per cent, of the total spindleage is Japanese, the capital involved being more than two and one-half times the Chinese capital. Out of a total of 4,516,898 spindles in all China, Great Britain owned three mills with 170,610 spindles. Foreign shipping in China comprises more than two thirds of the total tonnage and carries 80 per cent of the total freight.[11]

According to Clark,[12] the combined capital of 161 modern Chinese banks was 287,187,000 Yuan in 1930. There were, in 1930, 50 foreign banks doing business in China. Of these, 28, with head offices in China, had a combined capital of 43,206,000 Yuan, which is 13 per cent of all the banking capital in the country. But according to the 1933 *Shun Pao Year Book*,[12A] during 1925 24 foreign banks and Sino-foreign banks had a combined capital of 647,051,423 Yuan and were doing business with a combined financial power of 6,878,426,876 Yuan, while the 28 members of the (Chinese) Shanghai Bankers Association of outstanding importance had a combined financial power of only 2,503,006,000 Yuan in 1931.

5. *Unemployment.*

"According to Dr. Leonard Hsu's estimate, about 35 to 45 per cent of the male population and about 10 to 20 per cent of the female population in China are gainfully employed, which

---

[10]Remer, F. C., *Foreign Investments in China*, pp. 69, 70, and 76.
[11]*Shun Pao Year Book*, 1933, p. M232; Fong and Chen, *Op. cit.;* Ho, *Op. cit.*
[12]Clark, Grover, *Economic Rivalries in China*, p. 76.
[12A]*Shun Pao Year Book*, 1933, p. M157.

means that only 23 to 35 per cent of the entire population of China are gainfully employed. In a report on unemployment conditions in the leading countries of the world in March, 1926, Mr. Walter Leaf, then Chairman of the International Chamber of Commerce, estimated that on the basis of a total population of 436,094,000 China had at that time at least 168,322,000 who were without regular employment. The data collected by various philanthropic organizations in China, issued in Shanghai *Shun Pao* on September 5, 1929, revealed that in the whole country there were over 105,000,000 poor people who were depending upon charity for their living. . . . There should be about 280,000,000 industrial, handicrafts, and agricultural labourers among her 400,000,000 people. However, according to Ma Chao-chin's *China's Labour Problems,* there are only 121,260,000 labouring people in this country. This would mean that at least 158,740,000 people in China are without regular employment.

"According to the data of the National Famine Relief Committee, there were in 1927, 9,000,000 famine-stricken people; in 1928, 37,000,000; in 1929, 57,000,000; and in 1930, 71,000,000. The big flood in 1931 has served to increase this number by several tens of millions more.

"In 1931 the total number of overseas workers who had returned to China was 283,890.

"According to the figures of the All-China Labour Federation (Red), 60 per cent of the total number of industrial and handicrafts workers in China (or about 10,000,000) were unemployed in all branches of industry, commerce and trade in 1930.

". . . About 61 per cent of the total population of Peiping in November, 1932, have no regular occupations.

"Not more than 5 per cent of the graduates of 18 universities and colleges in North and East China were able to obtain jobs at the time they were graduated.

"In the large cities, like Shanghai, Peiping, Canton, Hankow, and Tientsin, public offices are practically haunted by jobless young men day and night."[13]

6. Concentration of Wealth. While the masses are reduced to a penniless condition, wealth and capital continues to flow disproportionately into the large cities and into a few men's hands. The influx of cash to

---

[13]Lowe Chuan-hua, *Facing Labour Issues in China*, p. 115.

Shanghai averaged $6,000,000 per month in 1932. According to Mr. Kann, an authority on finance in China, the minimum amount of silver currency in circulation in China is about $2,200,000,000. But the amount of dollars and tael deposits in Shanghai alone was about $350,000,000 at the end of June, 1932. The average for each of the 22 provinces would be about $100,000,000, with $5.5 per capita of population, while Shanghai alone has $160 per capita, or 21 times the average amount of deposits for the people in the interior regions in China.[14]

According to a certain estimate,[15] the total wealth of 70 selected war lords is about $700,000,000. Tsao Kuen and Chang Cho-ling had $50,000,000 each. Ni Sze-chung's property was reported to be worth $80,000,000 after his death. When Wang Chan-yuan was finally driven out of Hupeh Province, his ill-gotten fortune was said to be worth $50,000,000 to $60,000,000. There is no doubt that this wealth had been squeezed from the toiling millions, who can justly demand their return for educational and economic betterment.

It has been estimated that there is $1,000,000,000 in silver in hoarded wealth which has been only partially tapped by the sudden development of Chinese postwar native business.[16] In August, 1933, in Wuchang, Hupeh Province, a buried chest of carved jade, gold, and silver worth $1,000,000 was discovered under the houses of two inhabitants. The government had proposed to use the treasures for public purposes. This incident gives one an idea of the amounts of buried or hoarded wealth

---

[14]Chang Kia-ngau, General Manager of Bank of China, "Some Economic Symptoms in China," *The China Critic*, Volume V, No. 40, October 6, 1932.

[15]Nagano, Akira, *Chinese Social Organization*. (Translated by Chu Kia-ching), p. 187.

[16]Hodges, Charles, "Non-Political Factors Underlying the Chinese Problem." Preliminary Papers solicited by the data committee, Paper No. VI, Conference on American Relations with China.

The Ability of China to Support Education

in China. Education can rightly claim a share, if all these treasures can be unearthed.

Sources of the Wealth of China

Land Resources and Population. More than 82 per cent of China's wealth consists of land resources. From 1840 to 1931, China lost a territory of 3,369,747 square miles, or 26,305,644 square li.[17] At present, according to Woodhead,[18] she has a territory of 4,314,097 square miles, or 33,778,108 square li. Excluding the four lost provinces, her territory consists of 3,817,933 square miles, or 29,904,804 square li. There are five known estimates of China's cultivated land, as given in Table 62.

TABLE 62

ESTIMATES OF CHINA'S LAND AREA IN MILLIONS OF MOW, IN ORDER OF THEIR RECENCY AND ACCEPTABILITY

Authority	(1) Total Land Area	(2) Arable Area	(3) Cultivated Area	Per Cent (2) is of (1)	Per Cent (3) is of (1)	Per Cent (3) is of (2)
1. Liang Ching-chun*	11,824	3,301	1,311	25.4	11.0	41.0
2. Chang, C. C.**	12,049		1,249		10.3	
3. Lieu, D. K.***	10,966		1,687	29.0	15.4	
4. Buck, L. J.****			1,732			
5. Baker, O. E.***	8,995		1,186		14.9	26.0

*Liang Ching-chun, *The Relationship Between Population and Food Supply of China*. (In manuscript.)
**Chang, C. C., *An Estimate of China's Farms and Crops*, p. 11.
***The China Society of Economic Study, *China's Economic Problems*, pp. 37, 51–53.
****Tawney, R. H., *Land and Labour in China*, p. 28.

Table 6 gives the population figures for various years. To-day the population is generally estimated as 450,-000,000.

[17]Chiang Kung-chen, *A History of National Humiliation*, pp. 6–7.
[18]Woodhead, *China Year Book*, 1933.

"We have 83 per cent of our population thickly compressed in 17 per cent of our territory.... The average density is over 500 persons per square mile..., the remaining 17 per cent of the population in the remaining 83 per cent of our territory averaging only 35 persons per square mile."[19]

Only 46 per cent of the population, or about 150,000,000 persons, own land. The remaining 54 per cent, or about 235,000,000 persons, including tenant farmers are without land. Of the landowners, 44 per cent own only 6 per cent of the total cultivated land area, while 5 per cent own 43 per cent of the total cultivated land. Forty-four per cent of the landowners own less than 10 mow per family."[20] According to Chang,[21] 73 per cent of the total households are farming households. The Central Land Committee estimated that 80 per cent of the population are farmers (1927). Cheng Chang-heng, a member of the Legislative Yuan, estimated the average size of the farm family to be 5.2 persons. Tawney[22] wrote:

"In China as a whole 3 mow (.45 acre) per person, or 15 mow per family of five individuals, is required to supply the bare requirements of food alone, irrespective of housing, farm implements, clothing, fuel and other necessities."

Ho,[23] renowned rural educator, wrote that if a family owns 10 mow per person, it is on the creative level and its children can receive secondary education. With 7.5 mow per person, the family is on the cultural level, and its children can afford to receive elementary education.

---

[19]Wong, W. H., Director of the National Geological Survey of China, *The Distribution of Population and Land Utilization in China.*
[20]Ministry of Industry, *Industrial Statistics*, Volume I, Nos. 5, 6, December, 1933, p. 6.
[21]Chang, *Op. cit.*, p. 13.
[22]Tawney, R. H., *Land and Labour in China.*
[23]Ho Erh-ping (or Dr. W. C. Tao), "The Way Out for the Chinese Nation and the Way Out for Chinese Education," *Chung Hua Education Weekly*, Volume XIX, No. 3, September, 1931, p. 21.

With 6 mow per person, the family is on the insufficient clothing level and cannot afford to send its children to schools. With 5 mow, it is on the insufficient food level. Below that, the family is on the level of bankruptcy, death, and chaos.

Actually, according to Chang,[24] the farm land area per farm family is, on the average, only 21 mow or about 4 mow per person. According to the Ministry of Industry, 44 per cent of the landowners own less than two mow per person. Only 14 per cent of them own ten or more mow per person. Chen[25] concluded from many sample studies that no less than 65 per cent of the rural population is in dire need of land. Conliffe[26] wrote that overpopulation constitutes China's greatest, most fundamental, and most pressing difficulty, and stands in the way of all schemes for the betterment of her economic life. Liang[27] concluded from his intensive study of the relationship between population and food supply in China that the total food supply is 299,539,850 million calories. This averages only 2,409 calories per day per adult. The average of six dietary standards is 3,125 calories per adult per day. On this standard, China can feed only 342,000,000 people, or about four fifths of her population. If there is insufficient food, there is little hope for education for millions of people in China.[28]

Natural Resources and Industrialization. Although China is the world's largest producer of kaoliang, sweet potatoes, tea, cabbage, bamboo, and soy bean, and ranks second in the production of rice, wheat, tobacco, and

---

[24] Chang, *Op. cit.*
[25] Chen Han-seng, *The Present Agrarian Problem in China*, p. 1.
[26] Conliffe, J. B., *Op. cit.*, p. 17.
[27] Liang Ching-chun. (See his summary in manuscript.)
[28] Chen Kung-po, Minister of Industry, says that there is a shortage of food for 5 per cent of the people, or 25,000,000 persons. Chen Kung-po, "Two Years of Observation," *The Nation*, Volume I, No. 3, March 1, 1933.

fourth in cotton, she has, in recent years, constantly faced the problem of shortage and maldistribution of food and other agricultural raw materials in general. According to the geologist and economist, her basic metals and power resources are not overabundant. Table 63 shows her position as a producer of raw materials in the world. Table 64 shows her extent of industrialization as compared with the United States.

TABLE 64

STATISTICAL CONTRASTS BETWEEN CHINA AND THE UNITED STATES IN THE EXTENT OF INDUSTRIALIZATION

(Values are given in U. S. gold currency, and the figures are for the year 1930.)

Item	Amount in China	Ratio: China to U.S.A.
Railways (mileage)	11,000	1 to 23
Railway tonnage carried	40,000,000	1 to 34
Passengers carried on railways	60,000,000	1 to 13
Motor roads (mileage)	40,000	1 to 75
Motor vehicles (registered)	40,000	1 to 675
Electric railways (mileage)	5,734	1 to 8
Air mail lines (mileage)	2,500	1 to 18
Merchant marine gross registered tonnage	330,000	1 to 50
Telegraph wires (mileage)	97,000	1 to 24
Number of telephones installed	250,000	1 to 80
Number of post offices	12,300	1 to 4
Money orders issued in United States dollars	$60,000,000	1 to 28
Number of radio receiving sets	10,000	1 to 1,000
Electric power generated (in kilowatt-hours)	900,000	1 to 111,111
Number of cotton spindles	4,000,000	1 to 9
Number of cotton looms	35,000	1 to 21
Output of flour mills (barrels)	12,000,000	1 to 12
Coal output (long tons)	30,000,000	1 to 20
Pig iron production (long tons)	800,000	1 to 52
Value of all building construction	$60,000,000	1 to 133
Number of factory workers	1,200,000	1 to 9
Number of newspapers	100	1 to 23
Number of motion picture theaters	300	1 to 220
Aggregate capital and surplus of banks	$100,000,000	1 to 80
Per capita foreign trade	$2.30	1 to 24

Adapted from Arnold's *China Through the American Window*, pp. 25-27.

TABLE 63

THE STATUS OF CHINA'S RAW MATERIALS

Raw Materials	Unit of Measure	Year	Reserve	Production	Per Cent of World Reserve	Per Cent of World Production	China's Rank Among Countries
1. Rice	Bushels	1930		1,000,000,000			2
2. Wheat	"	1930		700,000,000			2
3. Cotton	Bales	1931		1,800,000		6.5	4
4. Leaf Tobacco	Pounds	1930		500,000,000			2
5. Kaoliang	L. Tons	1930		15,000,000			1
6. Soy Beans	Tons	1930		13,884,000		87.1	1
7. Tea	"	1930		400,000		49.2	1
8. Silk	"	1932		11,500		20.0	2
9. Silk Cocoons	Klgms.	1928		180,000,000		27.6	2
10. Coal	Tons	1928	a. 217,626,000,000 b. 236,287,000,000 c. 302,606,000,000	25,091,760	4	1.6	3(R)
11. Iron Ore	Tons	1928		2,003,800		.5	
12. Pig Iron	"	1928	a. 979,000,000	433,843	1.6		
	"	1931	b. 1,000,194,292	478,035		.86	
13. Copper				negligible		.02	
14. Lead	L. Tons	1930		15,000		.09	
15. Zinc	" "	1930		16,000		.09	
16. Tin	" "	1930		9,000			
17. Petroleum	Tons	1930	467,000,000	negligible		.00008	7(R)
18. Tungsten	Dollars	1927		8,366,000		64.3	
19. Antimony	Dollars	1927		7,004,550		77.0	
20. Hydroelectric Power	H. P.		a. 20,000,000 b. 25,000,000 c. 34,150,000	1,000 1,600	4.6		4(R)
21. Total Mineral Production	Dollars	1927	298,850,087				

Primary Sources: (1) *Economic Forces of the World*, Berlin, Dresdner Bank, 1930. (2) *Second, Third and Fourth Reports of the China Institute of Geological Survey,* up to 1932.

Secondary Sources: (1) Fong, H. D., *China's Industrialization, A Statistical Survey;* (2) Djang Siao-mei, *The Position of China as a Producer of Raw Materials and a Consumer of Manufactured Goods;* (3) Nieh, C. L., *China's Industrial Development: Its Problems and Prospects;* (4) Arnold, Julean, *China Through the American Window,* pp. 25–27; (5) *Shun Pao Monthly,* Volume II, No. 4, pp. 37–41, No. 7, pp. 87–96; and (6) *The Quarterly Journal of Economics and Statistics,* Volume II, No. 3, September, 1933, p. 693.

Note: (4)=reserve.

The Ability of China to Support Education   167

From data given on page 166 and in the Tables 63 and 64, the following points are obvious:

1. The shortage of foodstuffs can be remedied by scientific agriculture, and their maldistribution by more adequate transportation facilities.

2. China has more coal and iron reserve than many countries, and has adequate power resources, especially hydroelectric power. She can become an important manufacturing country.

3. China's industrialization on modern lines is confined to a few cities and counts for very little in her national economic life as a whole. She is essentially an agricultural country and tends, on the whole,to remain so.

"But China will be rapidly industrialized only from an oriental, not from an occidental, viewpoint, for she can scarcely aspire to the degree of industrialization that has been realized in the industrialized nations of the West. To raise China's present standards of living two or three times by means of industrialization, for instance, is feasible."[29]

Dr. Ku's energy estimate of China is shown in Table 65. The total amount of active energy or energy consumption per year is about 49,000,000,000 kilowatt hours, or 24,500,000 horse power. China ranks fourth among all the countries in this respect, although 82 per cent of her energy is human energy and only 18 per cent is mechanical energy. Modern wealth is based upon mechanical energy.

According to Arnold,[30] China has only .75 mechanical slave per capita, while the United States has 25 mechanical slaves per capita. However, Ku's estimate shows that China has abundant potential mechanical

[29]Fong, H. D., *China's Industrialization, A Statistical Survey*, 1931, p. 45.
[30]Arnold, Julean, *Some Bigger Issues in China's Problems*, Chart No. 2.

TABLE 65

SUMMARY OF KU YOU-CHUAN'S ENERGY ESTIMATE OF CHINA IN KILOWATT HOURS

I. Potential energy of coal, petroleum, and hydroelectric power	93,372,000,000,000
II. Active energy per year or energy consumption:	
Mechanical energy—	
Coal: 24,688,000 long tons, 1930	10,000,000,000
Oil and other fuels: 6,640,000 tung	1,500,000,000
Hydroelectric power: 1,000 H. P.	4,000,000
Total (or 4,510,000 H. P.)	11,504,000,000
(a) Electricity of all plants and factories 2,475,000,000	
(b) Locomotives (1,426 in no.). . 1,420,000,000	
(c) Automobiles (41,853 ,, ,,). . 1,390,000,000	
(d) Steamships (452,558 tons). . 620,000,000	
Total 5,905,000,000	
Human energy—	
Adult farmers (175,000,000 working 2400 hours) .	21,800,000,000
Working animals (31,700,000 working 100 days)	12,600,000,000
Factory workers (3,622,390 in 1930)	650,000,000
Handicrafts workers (1,000,000)	150,000,000
Ricksha men, etc. (400,000)	36,000,000
Other adults and minors	2,800,000,000
Total (or 20,000,000 H. P.)	38,000,000,000
Grand total of active energy (or 24,510,000 H.P.)	49,000,000,000

Source: Ku You-chuan, "The Development of Energy Resources and the Modernization of China." *Shun Pao Monthly,* Volume II, No. 7, July 15, 1933, pp. 87–96.

Note: One kilowatt hour equals 1.5 H. P. hour; 1 adult equals 1/10 H. P. (1/20 H. P. used).

energy of approximately 93,372,000,000,000 kilowatt hours. At the rate of consumption in Japan to-day (i.e., 166 kilowatt hours per capita), this reserve can last 1,400 years in China. This is more promising than the situation has been hitherto believed to be by the visionary defeatist.

It is seen, then, that China is potentially a wealthy nation. Yuan Shih-kai was right when, in his inaugural address as first President of China, he compared China to the rich man who has buried his riches under the ground and is complaining all the time of poverty. Chen Kung-po, present Minister of Industry, concluded

The Ability of China to Support Education 169

in his *China's Four-Year Industrial Plan* that her national weakness lies not in poverty but in economic stagnation.

"Our wealth and our treasures remain hidden in the ground awaiting the pick and shovel, the plough and the hoe. If we can make our dollars circulate faster, we shall be greatly enriching our financial resources."[31]

ESTIMATES OF CHINA'S NATIONAL WEALTH AND INCOME

There have been many attempts to estimate China's total wealth. Table 66 gives these estimates in various years. One is puzzled by the great variations and finds difficulty in trusting the reliability of the figures. The estimate of the Dresdner Bank for 1926 is probably fairly reliable in view of the German reputation for thoroughness. The officials of the Bank declared: "No figures have been taken into account that might give rise to real suspicion. . . . Not infrequently (the estimates) show rather considerable divergences and can only be compared in a limited sense . . . [the] following offers the best guarantee for their reliability."[32]

The lowest estimate of China's wealth is $40,183,000,000 in Chinese currency for the year 1922. The highest estimate is $200,573,000,000 in Chinese currency for the year 1929. The latter estimate was made by Doane.[33] According to this authority, China ranks third among all countries of the world, with 6 per cent of the total world's wealth of U.S.$1,401,809,000,000 in 1929, while the United States ranks first with 44.8 per cent, and Great Britain ranks second with 6.44 per cent (not including colonies).

The latest estimate of China's wealth was made in May, 1932, by China's largest and oldest newspaper, the

---
[31]*China Economic Journal*, Volume XIII, No. 3, Sept., 1933, p. 219.
[32]*Economic Forces of the World*, 1930. Notes on pp. 169 and 171.
[33]Doane, R. R., *The Measurement of American Wealth*, Table X, p. 35

170 *The Financing of Public Education in China*

Shun Pao. This figure, Yuan 106,351,987,446, is accepted by the writer for comparisons with figures of other countries. Of this total, land constitutes 82 per cent; houses, granaries, and other buildings, 5.2 per cent; commercial commodities in stock, 4 per cent; harbors, rivers, and so forth, 2.1 per cent; home furnishings and art articles, 1.6 per cent; domestic animals and other animals, 1.6 per cent; gold and silver moneys and bullion, 1.4 per cent; and salt production, 1.3 per cent. The remainder, including mining production, fishery products, shipping, railways and other public utilities, corporations and banks, libraries and electric plants, constitute only .8 per cent.[34]

CHINA COMPARED WITH OTHER COUNTRIES IN PER CAPITA WEALTH AND INCOME

Tables 66, 67, and 68, following consecutively, present the facts concerning per capita wealth and income of China and other countries.

TABLE 66

CORRECTED ESTIMATES OF CHINA'S WEALTH IN MILLIONS OF UNIT CURRENCY

YEAR	CHINESE CURRENCY	U. S. CURRENCY	OTHER CURRENCY	PER CAPITA IN CHINESE CURRENCY
High Estimates				
1913–14	$109,334	G$52,852(1)		
192?	106,133(2)	50,413		268
1926	126,360	60,026	ReM252,000(4)	301(600ReM)
1929	200,573	84,000(8)		413
1932	106,352(3)	50,517		224
Low Estimates				
1922	40,183	19,087	Yen 38,289(5)	106(101 Yen)
1922	40,183	19,087(6)		106
1926 (?)	40,619	19,294	ReM 81,000(7)	107

[34]*Shun Pao Year Book*, 1933, p. M47.

(1) Based upon Takahashi's estimate immediately preceding the World War and converted into U.S. currency by Charles Hodges in his "Non-Political Factors Underlying the Chinese Problem," Paper No. 6, *Op. cit.*
(2) From the *China Year Book*, No. 1, quoting from Takahashi, *The Wealth of China*, pp. 587–588 (in Chinese).
(3) Chinese estimate. The *Shun Pao Year Book*, p. M47 (in Chinese).
(4) German estimate. Dresdner Bank, *The Economic Forces of the World*, "The Development of National Wealth 1913–14," table facing p. 176.
(5) From table of "Wealth of Various Countries," published by the Japanese Cabinet Bureau of Statistics, April 19, 1929. Quoted by Chuan-Shih Li, "Ten Years of Chinese National Economy," Tenth Anniversary Issue of the *World Magazine*, August 10, 1931, p. 90 (in Chinese). Mr. Li mistook the figure for the 1929 estimate. This same figure appears in the Japanese *Ji Ji Year Book*, 1933 (in Japanese), in which the year for making this estimate is given as 1922.
(6) From Moody. See Edie, L. D., *Economics, Principles and Problems*, p. 273. This is found to be the Japanese estimate in U. S. currency at par exchange.
(7) Gourjon and Parkinson's computation. Quoted by Chuan-Shih Li under Note (5).
(8) Doane, R. R., *Op. cit.*, p. 35.

Remarks: The underlined figures appear in the original source. Those not underlined are freshly calculated by using the par of exchange taken from the U. S. Federal Reserve Bulletins for the respective years.

TABLE 67

A COMPARISON OF ESTIMATED WEALTH IN CHINA AND IN OTHER COUNTRIES IN MILLIONS OF CHINESE DOLLARS
(Corrected and Rearranged)

Countries	Year	Total Wealth	Per Capita Wealth
(1) China	1926	$ 126,360	$ 301
(2) China	1932	106,352	224
(3) India	1926	73,146	251
(4) Russia	1926	110,220	752
(5) Mexico	1926	14,028	951
(6) Italy	1925	44,738	1,117
(7) Japan	1924	102,343	1,731
(8) Japan	1928	107,404	1,287
(9) Germany	1926	165,320	2,455
(10) Belgium	1926	22,545	2,906
(11) France	1928	148,296	3,607
(12) United Kingdom	1925	236,330	5,247
(13) Canada	1926	56,112	5,962
(14) United States	1925	762,356	6,607
(15) United States	1927	879,275	7,515
(16) United States	1930	604,189	5,638

(1) See Table 66, Note (4).
(2) See Table 66, Note (3).
(3) Dresdner Bank, *Op. cit.*, Table facing p. 176.
(4) *Ibid.*
(5) *Ibid.*
(6) *Shun Pao Year Book*, *Op. cit.*, p. M47. Same figure appears in the Japanese *Ji Ji Year Book*, 1933. (Apparently the Chinese estimate assumes that the Yen and the Chinese dollar were approximately the same in value at that time.)
(7) *Ibid.*
(8) *The World Almanac*, 1933, p. 423. Converted from G$51,017,000,000.
(9) Dresdner Bank estimate.
(10), (11), (13) *Ibid.*
(12) and (14) *Shun Pao Year Book.*
(15) Dresdner Bank estimate.
(16) *Chicago Daily News Almanac and Year Book*, 1933, p. 280. Converted from G$329,738,000,000 and G$2,677 respectively.

Remarks: All computations are made by par exchange rates taken from the *U. S. Federal Reserve Bulletins* for the designated years.

TABLE 68

A COMPARISON OF THE ESTIMATED INCOME OF CHINA AND OTHER COUNTRIES IN MILLIONS OF CHINESE DOLLARS

Country	Year	Total Income	Per Capita Income
		$	$
(1) China	1928	12,525	29
(2) India	1922	17,335	54
(3) Russia	1928	24,800	163
(4) Russia	1931	26,316	
(5) Italy	1928	12,174	297
(6) Japan	1925	11,523	187
(7) Japan	1931	9,474	105
(8) Germany	1928	34,319	540
(9) France	1928	20,591	500
(10) United Kingdom	1928	35,822	785
(11) Canada	1927	12,024	1,263
(12) United States	1928	187,174	1,560
(13) United States	1931	113,684	926

(1) Dresdner Bank estimate. See Table 67, Note (4).
(2), (3), (5), (6), (8), (9), (10), (11), and (12) *Ibid.* Conversion from Reich Marks at par of exchange.
(4), (7), (13) From *Chicago Daily News Almanac and Year Book*, 1933, p. 276. Conversion from G$12,500,000,000, G$54,000,000,000, and G$4,500,000,000 at par of exchange.

There is only one estimate of China's income made by the Dresdner Bank for the year 1928 (see Table 68). Probably it is based upon the assumption that

"National income on the whole fluctuates between 10 and 20 per cent of national wealth and . . . it rises the more in its proportion to national wealth, the larger the latter is per head of population."[35]

Both China's per capita national wealth and her income rank the lowest among selected countries, while those of the United States rank highest despite the economic depression.

THE ABILITY OF CHINA TO SUPPORT EDUCATION, CONSIDERED IN RELATION TO ESTIMATES OF HER NATIONAL WEALTH AND INCOME

Wealth "is strictly a function of what other people than the owner are able and willing to pay for the possessions, hence the aggregate wealth is not a very good basis from which to start thinking out the financial foundations," says Morrison.[36] All taxes and other obligations of the people are paid out of their incomes. Income is the best test of ability to support education. However, there has been an attempt to measure the ability to support education by a combination of wealth and income as an index of economic power. Strayer, when Director of the Educational Finance Inquiry Commission in 1923, arrived at the following definition "after considerable study and consultation with the economic advisors":[37]

$$\text{Index of Economic Resources} = \frac{(\text{Taxable income}) + (1/10 \text{ Full value of real estate})}{2}$$

[35] Dresdner Bank, *Op. cit.*, p. 171.
[36] Morrison, H. C., *School Revenue*, p. 46.
[37] Strayer, G. D., and Haig, Robert M., *The Financing of Education in the State of New York*, p. 172. Report of the Educational Finance Inquiry Commission, 1923.

Norton used income plus one-tenth of the value of wealth as an index of economic resources in measuring the ability of the forty-eight states to support education.[38] It would be folly to apply this formula in China when actual figures of wealth and income of the provinces are not available. For the present, the writer shall content himself with a comparison between educational expenditure and the estimated wealth and income.

In the United States, the value of public school property was U.S.$7,143,803,297, or 2.21 per cent of the total value of wealth (U.S.$322,735,000,000) in 1930.[39] She spent in the same year U.S.$2,615,068 for public schools, or 3.35 per cent of her national income of U.S.$75,000,000,000.[40] For all levels of schools, public and private, she invested U.S.$11,216,704,000 in property and endowments, or 3.44 per cent of her wealth, and the current cost was U.S.$3,234,638,567, or 4.15 per cent of her national income in 1930.[41]

In China, the educational expenditure for 1930–31 was $217,877,611,[41a] or 1.77 per cent of her estimated income of $12,525,000,000. The cost of all public education was $155,042,788, or 1.26 per cent of this income. By comparison with the United States, China can afford to at least double her public educational expenditure, with, of course, full consideration of other limiting factors. Educational expenditure must be considered in relation to the proportion of taxes, to national income, and to the distribution of individual incomes. (See Table 69.)

---

[38]Norton, John K., *The Ability of the States to Support Education*, p. 19, Table 5.
[39]"Facts on School Costs." *Research Bulletin* of the National Education Association, Volume X, No. 5, November, 1932, p. 210.
[40]*Ibid.*, p. 208.
[41]*Biennial Survey of Education*, 1928–39, pp 11–12.
[41a]Table 15.

The proportions of the national income devoted to taxes in various countries in 1928 are as follows:[42]

Great Britain	22.0 %	Australia	18.4 %
Norway	20.0 %	Hungary	18.0 %
Italy	19.2 %	Austria	17.3 %
Canada	19.2 %	Japan	14.4 %
France	18.5 %	U. S. A.	10.2 %
China	10.4 %		

The proportions of national income and of taxes devoted to public education may be seen in the following tabulation:

TABLE 69

PROPORTIONS OF NATIONAL INCOME AND OF TAXES DEVOTED TO PUBLIC EDUCATION IN THE UNITED STATES AND CHINA

Country and Year	Per Cent That Tax Collections Are of National Income	Per Cent That Public School Costs Are of National Income	Per Cent That Public School Costs Are of Tax Collections	Per Cent That Total Education Costs Are of National Income
U. S. A.				
1900		1.20		
1913	6.61	1.57	23.77	
1922	11.80	2.49	21.07	
1928	10.39	2.44	23.51	
1930	14.46	3.07	21.24	4.15
1931	20.00?			
China				
1929–30	10.40	1.26		1.77

Figures for U. S. A.—adapted from Larson, *Op. cit.*, tables on pp. 7 and 10.

Figures for China—estimates per capita tax collection over per capita school costs and public school costs.

[42]Figures for China—per capita taxes, $3 Mex. divided by per capita ncome, $29. Per capita taxes estimated by the League of Nations' Mission of Educational Experts. *Reorganization of Education in China*, p. 50. Figures for other countries—Larson, Emil L., *School Finance and Related Problems in Arizona*, p. 9.

These facts do not mean that China can afford to increase the proportions given above to match the respective United States proportions. The principle underlying the progressive rates of taxation according to ability to pay operates here. Ability to pay involves the element of sacrifice and its amount. Its measure is what remains of the income after the taxes are paid. Larger incomes can produce higher rates of payment.

Most probably the tax rate is already high in China as compared with the proportion of tax collection related to national income in the United States in 1928 and previously. The problem in China is chiefly one of shifting the tax burden or finding new sources of revenue so that individuals with higher incomes may bear a larger share of the burden. It is certain that the proportion public school costs in China are of the national income can be increased at least twofold, and that this additional educational burden should rest upon the financially abler classes of the population, or should be taken care of by a reduction of the huge military expenditures and by more efficient systems of taxation so that the leakage of tax collections into private pockets may be checked.

This problem will be discussed in detail in the following chapter.

CHAPTER X

THE ABILITY OF CHINA TO SUPPORT EDUCATION

THE FINANCIAL FOUNDATIONS

Based on the estimate on page 142, with all factors considered as to its accuracy, the present educational program and the program of expansion and improvement during the next twenty years demands approximately $385,000,000 annually, or 3.04 per cent of the estimated national income (see page 172). This amount is still below the figure of 4.15 per cent of the national income of the United States spent for education in 1930 (see page 174), but the United States is certainly better able to pay a high percentage than is China.

However, if the educational budget is graduated, as shown in Table 58, the program of expansion and improvement would require $1,699,511,000 for the first decade, or about $170,000,000 annually. If the present cost of $155,000,000 for public education (see page 47) annually is added to it, then the total amount needed for both the present program and the program of expansion and improvement would be about $325,000,000 each year during the first ten years of the plan. This is approximately 2.6 per cent of China's national income. When the total national income is considered, this sum probably lies within China's ability to pay. The problem has now become one of the distribution of burden upon both the different classes of the population and the different levels and grades of government.

It has been shown that China has proven able to spend $155,000,000 yearly for public education. An increase of $170,000,000 for the expansion program would certainly raise the problem of how this sum should be distributed among the various levels of government, and the ability of the people to make such large cash payments.

The distribution of this increase in burden among the three levels of government has been proposed as shown in Table 58 (page 141). The central government would need to pay $728,883,000, the provincial governments $207,060,000, and the county governments, $763,568,000 during the first decade of the plan, or, in round numbers, $73,000,000, $21,000,000, and $76,000,000 per year respectively. This means that the central government would have to provide for an increase of at least four times its present educational budget. This is only 11.45 per cent (including the present cost) of the central government budget of $777,000,000 for 1934–35 (see page 80). This percentage is still below the 15 per cent provided by the Draft Constitution to be adopted in March, 1935 (see page 95). The provincial governments would have to provide for an increase of at least one half of their present educational expenditure. Including their present educational expenditure, the new sum would be about 25 per cent of their combined government budgets (see Table 34, Column 11). This percentage is still below the 30 per cent provided by the Draft Constitution.

Pending the development of a technique for the measurement of the relative ability of the different administrative units for supporting education, the writer arbitrarily suggests, for the time being, a ratio of 1:2:3 for three grades of governments in economic and financial ability. The ablest grade of government should pay at least three times as much as the poorest grade, and the medium grade should pay at least twice as much as the poorest grade.

Applying this tentative ratio, it is found that the eight poorest provinces should pay at least $437,500 each year during the first ten years for the expansion program; the eight medium provinces at least $875,000 each year; and the eight ablest provinces at least $1,312,000.

The 590 poorest counties should increase their educational expenditure at least $21,500 each per year; the 590 medium counties at least $43,000 each per year; and the ablest 590 counties at least $64,500 each per year, during the first ten years of the expansion program.

Are all these sums within the financial ability of the different treasuries? This question will be answered only after a careful analysis of the present status of the government treasuries.

THE FINANCIAL ABILITY OF THE CENTRAL GOVERNMENT

Since 1912 major or minor internecine warfare has been waged every year, and the Central Government has constantly faced deficits by borrowing. The writer has made a thorough study of the history of financial chaos in China, beginning with the Opium War and including the unequal treaties, the loss of tariff autonomy, and the enormous indemnities and increasing regressiveness of the tax system. A table has been constructed *showing internecine warfare* each year since 1912 paralleling the amount of foreign and domestic borrowings.[1] Space and time limitations prevent the inclusion of detailed data here. Only a few pertinent facts may be presented to indicate the seriousness of the financial situation.

Following 1916, the provincial war lords increasingly retained part or all of the revenues of the Central Government. It is not surprising that the impoverished Central Government from 1916 to 1922 incurred arrears of $195,716,000 for civil and military affairs, and arrears of

[1] Unpublished Document No. 3.

TABLE 70

STATUS OF CENTRAL FINANCE UNDER THE PEKING GOVERNMENT, 1916-22

Year	Estimated Actual Expenditure	Arrears of Civil Administration	Arrears of Military Affairs	Arrears of Central Education
	$	$	$	$
1915	139,036,455			
1916	98,455,000	283,000	1,374,000	18,000
1917	97,075,000	1,300,000	1,607,000	137,000
1918	97,937,000	504,000	1,559,000	6,000
1919	64,712,000	7,679,000	27,609,000	239,000
1920	59,225,000	14,161,000	26,603,000	173,000
1921	33,574,000	21,735,000	44,151,000	422,000
1922	20,000,000	18,048,000	29,103,000	1,758,000
Total		$63,710,000	$132,006,000	$2,753,000

Source: Chu Pian-yuan and Tang Tseh-yen, "Ten Years of Central Finance," *Tsing Hua Research Bulletin* (Tsing Hua Hsueh Pao), Volume 3, No. 2, January and February, 1926, pp. 967-997.

$2,753,000 for central education. It is not surprising that education was left to stagnate. What reliance could be placed upon the Central Government to aid the local governments in education and to take the initiative in promoting the cause of universal education?

From 1842 to 1895 China endured the crushing burden of indemnities amounting to 267,700,000 taels and 9,000,000 rubles, or approximately $410,550,000. The Boxer Uprising in 1900 placed her under the further obligation to pay an indemnity of 450,000,000 taels or $675,000,000. The total of principal and interest payments over a period of forty to forty-eight years is 982,238,150 taels, or $1,473,357,225. The actual yearly payments of this obligation from 1928 to 1931 were as follows:[2]

[2] *Annual Reports* of the Minister of Finance.

The Ability of China to Support Education 181

1928–29 $38,663,189.79, or 8.8 per cent of total central disbursements.
1929–30 $41,252,970.16, or 7.7 per cent of total central disbursements.
1930–31 $48,500,899.32, or 6.8 per cent of total central disbursements.
1931–32 $31,089,750.07, or 4.1 per cent of total central disbursements.

In January, 1934, the total of principal and interest payments still outstanding was $783,441,115.32, spreading over a period of fifteen years more.[3]

CHINA'S FOREIGN AND DOMESTIC INDEBTEDNESS

The financial situation in China has been characterized by the word, *chinoiserie*. Accurate financial statistics are lacking. Many estimates of China's total indebtedness have been made from time to time by the Finance Ministry and by foreign and native experts. These estimates vary widely, owing to the different rates of exchange applied, the inclusion and exclusion of unsecured loans and sundry loans and of communication loans not under the authority of the Finance Ministry, and also to the occasional lack of certain items of indebtedness outstanding for the year for which the total indebtedness has been calculated. Considerable time and care have been expended in arriving at the figures given in Table 71.

It is evident that in 1934 China's outstanding indebtedness had increased approximately 100 per cent since the end of the first year of the Republic. The obligation of the Ministry of Finance totals at present $2,523,890,000,000 (silver) as compared with $1,359,140,000,000 (silver) at the close of 1912. The total obligation of

---

[3] "A Summary of the Chinese Domestic and Foreign Loans and the Indemnity Funds for 1933," *Bank of China Monthly Review*, Volume 8, No. 3, March, 1934, pp. 1–6.

182 *The Financing of Public Education in China*

TABLE 71

TREND OF OUTSTANDING INDEBTEDNESS OF CHINESE CENTRAL GOVERNMENT, INCLUDING FOREIGN AND DOMESTIC SECURED AND UNSECURED LOANS AND INDEMNITIES
(In Millions of Silver Dollars)

Year Beginning—	Total Obligation of National Treasury Under Ministry of Finance (a)	Total Obligation of Central Government, Communication Loans not Under Finance Ministry Included (b)	Boxer Indemnity, Outstanding (Included in (a)) (c)	Amount and Per Cent that Debt Service of (a) Is of Total Central Expenditure (d)	
				Amount $	%
1. 1902, Jan. 1	501.4	574.40			
2. 190? ?		1,450.00			
3. 1913, Jan. 1	1,359.14	1,750.14		141.9	22
4. 1914, Jan. 1	1,292.09	1,683.90	618.4	29.4	21
5. 1917, Jan. 1	1,646.58	2,112.38		137.7	24
6. 1919				214.6	33
7. 1922, Oct. 1	1,981.73	2,618.13	576.25		
8. 1925				166.5	54
9. 1926, Jan. 1	1,813.91	2,463.23	396.52		
10. 1928, July	1,615.00	2,212.00		159.9	37
11. 1929, Jan. 1	2,663.79	3,313.12	554.59	200.3	37
12. 1929, April		3,028.48		289.5	46(1930)
13. 1931, Jan. 1	2,701.84	3,201.88	503.92	269.8	39
14. 1932, Jan, 1	2,074.76 ?	2,701.90 ?		223.9	26
15. 1932, Jan. 1	4,380.07 ?	5,308.02 ?			
16. 1933				241.8	29
17. 1934, Mar. 1	2,523.89	3,348.73	783.44		

Sources: 1. Remer, *Foreign Investments in China,* p. 135. Conversion at normal rate of $2 per U.S.$. Ching, Kia Chu, *Domestic Debts in China,* p. 2.
2. Chia, Shi Yi, *Financial History of the Republic of China,* p. 1182.
3. Ching, *Op. cit.,* p. 41; Chia, *Op. cit.,* p. 1202.
4. Remer, *Op. cit.,* p. 135. Conversion from U. S. $ at normal rate. Ching, *Op. cit.,* p. 41.
5. Chia, *Op. cit.,* pp. 1164 and 1179; Ching, *Op. cit.,* p. 41.
6. Chia, *Op. cit.,* Budget, p. 1179.
7. *First China Year Book,* 1924, p. 622. Rate of conversion at $8 per sterling as given.
9. Mayton, J. G., *Budgets of Far Eastern Countries,* p. 28; and Woodhead, *China Year Book,* 1928, p. 630.
10. Committee on National Indebtedness appointed by National Economic Conference, *China Year Book,* 1929-30, p. 657; and *Proceedings* of the Conference, p. 144.

The Ability of China to Support Education

11. Chia, Shi Yi, *China's Finances, the Public Debt* (Kuo Tzai Yu Ching Yung), pp. 1–6.
12. Estimate of Professor E. W. Kemmerer, *China Year Book*, 1931, p. 346.
13. *China Year Book*, 1931, p. 355. Compare with Clark's estimate of $2,524,538,930 and $3,786,808,395 for (b) at the rates of $10 and $15 per sterling respectively. See Clark, Grover, *Economic Rivalries in China*, pp. 44–45.
14. Based upon Wang's estimate of foreign debts (probably not including Boxer Indemnity) at the average rate between gold and silver for the past 30 years. See Wang, Kwo Chung, "Foreign Debts of Our Country," *Ta Kung Newspaper*, Jan. 24, 1934; and Ching, *Op. cit.*, p. 41.
15. E. Kann's estimate of foreign debts in sterling converted at $18 per sterling, as quoted in *China Year Book*, 1931–32, p. 447; also Ching's estimate of domestic debts, *Op. cit.*, p. 41.
17. "A Summary of the Chinese Domestic and Foreign Loans and the Indemnity Funds for 1933," *Bank of China Monthly Review*, Volume VIII, No. 8, March, 1934, pp. 1–6. Including communication indebtedness taken from Kann in *China Year Book*, 1931–32; also sundry loans and the recent $44,000,000 loan secured on the Italian Boxer Indemnity.

See also Unpublished Document No. 18, showing detailed calculations.

the Central Government, including communication loans, reaches $3,348,780,000,000 (silver) as compared with $1,750,000,000 at the close of 1912. The amount of debt service has reached approximately a quarter of a billion silver dollars, and constitutes about one third of the total central expenditure. However, the burden imposed by the Boxer Indemnity has almost reached an end, as the various countries have agreed to either return or renounce their shares of the indemnity. If this item is excluded as a foreign obligation, according to Remer[4] China's indebtedness at present is reduced to $1,470,-000,000 under the Finance Ministry, and the total indebtedness is reduced to $2,565,290,000,000, or $5.7 per capita of the population of 450,000,000. This amount is very small in comparison with the per capita debt of other countries, but the proportion that debt service is of central expenditure is higher in China than in all other countries studied, with the exception of France, as shown in Table 72 following.

[4]Remer, *Foreign Investments in China*, p. 145.

184 *The Financing of Public Education in China*

TABLE 72

RELATION BETWEEN DEBT SERVICE AND NATIONAL INDEBTEDNESS IN VARIOUS COUNTRIES, 1932-33

Country	Per Capita National Indebtedness 1931	Per Cent That Debt Service Is of National Expenditure, 1932-33
	(A)	(B)
1. United States	G$ 1,087	25 (1931-32)
2. France	G$ 940	40
3. Germany	G$ 772	12
4. United Kingdom	G$ 1,784	34
5. Italy	G$ 609	22 (1931-32)
6. Japan	Yen 63a	16
7. Soviet Russia	GR 395	2 (1931)b
8. China	S$ 7.44c	39 (1931)

A. *Chicago Daily News Almanac and Year Book*, 1933, p. 276.
B. Quoted from *Bank of China Monthly Review*, Volume VIII, No. 3, March, 1934, pp. 1-6.
    a. *The Third Financial and Economic Annual of Japan*, 1932.
    b. *The Unified Financial Plan*, V. O. K. S., published by the Soviet Union for Cultural Relations with Foreign Countries, Volume II, Nos. 7-9, 1931
    c. 1934—Total indebtedness including indemnity per capita of 450,000,000 population.

The chief difficulty in connection with China's increasing indebtedness lies in the nonproductive use of revenue from loans. The Nanking Government spent 85.6 per cent of the domestic loans for military purposes.[5] Another major difficulty lies in the heavy burden indebtedness places upon the national expenditure budget, leaving little for the constructive purposes of government. The recent financial crisis has revealed a deficit of $12,000,000 per month, and the Central Government has to depend upon further loans to maintain its existence. According to Ching,[6] there is hope of liquidating all domestic debts in 1953 if there is no further borrowing. However, the trend is toward more borrowing, especially from foreign countries for reconstruction. Evidently,

[5]Ching, *Domestic Loans of China*, p. 47.
[6]Ching, *Op. cit* p. 59.

The Ability of China to Support Education

there is little hope that the Central Government will allocate the $123,500,000 required yearly for education under the existing revenue system.

The Financial Ability of the Local Governments

The provincial treasuries are facing a crisis similar to that of the Central Government. These facts are shown in Tables 73, 74, and 75. Table 73 indicates that out of nine provinces reporting, four had deficits in the year 1931–32. Three provinces paid a debt service comprising 27.4 per cent, 29.7 per cent, and 38 per cent of their respective expenditures. In seven provinces military expenditure constituted 21.4 to 60.9 per cent of the total expenditure. In eight of them, approximately one half of the total expenditure was devoted to military expenditure and debt service. According to Wei,[7] the

TABLE 73

FINANCIAL SITUATION IN NINE PROVINCES REPORTING FOR THE FISCAL YEAR, 1931–32

Provinces Reporting	Actual Revenue	Actual Expenditure	Per Cent That Military Expenditures Including Public Safety Is of Total Expenditure	Per Cent That Debt Service Is of Total Expenditure
Kiangsu	$17,209,183	$17,176,820	21.4	27.4
Chekiang	32,443,823	32,405,287	10.2	38.0
Anhwei	8,473,790	8,520,219	29.6	3.5
Hopei	18,461,990	18,195,331	35.5	0.4
Honan	9,918,185	10,150,440	25.3	0.4
Shantung	21,410,780	22,896,603	23.4	0.0
Hupeh	24,502,056	24,502,056	24.2	29.7
Hunan	16,910,809	16,908,751	10.9	0.0
Ninghsia	2,534,112	2,715,133	60.9	0.0

Adapted from Table I, *Statistical Monthly*, No. 10, March and April, 1933. Percentages freshly calculated.

[7] Wei, Wung Tang, "The Status of Chinese Public Finance and Its Future," *New China Magazine*, Vol. 1, No. 3, Feb. 10, 1933, pp. 1–7.

TABLE 74

INDEBTEDNESS OF EIGHT PROVINCES AND FIVE MUNICIPALITIES, INCLUDING SOME SPECIAL LOANS, 1927–32

Year	Amount of Loans Floated	Outstanding Indebtedness
Before 1927	$ 37,301,294	
1927	4,530,736	
1928	9,500,000	
1929	20,137,425	
1930	44,563,828	
1931	26,014,672	
1932	64,730,000	
Total	$169,476,661a	
Total, Jan. 1, 1932	$140,500,000b	$87,318,000

Sources: (a) "Special and Local Public Loans," *Chinese Economic Journal*, Volume XIII, No. 5, Nov., 1933, pp. 495–514.

(b) "Chekiang Industrial Bank: A Survey of Special and Local Public Loans," *Shun Pao Year Book*, 1933, pp. M60–63 (not including loans floated before 1928).

TABLE 75

INDEBTEDNESS OF TWELVE PROVINCES AND MUNICIPALITIES, ACCORDING TO PURPOSES OF LOANS, FOR THE CALENDAR YEAR 1932
(In Thousands of Dollars)

Purposes of Loan	Amount of Issue	Per Cent of Total
Armaments	$45,000	41.6
Financial adjustment and payment of military deficit	23,000	21.3
Maintenance of paper currency	31,000	28.7
Bandit suppression	4,500	4.2
Aid to silk industry	3,000	2.8
Local public enterprises	1,500	1.4
Total	$1,008,030	100.0
January to June, 1933	$45,000	

Source: *Bank of China Monthly*, June 3, 1933, or *Shun Pao Monthly*, Vol. II, No. 10, Oct. 5, 1933, pp. 21–24.

budgets of Kiangsu and Chekiang (two of the wealthiest provinces in China) showed deficits of $8,635,000 and $6,000,000 respectively for the year 1932–33. The budgets of Hupeh, Hunan, Kiangsi, and Anhwei for the same year were sharply reduced.

The budget of Chekiang for 1933–34 showed a decrease of $1,467,629 below that of 1932–33, and carried a deficit of $1,360,000. The public debts of the provinces are steadily increasing. Table 74 reveals that 13 provinces and municipalities in 1932 had increased their loans to thirteen times their loans in 1927. The total amount of loans issued up to 1932 was $169,000,000 (or $140,000,000 according to two inquiries), and the amount of outstanding indebtedness was no less than $87,000,000. According to figures presented by the Bank of China, the total amount of loans issued reached $1,008,000,000 in 12 provinces and municipalities, with 45.8 per cent of this total used directly for military purposes, 50 per cent for financial adjustment, and only 4.2 per cent for productive enterprises. (See Table 75.)

This situation gives the politician plausible reasons for advocating the reduction of educational expenditures. But the school man sees the situation in a different light. He argues from the self-evident principle that school expenditure, and especially productive educational expenditure, is essentially a part of the national income and aids in increasing the sources of revenue, and that even under the present revenue system each large province can afford to spend $3,000,000 a year (as shown by the actual average of $2,601,086 in 1932–33 expended by each of the large provincial governments).[8]

Data for a study of county government finance are not available to the writer except in the case of Hupeh

[8] *Education and the Masses*, Volume V, No. 6, February 28, 1634. Table on Provincial and Municipal Educational Expenditure for the Fiscal Year, 1933–34, page 1068.

Province.⁹ It is perhaps safe to say that the county governments in all China are facing similar situations.

WHAT THE GOVERNMENT HAS DONE IN THE RECONSTRUCTION OF THE REVENUE SYSTEM OF CHINA

The problem has now become one of the preparation of the tax sheets and the mechanism of public finance. The school man cannot usurp the function of the tax experts, but certainly he should understand at least the essentials of a desirable revenue system in order to tackle the problem of financing schools more intelligently, with the coöperation of the tax experts.

General Standards for Judging Any State Tax System:

Authorities in the science of finance such as Seligman, Lutz, and others, have laid down criteria for judging a tax system. Some of these criteria are as follows:[10]

"(1) Adequacy—The tax system should produce sufficient revenues to meet all the legitimate needs of the state.

"(2) Economy—Taxes should involve low percentage of overhead cost for their collection.

"(3) Convenience—Installments, places, and dates for payment should be arranged to meet the convenience of the public.

"(4) Certainty—The revenue of a state should be stable and dependable.

"(5) Adaptability—The tax system should be susceptible of ready modification in time of need.

"(6) Diversity—Taxes should tap more than one source.

"(7) Conformity—The tax system should be unified and in accord with the political ideas of the time.

"(8) Conservation—The tax system should discourage squandering the patrimony of the state.

---

[9] See Table 86, pages 241 *sqq.*

[10] National Education Association, Research Division, "School Revenues and New Methods of Taxation," *Studies in State Educational Administration*, No. 2, January, 1930, p. 2. See also National Tax Association, *Second Report on a Plan of a Model System of State and Local Taxation.* National Tax Association, 1933, pp. 9–10.

"(9) Equitableness—A sound tax system must be equitable; that is to say, the burden of paying taxes should be distributed fairly among the people of the state."

In 1933 a committee of the National Tax Association in the United States outlined a new plan for a model system of taxation. The three fundamental principles mentioned in its report are:

"(1) Every person having taxable ability should pay some sort of a direct personal tax to the government in which he is domiciled and from which he receives the personal benefits that government confers.

"(2) Tangible property, by whomsoever owned, should be taxed by the jurisdiction in which it is located, because it there receives protection and other governmental benefits and services.

"(3) Business carried on for profit in any locality should be taxed for the benefits it receives."[11]

Shaw Kinn-wei, in his doctorate dissertation at Columbia University in 1926, has worked out a set of underlying principles for the reconstruction of the Chinese financial system, based upon a thorough study of the philosophical and historical background of Chinese public finance in the light of the teachings of Western authorities in the science of finance. These are briefly summarized as follows:[12]

1. Finance of the people.
(a) Fiscal autonomy. There should be tariff autonomy.
(b) Civil control as opposed to military control.
(c) Finance by taxation instead of by loans.
(d) Direct taxation more emphasized than indirect taxation.
(1) The ethical principle of justice.
(2) The economic principle of protection.
(3) The sociological principle of progressive rates.
(4) The regional principle of local tradition and expediency.

[11] National Tax Association, Op. cit., pp. 10–11. See also "Critical Problems in School Administration," Twelfth Yearbook of the Department of Superintendence of the National Education Association, February, 1934.
[12] Shaw Kinn-wei, Democracy and Finance in China, 1926, pp. 169–194.

(5) The political principle of avoiding double and multiple taxation.

(6) The administrative principle of honesty, economy, and efficiency.

(7) The technical principle of practical experts.

(8) The psychological principles of increasing governmental functions and maximum social advantage as opposed to minimum taxation as the best taxation; of taxation as a way of coöperative living as opposed to the old concept of taxation as a tribute; and of the right conception of direct taxation as opposed to the old concept of indirect taxation as less burdensome.

2. Finance by the people.
(*a*) Taxation with representation.
(*b*) Publicity of accounts.
(*c*) Efficient budget-making.

3. Finance for the people—promotion of general welfare.
(*a*) Finance for peace versus war.
(*b*) Government by wise economy versus parsimony.
(*c*) The operation of government industries according to the principle of maximum welfare versus maximum revenue.
(*d*) Expenditure for constructive social development.

No facts are needed in addition to those presented in Chapter VII to prove that the Chinese tax system and the entire financial mechanism is very antiquated and unjust in the light of the above-mentioned principles and standards. It is true that a new pump is no cure for a dry well, but a new drill can penetrate the hard crust of special privileges and vested interests, and open an artesian well to reach the values hidden beneath. Though China's resources are known to be limited, yet they are sufficient to keep the ship of state sailing from the isle of scarcity to the port of plenty.

The problem of taxation in China is too technical and complicated to be handled in the present study. It demands monumental volumes of facts and the coöperative research of numerous specialized scholars in the field in order to arrive at any practical and workable recommendations. This study will merely show what the

Chinese Government has done and proposes to do in providing for an embarrassed treasury and developing a national economy; it will limit itself to those issues that directly affect educational support.

Due to the efforts of the Nationalist Government, China has made some real progress in reforming her financial system. Numerous Chinese authorities in the science of finance have sown the seeds and are persistently battling for the cause.

The First National Finance Conference and Its Effects

The First National Finance Conference, which convened in July, 1928, adopted the following measures:[13]

A. Financial Measures:

(1) The demarcation of central and all local sources of revenue and items of expenditure.

The central sources of revenue are: salt tax, maritime customs duty, native customs duty, tobacco and wine tax, rolled tobacco tax, kerosene oil tax, Likin or transit duty (before it was abolished), parcel post duty, stamp tax, exchange house tax, corporation and trade-mark registration tax, maritime fishery tax, income tax and inheritance tax, etc.

The local sources of revenue are: land or farm tax, title deeds tax, brokerage tax, pawnshop tax, butchery tax, interior fishery tax, business tax, urban land tax, surtax of the national income tax, boat tax, house tax, and the like.

(2) The unification of national fiscal administration and the separation of the four powers of receipt, disbursement, depository, and audit.

(3) The overhauling of the tax system and the abolishment of the exorbitant miscellaneous levies.

(a) Tariff autonomy.

(b) Improvement of the regressive tax on salt which cannot be abolished abruptly at present.

(c) Cadastral survey of farm land, and the introduction of the land value tax.

(d) Introduction of new taxes:

1—Income tax at a progressive rate.

2—Inheritance tax at a low rate in the beginning.

[13]Ministry of Finance, *Proceedings of the National Conference on Public Finance,* 1928, *passim.*

3—Special consumption taxes on articles of luxury and the abolishment of the obnoxious Likin.

(4) The consolidation of national indebtedness so as to maintain China's credit.

(5) The reduction and regulation of military expenditure at 40 per cent of the national budget.

(6) The enforcement of the budget system, and the supervision of the budgets of all local governments.

B. Economic Measures:

(1) A definite policy for reforming the currency of China; the concentration of the power to issue paper money in the national banks and the introduction of the gold exchange standard.

(2) The development of banking enterprises; the establishment of a powerful central bank, exchange banks, and agricultural and industrial banks, and the encouragement of savings enterprises.

(3) The extension of maritime, land, and air communication.

(4) The employment of soldiers in material reconstruction.

(5) The protection of native industries and commerce.

(6) The development of production through the carrying out of Dr. Sun Yat-sen's industrial plan.

This Finance Conference was called by T. V. Soong, former Minister of Finance, and the above measures have been his actual fiscal policies during the Political Tutelage period.[14] Six years have passed. Although the dark clouds are still in existence, yet the silver linings may be seen, as shown by the following reforms:

1. The national and local sources of revenue have been demarcated.[15]

2. Tariff autonomy has finally been restored by the National Government (in 1931).[16]

[14]Ministry of Finance, *The Finance Monthly*, all numbers, 1928–29. See also, Chia Shi-yi, *Financial History of the Republic of China* (continued), November, 1932, pp. 202–36.

[15]The Directorate of Budget and Statistics, *The National Revenue and Expenditure Budget of the Republic of China for the Fiscal Year 1931–32.* "Standards for the Classification of the Revenue and Expenditure Budgets," pp. 423–27.

[16]Ministry of Finance, *Annual Report for the Fiscal Year, July 1929 to June 1930*, p. 3.

3. Military control of finance has been decreasing.

4. Borrowing actually ceased in the fiscal year 1931–32, although only in that year.[17] The national internal debts were consolidated and converted into longer periods at a lower rate of interest in February, 1932.[18] If no more internal debts are floated, internal indebtedness could be wiped out by 1953.[19] The credit of the Central Government has been enhanced.

5. The obnoxious Likin was officially abolished in January, 1931, although the abolition has never been complete.[20]

6. There has been a marked increase in the amount of yield of the three chief central sources of revenue, namely, the customs duty, the salt tax, and the consolidated taxes.[21]

7. The unification and centralization of central fiscal administration has made marked progress.[22]

8. The Directorate of Budget and Statistics was established in April, 1931. The first real budget of the Republic of China was prepared for the fiscal year 1931–32. A budget law governing the supervision of local budgets was promulgated at the same time.[23]

9. The Ministry of Finance has been trying to maintain and extend whatever basis for a civil service system already exists among its departments.[24]

10. Military expenditure has decreased both in amount and in proportion to the total national budget.[25]

11. The Central Bank of China was established in 1928 and has made steady progress.[26]

12. The silver tael has been abolished as a unit of currency and the dollar adopted instead.

[17]Ministry of Finance, *Report for the 19th and 20th Fiscal Years, July 1930 to June 1932*, p. 2.
[18]*Ibid.*, p. 10.
[19]Ching Kia-chu, *Domestic Debts in China*, 1933, p. 59.
[20]Ministry of Finance, *Op. cit.*, p. 5.
[21]Li, Rei, "Four Years of Tax Reform under the Central Government," *The Economic Statistics Quarterly*, Volume II, No. 1, March, 1933.
[22]Chia Shi-yi, *The Financial History of the Republic of China* (Continued), 1932, pp. 237–314.
[23]The Directorate of Budget and Statistics, *Op. cit.*, pp. 410, 415–22.
[24]Ministry of Finance, *Annual Report for the Fiscal Year, July 1928 to June 1929*, p. 9.
[25]Ministry of Finance, *Report for the 19th and 20th Fiscal Years, July 1930 to June 1932*, p. 12.
[26]Chen, Gideon, *Chinese Government Economic Planning and Reconstruction Since 1927*. China Institute of Pacific Relations, 1933, *passim*.

13. There has been marked progress in material reconstruction.[27]

Reforms which have been attempted but are not yet in effect are not mentioned in the above list.

The Second National Finance Conference

The Second National Finance Conference, under the leadership of the new Minister of Finance, H. H. Kung, convened during the week of May 21-27, 1934.[28] The central themes of the Conference were:

1. Farm tax reduction to alleviate the sufferings of farmers.
2. Abolition of exorbitant taxes and miscellaneous levies.
3. Improvement of the tax system.
4. Determination of local budgets.
5. Productive reconstruction.
6. Mutual coöperation between the central and local governments.

The underlying principle or policy of government finance in the near future was announced to be "the tapping of new sources and the economizing of current expenditure," or "the amount of expenditure to be measured or governed by the amount of revenue."

Though no mention was made of the problem of school finance, some of the important resolutions adopted affect educational support in various ways. They are as follows:

1. The exorbitant taxes and miscellaneous levies shall be abolished during the period, July 1 to December 31, 1934. These include those taxes and levies that:[29]

---

[27]Chen, Gideon, *Chinese Government Economic Planning and Reconstruction Since 1927*, passim.
[28]The International Relations Committee, *Chinese Affairs* (monthly), Volume VI, No. 1, June 15, 1934, pp. 21-36. Cf. *Shun Pao*, May 28, 1934.
[29]*Ibid.*, p. 30.

(a) Harm the welfare and the interests of the public and society.
(b) Injure the sources of revenue of the Central Government.
(c) Are based on multiple taxation.
(d) Are detrimental to communication.
(e) Are unfair and discriminating taxes of goods from other localities.
(f) Transit dues on commodities transported from one place to another.

To make up the deficits of the local governments caused by such abolishment, 30 per cent of the estimated increased annual yield of $60,000,000 of the stamp tax shall be given by the Central Government to the county governments, 10 per cent to the provincial governments, and 20 per cent to the border provinces. The tobacco and wine license tax (the tobacco and wine tax yields $23,545,055, according to the 1933–34 budgets) shall be given to the provincial governments for collection. All the expenses of judiciary of the provincial governments shall be disbursed from the central treasury.

2. The inheritance tax shall gradually be enforced.

3. The land value tax shall be introduced after land registry and land survey, and all surcharges must be abolished. A single uniform tax rate of 1 per cent of the value of land shall be enforced with the division of yield, 60 per cent to the provincial government and 40 per cent to the county local government. Before the land value tax is in effect, pending the cadastral survey of land, the farm tax shall have a new schedule. All surtaxes shall not exceed the regular tax and the total amount of regular tax and surtax collection shall not exceed the 1 per cent rate. The latter surtaxes refer to taxes whose authorized period of collection has not expired or to those which are justified because the purpose for which they were levied still exists. "It is expected that increased revenue to be derived from the levy of the farm tax after the cadastral survey will be sufficient

to make up for the deficit caused by abolishing surtaxes."[30]

4. The rates of title deeds tax shall be reduced, with the maximum set at 6 per cent of the value of property sold and 3 per cent of the value mortgaged.

5. The salt surtaxes shall not be allowed to be collected by the provinces, but subsidies now granted from their yield shall be remitted as usual and special arrangements now in force will be continued as usual.

6. The demarcation of provincial and county or municipal revenues by sources shall be effected, but not by the division of one single source into regular and surtaxes, except those sources the yield of which is quite large; the division shall be according to percentage ratios. Whenever necessary, there should be coöperation between the two levels of government through subvention and contribution.

7. The readjustment to business taxes. The method of collecting business taxes shall be improved. Foreign business shall be taxed. The brokerage tax shall be limited to the minimum of 3 per cent of the amount of brokerage fee.

8. Corrupt practices shall be eradicated.

9. The tax collection organs shall be unified.

10. The peace preservation expenses of county governments shall be disbursed by the provincial government.

11. The expenses of local autonomy in the counties shall be reduced in order to lighten the burden of the people.

12. There shall be rural relief.

13. Two of the important committees to be created to effect the carrying out of all these measures are the Committee for the Readjustment of Local Levies, and the Committee on the Supervision of Taxation.

---

[30] *Ibid.*, p. 31.

A mandate has been promulgated by the National Government on June 8, 1934, to prohibit tax increases and the abolition of exorbitant taxes and miscellaneous levies.[31]

The effects of this conference remain to be seen. Forced by the huge deficit of the national budget and by the circumstance that the rates of indirect taxes which constitute more than 90 per cent of the national revenue can no longer be increased as they have been continuously increased in the past few years, Minister Kung began to take up the proposed income and inheritance taxes.[32] He presented a plan of action in December, 1933,[33] but it still exists as a plan only.

THE EFFECTS UPON EDUCATIONAL SUPPORT AND WHAT EDUCATION CAN EXPECT

The Effects upon Educational Fiscal Control

The policy of unification of government treasury, centralization of fiscal administration including tax collection, and the centralized supervision of all local budgets under the government fiscal authorities, definitely limits the extent of educational fiscal independence almost to a mere allocation policy. For example, the provincial departments of education of Hunan, Fukien, Kiangsi, and so forth,[34] that depend upon the earmarked salt tax for support are, or would be, left without any control of its yield for education and must depend upon the national tax collection agencies or the Ministry of Finance for remittance. Hupeh has proposed to use the salt surtax as an independent source of revenue for the provincial schools, but the Ministry of Finance has never

---

[31]*Ibid.*, pp. 34–36.
[32]Chang Jo-jen, "China's Finance in 1933," *Chinese Economy* (monthly), Volume II, No. 1, January, 1934, pp. 6–7.
[33]*Central Daily News*, December 9, 1933, Nanking.
[34]See Table 50.

been willing to let it go. In that case, independence of source would be merely nominal.[35]

In the counties, educational fiscal independence would be reduced to the same nominal status, if the resolution of unification of collecting organs and the like is carried out without reservation.

The Effects upon the Existing Sources of Educational Revenue

The existing sources of educational revenue have been shown in Chapter VII. The earmarked tobacco and wine surtax would be abolished and new adjustments for the division of yield between the provincial government and educational department must be made. The grain tribute surtax and various types of land taxes earmarked in Kiangsu would be abolished, also, and a new adjustment must be made for the division of yield of the new land value tax. The same situation would occur in the counties in which 45 to 75 per cent[36] of the educational budget is provided from the yield of the various forms of land or farm tax.

In Chapter VII, in Tables 54, 55, 56, and 57, it has been shown that county education is partly supported by multifarious exorbitant taxes and miscellaneous levies. Their yield constitutes about 8.7 per cent and 13.3 per cent, including commodity taxes, of the county educational budgets of Shantung and Kiangsu respectively (see Tables 51 and 52). To make up this deficit caused by the abolition of these earmarked petty levies, a new source must be provided from a part of the yield of stamp and tobacco and wine license taxes donated by the Central Government. It then becomes a problem of distribution and unless certain reservations are made,

---

[35]Jen Ho-sheng, "The Problem of Educational Fiscal Independence in Hupeh," *Hupeh Education Monthly*, Volume I, No. 8, August, 1934, p. 54.

[36]See Tables 51, 52, and 53.

the independence of the source is thereby lost. Hence local educational support would become unstable and critical during the period of reorganization of the revenue system.

The lowering of the rates of title deeds taxes would reduce the amount of yield for education in Honan Province and additional sources must be provided.

The method of demarcation of the sources of revenue between the provincial and county governments would affect one independent source of education revenue, namely, the sacrificial metallic paper sales tax of the Chekiang Provincial Department of Education, if it were given to the counties.

Of course, such reforms are ultimately good for the people as well as for educational support, in view of the facts concerning the unnecessarily complex procedure and high cost of collection involved, as shown in Table 57. Temporary dislocation, instability, and chaos must be tolerated. All this inconvenience is possibly due to the lack of foresight and of research in finance on the part of school men in their demands for fiscal independence.

The Effects upon the Proposed Sources of Educational Revenue

In order to finance the twenty-year program of expansion and improvement, the Second National Conference on Education proposed the following sources for the expansion of educational revenue.[37] Since the Ministry of Education initiated this conference and had prepared all important proposals in advance, these measures may be considered as the actual policies of the Ministry:[38]

---

[37]*Proceedings of the Second National Conference on Education*, 1930, Section VI, pp. 78–79.
[38]*Ibid.*, Section II, p. 6.

A. Sources completely earmarked for education:

(1) The income from sand lands and government waste lands—50 per cent to go to the central educational authority, 30 per cent to the provinces, and 20 per cent to counties and cities.

(2) Inheritance tax—50 per cent of the revenue to go to the Central Government, 20 per cent to the provinces, and 30 per cent to the counties and cities (30 per cent to the special municipalities and the rest to the Central Government).

(3) Butchery tax and business middleman license tax to go completely to the counties and cities.

(4) Temple property to go to the county, city or local authorities according to situs.

(5) Land surtax to go completely to the counties and cities.

(6) Tobacco and wine surtax—50 per cent to go to the provinces and 50 per cent to the counties and cities.

(7) All existing local surtaxes, unless there are other legal provisions affecting them, shall continue as they are.

B. Sources partly earmarked for education (the proportions allocated to the different levels of authority will be fixed later):

(1) The Boxer indemnity remissions and the income from their investment.

(2) Production taxes (tea, cocoons, etc.)

(3) Consumption taxes (feast tax, amusement tax, etc.)

(4) House tax and business shop taxes.

(5) Business taxes.

(6) Income taxes.

NEEDED READJUSTMENT AND EDUCATION'S EXPECTATION

1. The National Government, however, has provided little legal basis for developing the above proposals. The attitude of the Second National Finance Conference gives no indication of earmarking the inheritance tax for education. The financial authorities are interested in their yield for meeting the present deficit of the Central Government.[39] It is doubtful whether the complete yield of these two new sources

[39] *Central Daily News,* December 9, 1933.

would be used for education. Furthermore, it is doubtful whether these taxes can be effectively levied in China at present and whether the yield would be significant enough. The Kemmerer Commission of Finance Experts were unable to recommend the income and inheritance taxes because the conditions essential to satisfactory operation of the income tax were lacking, and the justification of the inheritance tax—the sudden increase in the heir's ability to contribute to the support of the state—seems to them to be wanting in China except in rare cases.[40] Dr. Li Chuan-shih is strongly in favor of the inheritance tax and shows how its obstacles may be overcome.[41] At any rate, China must try these new sources of revenue, and public education has a legitimate claim to their proceeds.

2. The land surtax will be abolished. The land value tax has been estimated to have a very much larger yield even at a lower rate. For example, it is estimated that after a cadastral survey of land, in Hupeh, a single tax on land at a rate of only 30 cents per mow, or at about 1 to 1.5 per cent of the value of the land, would yield $47,299,543 annually, which is 16 times the present revenue from all forms of land tax in the province.[42] Probably there will be no more need of levying the proposed local surtaxes, for education, even if they were permitted.

3. There is need for much adjustment in supporting education in the cities. The business tax, urban real estate tax, and so forth, would be good sources of educational revenue.

4. Finally, the reduction of military expenditure, the payment of provincial judicial expenditure by the Cen-

[40] Commission of Financial Experts, *Report on Revenue Policy*, Dec. 10, 1929.
[41] Li Chuan-shih, "My Views of Inheritance Taxation," *Bankers' Weekly*, Volume XVII, No. 50, Dec. 26, 1933, pp. 1–2.
[42] Hupeh Department of Civil Affairs, *Report of Hupeh Provincial Civil Affairs*. Wuchang, 1930, p. 45, Table 6.

tral Government, would leave much leeway for the claim of education. The reduction of local autonomy expenditure and the payment of county peace preservation expenses by the provincial treasury would also leave a large leeway for the claim of education in the counties. For instance, in Hupeh the combined expenditure budget for self-defense or peace preservation constituted an average of 54.73 per cent of the combined county government budget of 58 counties reporting in 1932–33. The combined amount was $3,570,225, which was almost three times the expenditure budget for education.[43] If it can be used for education, it is enough to provide for the increase for the expansion program shared by the counties of Hupeh.

5. The eradication of corrupt practices would lead to an increase in tax collections at least twofold, if this plan could be rigidly carried out. For example, it has been pointed out by fiscal authorities that for each tax dollar reaching the public treasury no less than three dollars have gone into private pockets. Cheng[44] has estimated the leakage into private pockets to be $224,-255,633 in the collection of Likin, the business brokerage license tax, the pawnshop tax, and the butchery tax, in sixteen provinces. This is about three times the amount of $76,418,547 actually reaching the public treasuries. Education has a legitimate claim to such increases.

To summarize the progress of financial reform,

"The financial position of the Chinese government, in spite of floods and famine and external troubles, has shown a marked improvement since 1932. In many respects, China appears at present to be in a better position financially than at any time since the establishment of the Republic."[45]

[43] See Table 57, Columns 32 and 33, pages 134–35.
[44] Cheng, Cheng Yi, "Our Business and Sales Tax Heretofore," in *Chinese Economic Problems*, pp. 103–04.
[45] American Council of the Institute of Pacific Relations, *Memorandum on China's Government Finances*, Volume II, No. 3, Feb. 10, 1933.

Former Finance Minister T. V. Soong concluded his report with the statement:

"But in view of the accomplishments during the period under review, a continuation of steady improvement may justifiably be hoped for, given comparative peace and the lifting of the world economic depression."[46]

The continuation of this steady improvement will eventually enable the government to increase the educational budget. It is impossible at present, however, to estimate the exact amounts education can expect from the new tax sources of school revenue suggested above.

6. *The Use of Waste Land for Education.* This subject has been discussed in Chapter VII (see pages 113–116).

7. *The Use of Temple Property for Education.* The movement for the use of temple property for education, under the leadership of Dr. S. C. Tai, has won universal recognition and support by educators as well as by many political leaders. The story of the movement has been adequately told in Dr. Tai's book entitled, *The Problem of Using Temple Property for Education.*[47] He maintains:

"I have carefully pondered over the problem of Chinese educational finance and found that there are only three roads to its solution: (1) the use of temple property, (2) the levying of inheritance taxes, and (3) the reconstruction of the tax system. For the increase of the sources of school revenue, the first road is the most important."

As yet there has been no effective legal instrumentation for putting this plan into effect. The government seems to have allowed the matter to drift. The writer

---

[46]Soong, T. V., *Report for the 19th and 20th Fiscal Years, July 1930 to June 1932*, p. 12.
[47]Tai Shuan-chiu, *The Problem of Using Temple Property for Education*, 1929, pp. 1 and 16–58.

is chiefly interested in knowing just how much educational finance can expect if the movement is successful. Dr. Tai roughly estimated the temple property of Tan Tu County of Kiangsu Province alone to be worth $50,000,000. The total value of temple property in all China is at least $2,000,000,000. The government at one time had decided to use 20 per cent of it for education; therefore, at least $400,000,000 can be expected from this source. The Ministry of Industry hs begun an economic survey of each province of China. It is suggested that a survey of temple property be included, and that laws be promulgated to prevent the illegal disposal and concealment of temple property by the priests. Speedy and consistent governmental action is imperative to make the movement a success.

8. *The Proceeds of the Boxer Indemnity Remissions.* It has been seen (page 181) that the Central Government paid from $30,000,000 to $50,000,000 annually for the Boxer indemnity service. In January, 1934, the total of the principal and interest for this service still outstanding was $783,441,115, spread over fifteen years or more. An average annual payment of $55,960,079 is required to meet this obligation. Theoretically, this entire amount should be devoted to education. Article 4 of the External Policies of the Kuomintang platform is the basis of this theory. It reads as follows:

"The payments due on the Boxer Indemnity shall be entirely devoted to educational purposes."[48]

But in practice this cannot be realized. First, the attitude of the Ministry of Finance is not favorable. For instance, immediately after Minister Kung came to office, he used the Italian share as a security for a new loan

[48]Tyau, M. T. Z., *Two Years of Nationalist China*, 1930, "The Kuomintang Platform," p. 29.

TABLE 76

STATUS OF BOXER INDEMNITY REMISSIONS AND THE AMOUNT AVAILABLE FOR EDUCATION

Countries	Original Share, Principal and Interest A	Amount Remitted B	Amount Outstanding Jan. 1, 1934 C	Proportion of Remission for Education, Culture, and Philanthropy According to Agreement D	Estimated Amount Available for Education, Culture, and Philanthropy 1934—Last Year of Payment E
1. United States	G$53,348,145	G$42,647,486	G$10,407,713.5 or $62,842,650	100% for Tsing Hua University and students in U.S.A. and education and culture with special attention to scientific requirements.	$62,842,650
2. Great Britain	£16,573,810:3:2	£11,362,517:14:0 or $200,000,000	£9,241,008:7:8 or $99,216,134	50% for railway construction and 50% for education after 1931.	$49,608,067
3. France	Fr.580,160,927.78	G$75,556,964.46	G$47,734,205.89 or $182,825,220	About 1/8 of loan floated for rehabilitation of the Banque Industrielle de Chine to be used for Franco-Chinese education and philanthropy.	$19,000,000
4. Belgium	Fr. 69,447,061.13	G$9,044,402.68	G$3,709,832.22 or $14,208,908	75% for railways and 25% for Sino-Belge education and philanthropy.	$3,552,227
5. Soviet Russia	G$211,149,270.86	Renounced $100–150 million less liability	£12,527,668:19:6 or $200,443,000 including liability	100% for the promotion of education among the Chinese people.	$125,000,000
6. Netherlands	Fl.3,066,005.32	Fl.1,451,642.33	Fl.772,405 or $1,526,251.8	65% for water projects and 35% for cultural purposes.	$534,188.3
7. Spain	Fr.1,107,596.29		Fr.279,031 or $53,473.12		—
8. Portugal	£30,203:16:6		£11,373:9:10 or $181,976		—
9. Sweden and Norway	£20,568:1:4		£5,181:7:4 or $11,843		—
10. Germany	M 600,617,725.23 or 196,601,546.72 HK. Tls.	Canceled but used as security for loans	M49,538,985.59 or $77,166,160	100%—For security of government debts	—
11. Austria	Kr.31,418,725.97 or 8,739,562.16 HK. Tls.	Canceled but used as security for loans	£329,524:7:4 or $5,272,390	100%—For security of government debts	—
12. Italy	Fr.147,051,159.76	G$28,374,012.9	G$19,060,890.6 or $73,004,497	50% for railways and 50% for education and philanthropy but in 1934 used as security for a domestic loan of $44,000,000.	—
13. Japan	Yen 106,854,177.8	No remissions	£4,121,460:6:2 or $65,943,365	For cultural work for China but not under control of China	—
Total	982,238,150 HK. Tls. including 149,670 HK. Tls. of international claims.		$783,441,115.32	Approximately 33% of total amount outstanding Jan. 1, 1934. (Not of amount of remission.)	$260,637,132

Source: A, B, D. See Dr. Yam Tong Hoh, *The Boxer Indemnity Remissions and Education in China*, Table 35, p. 442 (Mss). With additions and minor revision.
C. "A Summary of Chinese Domestic and Foreign Loans and the Indemnity Funds for 1933," *Bank of China Monthly Review*, March, 1934.
E. Freshly calculated.

The Ability of China to Support Education

of $44,000,000 for central expenditure.[49] Second, the leaders in material reconstruction demand that the remissions be applied first to railways and capital investments.[50] Third, the powers concerned demand the fulfillment of certain conditions that complicate the situation (see Table 76, Column D).

Both the gross amounts available and the amounts available for educational purposes after the above conditions have been considered are presented in Tables 76 and 77, following.

TABLE 77

ESTIMATED AMOUNT OF BOXER INDEMNITY REMISSIONS PROPOSED FOR RURAL EDUCATION

Countries	Average Annual Payments of Amount Outstanding According to Bank of China (A)	1/3 of Remission to be Used for Rural Education According to Dr. Hoh (B)	Remarks About Total Yield for Proposed Rural Education (C)
1. United States	1934–40 $ 7,353,603.6 1941–48 1,420,928.1	$2,451,201.2 473,643.7	1. Proposed annual yield for rural education during first 7 years, 1934–40 is $19,716,683.1. The total is $138,016,781.7
2. Great Britain	1934–40 9,543,701.7 1941–45 6,610,044.2	3,181,233.9 2,203,348.0	
3. France	1934–40 15,730,558.6 1941–47 10,687,330.0	5,243,519.5 3,562,443.0	2. Total yield for 1941 is $8,614,936.7
4. Belgium	1934–40 1,847,086.0 1941 1,279,307.0	615,695.0 426,436.0	3. Annual yield for 1942–45 is $8,188,500.7. The total is $32,754,002.8
5. Soviet Russia	1934–40 24,458,142.8 1941–45 5,847,200.0	8,152,714.0 1,949,066.0	4. Annual yield for 1946–47 is $4,036,086. The total is $8,072,172
6. Netherlands	1934–40 218,036.0	72,679.0	
7. Spain	1934–40 7,639.0	?	5. Annual or total yield for 1948 is $473,643

[49] Unpublished Document No. 18; Cf. *Bankers' Weekly*, Vol. XVIII, No. 11, March 27, 1934.

[50] Tai Chi-tao, "Chinese Economic Reconstruction and Educational Reconstruction," *The New Asia*, Volume IV, No. 3, July 1, 1932, pp. 1–9.

TABLE 77 (*Continued*)

Countries	Average Annual Payments of Amount Outstanding According to Bank of China (A)		1/3 of Remission to be Used for Rural Education According to Dr. Hoh (B)	Remarks About Total Yield for Proposed Rural Education (C)
8. Portugal	1934–40 1941–45	$17,392.0 12,046.0	?	
9. Sweden & Norway	1934–40	1,692.0	?	
10. Germany	1934–40	11,023,737.0		
11. Austria	1434–40	753,199.0		
12. Italy	1934–40 1941 1942–48	5,794,659.7 4,347,881.0 4,013,428.3		
13. Japan	1934–40 1941–45	6,302,581.0 4,365,060.0		
Total	1434–48	$783,441,115.32		1934–48 $187,931,536.2 or 24 per cent of A and 67.2 per cent of E in Table 76.

Source: (A) See Table 76 note C.
(B), (C) Freshly calculated.

Table 76 shows that, according to an agreement between China and the respective powers, only $260,637,-132, or 33 per cent, of the amount outstanding on January 1, 1934, is available for education, culture, and philanthropy. As Dr. Y. T. Hoh has treated the subject most thoroughly and in a scholarly manner, the writer needs only to quote some of his findings and recommendations.

Hoh[51] finds that emphasis has been placed overwhelmingly upon phases of higher educational activities such

[51]Hoh, Yam Tong, *The Boxer Indemnity Remissions and Education in China.*

as sending students abroad, and subsidizing institutions of higher learning, scientific researches, and cultural projects.

"People in the coastal and riverine provinces, especially the wealthier class in the big cities, have been unduly favored at the expense of the 300,000,000 or more rural population. While these activities, on account of their tested merits, should be continued, the interest of the forgotten millions must be duly considered on the principle of justice and for political, economic, and humane reasons."[52]

He proposed that with the number of remissions and the funds thereof greatly increased, from one third to one half of the total should be spent for the Chinese farmers by starting a program of rural education. It is improbable that one half of the total will be used for Hoh's proposal, owing to the complications indicated in Table 76. Furthermore, in 1934 the Italian share, which yields from 1934 to 1948 $73,004,497, has been set aside as security for a new government loan.

Table 77 shows that from 1934 to 1948 the total amount available for education and culture would be $187,931,536.2. If this amount is to be used for rural education within the general program of expansion and improvement, only about $19,716,683 will be available annually during the first seven years of the period. This is but 16 per cent of the $123,500,000 required annually by the Central Government. Even this amount may not easily be realized because the agreements with the powers restrict the use of the funds to enterprises of mutual benefit, including philanthropic objectives. The only portion of the indemnity which is not so restricted is the Russian share. According to the estimate of Shih Tung,[53] based upon the prevailing rate of exchange, up

---

[52]*Ibid.*, Digest of Dissertation, p. 7.
[53]Shih Tung, "The Status of the Russian Boxer Indemnity and Educational Finance," *Education of Tomorrow*, Vol. II, No. 9, May 16, 1933, Table 7, p. 13.

to 1940, the last year of payment, the Russian share can yield $213,163,533.03, at a compound interest rate of 6 per cent, after the liabilities of government debts secured upon it and the claims of the national universities of Peiping are deducted. If the principal of this fund is left untouched, the interest alone would yield annually an average of $12,789,813. Since this fund is in the control of the Ministry of Finance, there is grave danger that it may be diverted to other purposes. Already proposals have been made that it be used in building railroads.

The interests of the "forgotten millions" must be considered first, and it is high time that educators of the country see to it that this fund, legitimately available for education, is not squandered by the government.

Other Possibilities

The Support for Productive or Vocational Education in China:

Productive education, as it concerns specific technical and industrial schools, directly benefits industry and should be financed, at least in part by the industries concerned. This type of productive education differs from citizenship training which benefits the civic state as a whole. As the proposed program of improvement emphasizes the establishment of vocational schools, its financial burden can justifiably be distributed in three channels, namely, the industries themselves, the government agencies of industry, communications, and reconstruction, and the budgets of the industrial or economic planning bodies. It is needless to state that in the initial stages a predominant part of the burden should be borne by the second and third channels.

1. The Industries Themselves. In industrial countries, the industries play a large part in the support of vocational education. Great Britain may be used as an example. British industries aid education by:

(a) Donating buildings and sites. For instance, the textile industry has met the cost of building and equipment of the textile department of the Technical College at Huddersfield.

(b) Giving scholarships and annual grants. For instance, the Manchester Cotton Goods Export Trade provides numerous scholarships. The Chemistry Department of Carlisle and the London School of Printing are supported by trade bodies.

(c) Furnishing equipment. During the three years preceding March, 1925, the industries presented to 92 schools equipment valued at over 120,000 pounds.

(d) Maintaining continuation schools, such as those established by Messrs. Boot, Cadbury, Clark, Fry, Lee, and other companies.

(e) Reorganizing employment to facilitate the "Sandwich System." Students spend alternate periods in the schools and the works. This plan is very well organized in the engineering industry. Some firms open work schools. The dockyard apprentices, the engine-fitter, and electrical-fitter schools are notable examples.

(f) Giving rewards to students. The reports of students' school records are emphasized by employers in considering promotion. Prizes in the form of textbooks and instruments are distributed to successful students.[54]

Even the collective economy under state control prevailing in Soviet Russia has to depend upon the industries for educational support, in addition to the budget of the unified financial plan of the five-year plan. From

---

[54]Cheng, Ronald Y. S., *Technical Education or Education for Industry in England and Its Lessons for China*, 1932 (Mss.). Unpublished Document No. 19.

1928 to 1932 the Soviet economic organizations spent 2,080,900,000 rubles on capital construction for social and cultural needs.[55]

Chinese industrial and commercial bodies should organize themselves to aid productive education along similar lines. For centuries, the guild system and individual trades and businesses in China have preserved their existence through an independent form of apprentice training neglected by the educational system of the scholars. With the new emphasis on productive education, this old traditional system can be modernized and combined with the "white collar" educational system. Here is an important source of school revenue which must be systematized and tapped as soon as possible.

The Government Agencies of Industry, Communication, and Reconstruction

If the educational function of the Ministries of Industry and Communications and of the provincial departments of reconstruction is broadened, then the financial burdens faced by the Ministry of Education and the provincial Departments of Education will be lightened. The Ministry of Communications and the Ministry of Railways have so far maintained commendable technical education on the higher level and some general education for the children of the employees. The Ministry of Industry also should share a part of the burden of financing vocational education. There will be a great advance along these lines if all these ministries coöperate closely in setting up a coördinating agency with the Ministry of Education, similar to the United States Federal Board for Vocational Education, for the purpose of planning and financing a comprehensive program of productive education. The provincial departments of reconstruction should follow the same pattern

[55] See Table 35, Source for U. S. S. R.

in coördinating technical and financial resources. Recently the provinces of Chekiang and Anhwei have initiated such plans, but it is not known whether or not a definite part of the budgets of these provincial departments of reconstruction has been assigned to technical and vocational training. Economic reconstruction rests upon the foundation of technical skill, scientific knowledge, and informed labor; it is needless to repeat that the budgets of economic reconstruction should assure the support necessary for such training.

The United States Department of Agriculture provides the best example of provision for productive education. Its budget in 1933-34 totaled G$116,000,000, and ranks fourth among the ten departments of the Federal Government (excluding other establishments and the executive office). Its purpose is mainly educational. The agencies of research, experimentation, and extension activities consume the bulk of this budget.[56]

Agricultural education in Great Britain is financed by the Ministry of Agriculture. In Belgium, the Ministry of Agriculture spent one third of its budget for education, and the Ministry of Industry and Work spent 11.9 per cent of its budget for education.[57]

These are but examples of how productive education is financed in an unplanned economy. The Soviet experiment has stimulated world-wide interest in economic planning instead of the *laissez-faire* policy of uncoördinated competing and duplicating enterprises. China has talked about economic planning for many years; but unless there are present certain fundamental factors necessary for a planned economy, such as the unification of the country, a stable government, a sound financial system, control figures, or detailed and accurate

[56]National Committee for Economy in Government, *Federal Appropriations of 1932-33-34*, Chart VI. Unpublished Document No. 20.
[57]Abel, J. F., *Education in Belgium*, p. 6.

statistical information concerning the social and economic scene, it will be a long time before China can aspire to the Soviet scale of planning. Pending the realization of such a plan even partially, China for the immediate present must rely upon the separate government agencies of reconstruction for her economic development. It follows that the training of the functionaries for such economic development and for productive education may justifiably claim a share of the annual budgets.

It was Dr. Sun Yat-sen who initiated the idea of planning in the modern sense of the word. About the year 1919, when the Supreme Economic Council of Russia was drafting its first industrial plan for the Metal Industry in the Ural region, and the idea of economic councils as planning bodies became a live issue throughout Western Europe, Dr. Sun outlined his ten-point industrial plan for the "International Development of China." This has been used as a guide by the National Government in its program of economic reconstruction. Following 1927, many industrial plans have appeared, as follows:

(1) Sun Fo's Ten-Year Plan for communication, commercial harbors, modern cities, water power development, basic industries, mineral development, agricultural development, irrigation work in Mongolia and Sinkiang, reforestation in Central and North China, and colonization.

(2) The 1929 Program and Budget for Material Reconstruction, passed by the National Congress of Representatives. It followed the main principles and policies of Dr. Sun Yat-sen's "Plan of National Reconstruction," of which the ten-point industrial plan is a part.

(3) Six-Year Plan, passed by the National People's Convention in 1931.

(4) The Ten-Year Plan announced by the League of Nations in August, 1931.

(5) The three-year plan worked out by the National Economic Council, which was formally organized in November, 1932.
(6) Specific and regional plans:
  (a) H. H. Kung's plan for developing basic industries, including iron, steel, electrification, machine shops, salt refineries, acids and alkaline manufacture, cotton spinning, paper, and alcohol industries.
  (b) Chen Kung-po's Four-Year Plan of twelve separate industries for the Yangtze region.
  (c) Sun Fo's separate plans for railways and highway construction.
  (d) Four-year plan for Northwest development by the Ministry of Industries.[58]

The Soviet experiment has been overwhelmingly successful, owing chiefly perhaps to their inclusion of the educational plan in the Five-Year Plan. The unflinching popular zeal and the speed of accomplishment can easily be traced to the marvelous system of mass education and propaganda developed, and especially to the training of technical experts and skilled labor. The system is better named "social-economic planning" than economic planning.

Fortunately, China has just started to think along these lines. The National Economic Council, organized in 1932, has created five technical committees. The Educational Technical Committee is one of these. The membership of the Economic Council is composed of the President and the Vice President of the Executive Yuan, the Ministers of Interior, Finance, Railways, Communications, Industries, and Education being considered as ex-officio members. Through such an organization, a unified and coördinated plan of economic, social,

[58]Chen, Gideon, *Chinese Government Economic Planning and Reconstruction Since 1927.*

and cultural reconstruction can be more fully realized. The Council's Three-Year Plan includes a definite educational scheme. The League of Nation's Mission of Educational Experts was invited to make a survey of education in China and its recommendations were to be "considered with particular care by the National Economic Council," as announced by General Chiang Kai-shek. He said:

"The Ministry of Education will make a special proposal to the council in this respect. The National Government suggests that future reforms be made in the light of the needs of the development of the country as revealed by the studies and the plans of the Council whose opinion will be asked in regard to any expenditure of money on new projects in this domain."[59]

Thus, education is now legally recognized as a definite part of economic planning, and educational support has been promised from the budget of the Economic Council.

How Much Can Educational Finance Expect from the Budget of Economic Planning?

The appearance of plan after plan and their lack of consistency indicates that no single plan has been adhered to steadfastly thus far and that there has been no coördination among the various plans.

"The necessity of making provisions for machinery to carry out these plans is generally overlooked. Then there is the habit of drawing up plans without considering the question of finance."[60]

"Reflecting the widening requirements of the public, we have seen each department of the Government proposing its own petty projects, all of them involving huge expenditures. Doubtless many of these projects are in themselves sound but they must be unrealized because of the known lack of funds and the fact that they are not coördinated with the projects of other departments."[61]

[59]Chen, Gideon, *Ibid.*, p. 16. Opening address of General Chiang.
[60]*Ibid.*, p. 25.
[61]Soong, T. V., *Financial Report of the Eighteenth Fiscal Year of the Republic of China.*

The Ability of China to Support Education 215

Hence, there has been created the National Economic Council for the unification and control of the haphazard, unrelated, and clashing programs of the various departments of government.

Most of the plans make no mention of the rôle of education in training informed and skilled labor and technical experts which is basic to their successful propagation and execution. So long as the Ministry of Education draws its own educational plan without close coördination and adjustment with the machinery of economic reconstruction, the result is bound to be ill-adapted to the stark reality of the specific vocational needs of the nation. In Dr. Sun's original "Plan of National Reconstruction," he had this point in mind and had outlined a program of psychological reconstruction.

The Unified Financial Plan of the First Five-Year Plan of Soviet Russia, as realized in four and a half years, actually provided 14,500,000,000 rubles, or 11.7 per cent of the total expenditure of 120,100,000,000 rubles, for education. This does not include local educational expenditures and the expenditures of economic organizations on capital construction for social and cultural needs, including educational needs.[62] The emphasis upon education in Soviet planning is shown in the following statement:

"In view of the necessity of solving the greatest economical, technical, and organizational problems of socialist construction, the Fifth Congress of the Soviets charges the U. S. S. R. with the duty of giving the maximum attention to the questions of culture and of attaining the fulfillment of the most important tasks of the cultural revolution by introducing universal obligatory elementary education, by eliminating illiteracy, by raising the level both of the general and of the technical vocational education of the masses, by developing cadres of specialists and scientific workers from the ranks of the working class

[62] *Summary of the Fulfillment of the First Five-Year Plan for the Development of National Economy of the U. S. S. R.*, Table 28, p. 291.

216 *The Financing of Public Education in China*

and the toiling masses in general, and by adapting the entire system of public education to the tasks of socialist reconstruction of economy."

"The enormous program which is to change radically the types and conditions of production in our country, the program based upon the most extensive mastery of the latest achievement and best models of the world's technique, squarely puts the question of new cadres, of a new generation of builders who are to become the protagonists of the technical and social reconstruction of our country."[63]

Let us consider the productive personnel alone which the unified financial plan has provided for training. In 1928, at the beginning of the Five-Year Plan, there were in Soviet Russia only 493,000 specialists including trained technicians and cadres in all branches of national economy. In 1932 the number had increased to 973,200. There were 6.9 specialists, including graduate engineers and technicians and those with practical training, per 100 workers in industry. Vocational education has been increasingly extended. The rapid need for and growth of new institutes for training cadres is shown in Table 78.

TABLE 78

ENROLLMENT IN NEW INSTITUTIONS FOR TRAINING CADRES IN SOVIET RUSSIA

Types of Productive Schools	Number of Students	
	1928	1932
Academies	200	9,000
Higher technical institutions	159,800	492,300
Workers' colleges	49,200	444,400
Factory schools	178,300	1,177,300
Technicums (secondary)	253,600	949,200

From *Ibid.*, p. 295.

[63] *Ibid.*, p. 76.

The Ability of China to Support Education 217

In China the dearth of trained labor and specialists has been the constant cry of all industries. Table 4 gives the figure to show that students enrolled in productive education on all levels totaled only 55,226, or .44 per cent of the total enrollment in 1930–31. Table 4 shows that students in vocational secondary schools in 1930–31 constituted only 10 per cent of the total enrollment of all secondary schools. This situation presents one of the most pressing problems the National Economic Council has to face in the execution of its industrial and agricultural plans. Both from the example of the Soviet Union and the actual needs of China, there is absolute necessity for financial provision for specific productive education by the budget of economic planning. From the Soviet experience (see Table 78) it appears that education's proportion of the total budget of economic planning should be at least 10 per cent. If the general educational program is to be financed by the Ministry of Education, 5 per cent of the budget of the industrial plan may arbitrarily be claimed for productive education.

The total budget estimates of the various industrial plans are exhibited in Table 79.

TABLE 79
BUDGET ESTIMATES OF THE VARIOUS INDUSTRIAL PLANS

Plan*	Total Budget Estimate of Industrial Plan	Proposed Education Budget**
Plan 1	$500,000,000 a year for 50 years	$25,000,000
Plan 2	No estimate available but source of revenue assured	
Plan 3	No estimate available but source of revenue assured	
Plan 4	$1,120,489,000 for 10 years for machinery, or $112,048,900 a year	$5,602,445 a year
Plan 5	No estimate available	

TABLE 79 (Continued)

Plan*	Total Budget Estimate of Industrial Plan	Proposed Education Budget**
Plan 6:		
(a)	$200,000,000 for 8 industries	$10,000,000
(b)	$600,000,000 for industry, mining, and agriculture, or $150,000,000 a year	$7,500,000
(c)	$800,000,000 or $80,000,000 a year for railways	$4,000,000
	$364,000,000 or $36,400,000 a year for highways	$1,820,000
(d)	$920,000,000, or $230,000,000 a year	$11,500,000

From Chen, Gideon, *Op. cit.*
* The plans are listed in the same order as they appear earlier in the text.
** These amounts are calculated as 5 per cent annually for education.

It is evident, therefore, that productive education should claim at least $25,000,000 a year from the budget of the inclusive industrial plan for all China, and at least $5,000,000 to $10,000,000 a year from the budgets of particular or regional plans. Actual figures must be worked out by the Educational Technical Committee.

2. *Borrowing Money for Education*

"Adams classifies the conditions under which a governmental unit may justify 'public credit' in the name of 'public economy.'

"(1) A want of coincidence between estimated and actual revenue, if the error comes in in the form of a deficit, calls for a temporary loan.

"(2) The advent of some unforeseen financial emergency, as war, famine, fire, flood, and the like, when the government is called upon to act promptly, if at all, is regarded as a just occasion for a resort to the money market.

"(3) A determination on the part of the government to undertake some public work of such a nature that some considerable time must intervene between its beginning and its completion, presents a necessity for the employment of state credit.

"It can readily be seen how these principles may be applied and may result in unsound financial conditions. . . ."[64]

[64] Engelhardt, N. L., and Engelhardt, Fred, *Op. cit.*, 1927, p. 409.

"Irrespective of opinion, borrowing is a legalized government business procedure and will continue."[65]

All three principles cited above have been applied in Chinese government borrowing. But the government fiscal authorities have rarely considered the financing of public education by means of loans, except for the school men. Tables 71, 73, and 75 have shown the enormous loans squandered for destructive purposes. The lesser of the evils of borrowing would be the use of the loans for education.

The economist, H. G. Brown maintains:

"Could funds be borrowed for this purpose [education] at the current rate of interest charged on well secured loans, the investment might pay much better than investment of other kinds...."[66]

That education is a worth-while economic investment can be further supported by the following quotations from other economists and educators:

Professor H. F. Clark[67] made a collection of the statements of the economists of the world on the economic effects of education.

A few quotations are selected here:

"Adam Smith included under the fixed capital of a nation, the natural and acquired abilities of its inhabitants."

"All expenditure in the instruction of youth is consumption of present values for the behalf of the productive powers."[68]

List corrected the erroneous philosophy that "The man who breeds pigs is, according to this school, a productive member of the community, but he who educates men is non-productive," by stating:

[65]*Ibid.*, p. 407.
[66]Brown, H. G., *Economic Science and the Common Welfare*, 1923, p. 187. Cf. Clark, H. F., *The Economic Effects of Education*, 1928, *passim*.
[67]Clark, H. F., *The Economic Effects of Education*.
[68]List, Friedrich, *The National System of Political Economy*. Translated by S. S. Lloyd, 1922.

"The more the mental producers succeed in promoting enlightenment, and increase of knowledge, so much greater will be the production of material wealth."[69]

"Have we, for instance, carried as far as we should the collective ownership of the means of instruction? Living economists with one consent maintain that such expenditure is a true economy."[70]

"Education, in short, all those qualities which differentiate, advanced from low grade communities, tend to raise wages because they increase production."[71]

"Nevertheless, the economic effects of public education are scarcely capable of exaggeration. As producers and claimants of their respective shares of the product, and as consumers of wealth, the whole character of a people is governed by the degree and the nature of education which it enjoys. The economic superiority of the United States and the other leading nations of the world, or equally the economic inferiority of such nations, as China and India, is without a doubt largely to be ascribed to difference in education. With such understanding as the reader already possesses of factors of production, and the principles which govern the distribution and the consumption of wealth, the immense significance of education in the realm of economics will scarcely need further demonstration."[72]

Strayer and Haig have pointed out even a larger conception of the economic value of education by saying that:

"The system of education generates technical skill, and increases productive capacity. It tends to raise the intellectual and moral standards of the people, and prepares them to participate intelligently in the government of the country. In recent years, it has been effectively used to improve social qualities of great economic significance in such fields as: health and thrift. Finally, it makes important contributions in cultivating powers of appreciation, which determine the character of economic goods and services demanded and consumed by the community."[73]

[69] *Ibid.*, p. 129.
[70] Marshall, Alfred, *Principles of Economics*, 1922, pp. 42–47.
[71] Seligman, E. R. A., *Principles of Economics*, 1926, p. 423.
[72] Fairchild, F. R., and others, *Elementary Economics*, 1926, Vol. II, p. 201.
[73] Strayer, G. D., and Haig, R. M., *The Financing of Education in the State of New York*, pp. 142–45.

"The support of scientific research . . . holds forth the possibility of undreamed-of expansions of productivity. . . . According to Huxley, Pasteur's discoveries for preventing anthrax, silkworm disease and chicken cholera, added annually to France's wealth, a sum equivalent to the entire indemnity of the war of 1870."[74]

Norton[75] summarized the rôle of education in diminishing the gap between potential and actual productivity with the following points:

1. Reduction of the economic illiteracy of the individual, according to such economists as Veblen, King, Carver, and Haig.

2. Development of social purposes and laying the foundation for increased social planning.

3. Modifying standards of value in economic consumption.

Hence, from the basic assumption of the third principle of Adams regarding public credit, education may justify borrowing.

Based upon his second principle of emergency, borrowing for the support of education has even a greater argument in the case of China. The necessity of education is no less emergent than war, and in fact it is the basic preparation for war, in view of the most probable Pacific war and the economic crisis. Professor Tawney, noted British economist and educator, concludes in his recent book on China:

"Any great economic improvement on her part must be preceded by the development of an adequate system of public education."[66]

There is needed immediate mobilization for a war against ignorance and poverty, through supreme sacrifice.

[74]Strayer, G. D., and Haig, R. M., *The Financing of Education in the State of New York*, pp. 142–45.
[75]Norton, John K., *Major Issues in Public School Finance* (manuscript), pp. 6–9.
[76]Tawney, H. H., *Land and Labour in China*, 1932.

Viceroy Chang Chih Tung a long time ago discerned the necessity for immediate sacrifice when he presented his memorial for raising huge funds for the carrying out of important government affairs, including his ambitious educational enterprises, as shown by his record in Hupeh.

"Since the payments of this enormous indemnity have been raised with great difficulty, many maintain that all affairs should be economized and no new expenditure should be added, on the ground of the distress of the national treasury, and consequently hesitation and reluctance and delay cannot be avoided. Your servant, though stupid, maintains that this cannot do. If we only comb the nation for funds to pay this indemnity without further effort of achievement, foreign countries will think that China is a nation of happy-go-lucky weaklings, and her scholars without the spirit of struggle, and her masses without an invincible will. Their contempt and arrogance would grow degree by degree, and before the indemnity is paid up China would no longer exist as an independent country."[77]

How much more true this is to-day!

A Precedent in the United States

In the United States the school bonds outstanding and other forms of debt of the state school systems totaled G$2,425,796,439 in 1929–30.[78] This amount is almost equal to the total current expenditure for public education, G$2,656,420,316, for the same year in that country.[79] The debt service in interest payment was G$92,535,800, or about 3.6 per cent of the current expenditure. The debt service in payment of principal and interest including transfers to sinking funds was G$251,466,228, or 9.5 per cent of the current expenditure

---

[77]*The Complete Works of Chang Wen Hsiang Kung*, Volume 54, "Petition for Raising Huge Funds for Carrying Out Important Government Affairs," Fifth Day of Sixth Moon, 1901.
[78]U. S. Office of Education, *Biennial Survey of Education*, 1928–30, p. 61.
[79]*Ibid.*, p. 11 and p. 61, Table 17, Columns 4–7.

The Ability of China to Support Education

mentioned above. This does not mean that China should follow the American example in borrowing to such an extent; it only shows that borrowing for education has a precedent. Furthermore, American long-term borrowing is perhaps exclusively for financing school buildings and other permanent capital investment for the schools. Temporary loans are allowed to tide over periods in which income is anticipated.[80] If borrowing for education is allowed in China, the same principle governing the use of borrowed capital can be followed.

The Amount of Borrowing Proposed by the First National Conference on Education in China

The First National Conference on Education adopted the following resolutions:[81]

(1) A $30,000,000 serial bond secured on the Customs Tonnage Duty shall be issued, beginning with 1929 and expiring in 1944. Each year $3,000,000 is to be allocated from the said revenue to the Permanent Funds Custody Committee, to be deposited in a national bank to the credit of the fund for the payments of principal and interest. The issue shall be completely used to build a permanent educational fund for the use of all provinces.

(2) A $50,00,000 issue of treasury notes secured on the remainder of the Russian Boxer Indemnity, shall be paid to the permanent educational fund. The issue shall begin in 1929 and expire in 1938.

(3) A $20,000,000 issue of treasury notes secured upon the Belgian and Italian Boxer indemnities shall be paid to the permanent educational fund.

Thus the total amount of borrowing would be $100,000,000 for a permanent education fund in China. Five

[80]Engelhardt, Fred, *Public School Organization and Administration*, p. 503.
[81]*Proceedings of the First National Conference on Education*, 1929, Section B, pp. 259-64 and 276-80.

years have passed, but the proposals still exist on paper. Moreover, the Italian share has already been used as security for a different governmental purpose. It is difficult to say how much education should and can borrow at present. It is a matter that demands adequate factual information and concerns the entire political and economic fabric of the country. It is largely a task of the finance experts. For this reason, this study should close at this point.

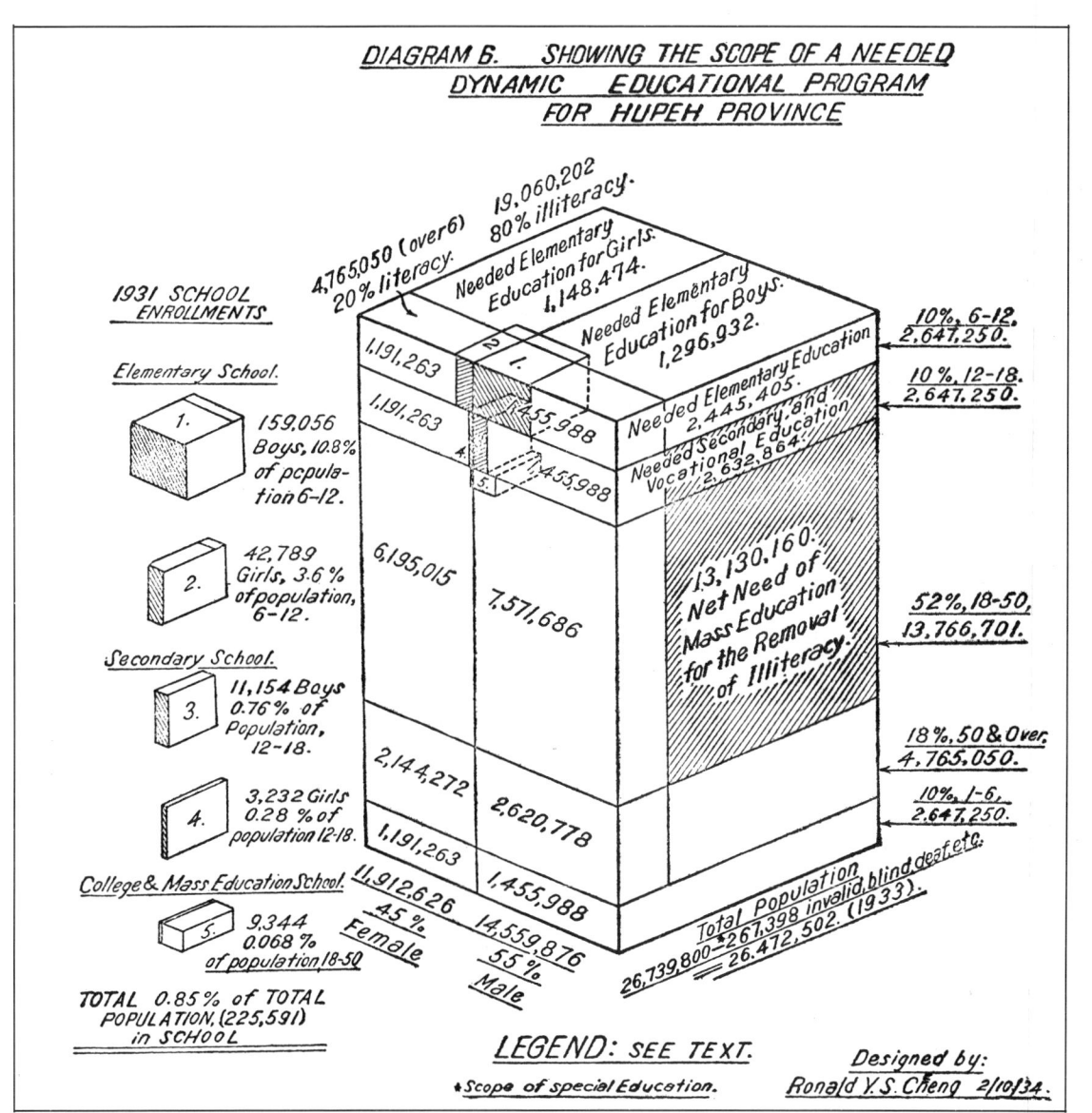

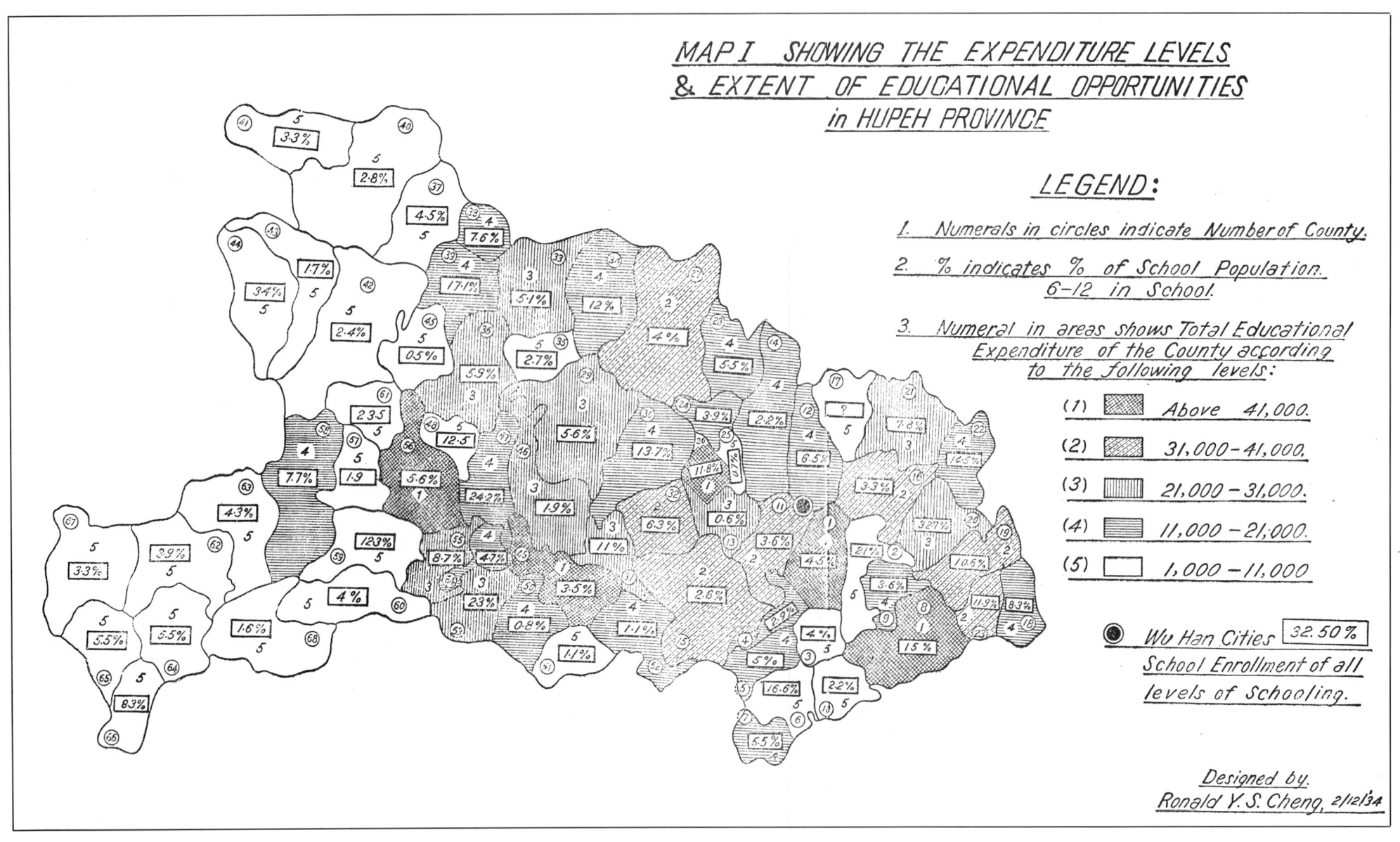

APPENDIX

A STATISTICAL ANALYSIS OF SCHOOL SUPPORT IN HUPEH PROVINCE AND ITS PROBLEMS OF RECONSTRUCTION

The Position of Hupeh Province

In normal years Hupeh is one of the wealthiest provinces of China. It is situated in central China, occupying a strategic political and economic position in the Yangtze Valley, which has a population of 206,000,000. The area of the province is approximately equal to the combined areas of the States of New York, New Jersey, Connecticut, Massachusetts, and Rhode Island, in the United States. Its population is approximately equal to that of these five states and Michigan combined, and is twice the population of either Turkey or Czechoslovakia.[1]

Hupeh's economic importance is due chiefly to its industry, commerce, and cotton fields, and to the trading port of Hankow, commonly called the "Chicago" of China. The trading ports of Shasi and Ichang will become increasingly important, if normal conditions are restored. With railways extending to North and South China and steamship lines traversing six provinces, and with Hankow as the commercial center of more than nine provinces of China, Hupeh holds the key to the solution of the livelihood problems of at least one-half the population of China.

[1] *Shun Pao Year Book*, 1933, pp. B2 and D4 *sqq*. *Statesman's Yearbook*, 1933.

The Present Educational Program

The present modern school enrollment and its trend are shown in Table 80.

TABLE 80

TREND IN MODERN SCHOOL ENROLLMENT, PUBLIC AND PRIVATE, HUPEH PROVINCE, 1902–32

Year	Elementary Education Enrollment (A)	Secondary Education Enrollment (B)	Higher Education Enrollment (C)	Total Enrollment (D)	Index (E)	Roll in Teacher Training (F)	Roll in Productive Education (G)
1. 1902	—	200	200	400		200	—
2. 1903	1,028	697	200	1,925		390	—
3. 1904	1,797	147?	240	2,184		—	—
4. 1905	9,735	2,111	304	12,150		1,864	—
5. 1906	13,544	2,468	300	16,312		1,932	—
6. 1907	51,437	3,794	1,138	56,671		2,403	803
7. 1908	66,227	4,665	1,741	72,633		1,494	1,909
8. 1909	92,037	5,769	1,258	99,064		1,702	1,751
9. 1912	196,918	4,159	2,135	203,212		458?	2,604
10. 1913	255,812	5,636	2,898	264,346	100	1,769	2,493
11. 1914	231,277	4,298	2,723	238,298		1,199	3,556
12. 1915	233,206	3,791	954	237,951		1,126	1,896
13. 1916	221,469	3,670	1,487	226,626		923	1,897
14. 1922	236,789	8,441	2,577	247,777		943	1,620
15. 1928	—	7,251	314?				
16. 1929a	111,662	10,041	624	127,342		482?	(752)
17. 1929b	136,952	10,041	624	152,632		—	—
18. 1930	175,368	10,041	624	191,048		—	—
19. 1931	201,894	14,386	816	224,539	85	952	(535)
20. 1932	159,670	16,422	869	176,961	68	1,096	1,033

Sources:
1902–09, from official reports, A, B, C.
1912–16, from official reports, D, E, F, G, H.
1922, from I.
1928–29, from J, except (A) 17b.
1930 from report of Hupeh's representative. See *Proceedings of the Second National Conference on Education*, Section VIII, p. 25.
1931, from *A Glimpse of Recent Education in Hupeh*, Section II, pp. 2–5; Section III, p. 4.
1922 figures include missionary school enrollment. The elementary and secondary rolls in missionary schools for 1922 are respectively, 10,235 and 852, according to Stauffer, M. T., *The Christian Occupation of China*, section on Hupeh.

Appendix

(A) 17. Freshly computed and corrected from Tables on School Statistics by districts. See *The Status of Education in Hupeh*, 1929–30, Section IV. The original figure is 145,090 not including Hankow, and probably not including the roll in provincial elementary schools which is 12,657 in 1931.

(B) includes (E). B–14 is 7,437, if missionary roll is not included.

(C) probably does not include national and missionary college roll in recent years except 1922. C–16–18 includes 86 students studying abroad.

(D) 16–18, includes roll in mass education and adult continuation schools (5,115).

(D) 19, includes roll in mass education and adult continuation schools (7,443).

(F) includes roll in independent normal schools and probably does not include roll in normal courses in high schools, especially after 1922.

(G) includes roll in vocational schools of all levels.

(G) 16 and (F) 19 do not include roll in the Provincial High Schools, No. 2 and No. 3, which are vocational in the main.

1932, Hupeh Provincial Department of Education, *Hupeh Education Status and Statistics for the Year 1933*, Table B, pp. 12–13 (not including 14,886 in social education).

Table 80 shows that in 1931 the public and private schools of all levels in Hupeh Province enrolled a total of 224,539, which dropped sharply to only 176,961 in 1932 owing to the effects of the flood of 1931. There were, in 1932, 159,670 pupils in the elementary schools, 16,422 students in the secondary schools, and 869 students in higher education institutions. There were 1,096 enrolled in normal schools and only 1,033 in vocational schools.

In 1902 Hupeh had only 400 students in the modern schools. It increased steadily to 99,064 in 1909, and suddenly to 203,212 in 1912. The years between 1912 and 1922 showed a larger enrollment than that between 1929 and 1932, except 1931. The educational program has gone backward instead of making any progress.

The Extent of Educationl Opportunities

The extent of educational opportunities is shown in Diagram 6 and Map 1 following consecutively.

Diagram 6 is at once striking in illustrating the vast proportion of the population without modern educational opportunities. The total school enrollment is 225,591 (the 224,539 given in Table 80 does not include students studying abroad). It dropped to 176,961 in 1932, a decrease of 17 per cent below 1931.

The proportion of boys and girls in school at each level with respect to total population of the corresponding age group is shown by the shaded blocks. The girls of Hupeh are given far less opportunity than the boys. Approximately 2,445,405 children of school age need schooling. The net need of mass education for the removal of illiteracy is a program for 13,000,000 persons between the ages of 12 and 50 years. One per cent of the total population belongs to the special education category. This is estimated on the basis of the American figure of .77 per cent.[2]

Due to the lack of an actual school census, the proportion of school children 6 to 12 years of age is estimated to be 10 per cent of the total population. A great deal of labor has been expended by the writer in arriving at this approximate percentage from 16 sources, including 95 instances of total populations of various counties, with age groups specified. The details are shown in Diagram 7.

In 1929-30 Hupeh ranked twenty-third among 34 provinces and municipalities in having only 5.2 per cent of the children of school age in school. In 1931 the percentage had increased to 6.9, or only .69 per cent of the total population. (See Table 90, Column 35.)

The data presented in Map 1 are derived partially from Column 35 in Table 90. It illustrates that in the 68 counties, the proportion of children of school age in school varies from .6 per cent in Han-Chuan to 32.7 per cent in Chi-Shui. The 32.5 per cent in Wu-Han cities includes the enrollment of secondary and higher schools. The county enrollment also includes secondary

---

[2] White House Conference on Child Health and Protection, *Special Education, the Handicapped and Gifted*, pp. 4, 5, and 538.

Appendix 229

enrollment. Neverthless, it is safe to say that educational opportunities are concentrated in the large cities. Only 15 counties have more than 10 per cent of the children of school age in school, or more than 1 per cent of the total population in school.

In 1932, the enrollment dropped sharply, as shown in Table 80. The proportion of children in school probably decreased to the same extent.

THE RANK OF HUPEH IN EDUCATIONAL OPPORTUNITIES AMONG THE PROVINCES AND SPECIAL MUNICIPALITIES

To show how Hupeh compares with other provinces and special municipalities in providing educational opportunities, Table 81 is prepared. Nine educational factors and nine financial factors on a comparable basis are presented.

TABLE 81

RANK OF HUPEH PROVINCE IN EDUCATIONAL OPPORTUNITIES AMONG TWENTY-NINE PROVINCIAL UNITS AND SEVEN MUNICIPALITIES, 1929–30

Factors	Average for China	Range	Hupeh	Rank	No. of Admin. Units Reporting
I. *Educational Factors:*					
1. Per cent of population in elementary schools	1.93	.05–7.52	.52f	29	34
2. Per cent of children of school age in elementary schools .	17.1	1.4–65.4	5.2f	23	27
3. Per cent of population in secondary schools	.0733	.0007–.98	.0385	26	36
4. Per cent that public elementary school enrollment is of total elementary enrollment	77.32	27.77–100	80.53	16	28
5. Per cent that girls are of total elementary enrollment	16.58	4.61–41.5	17.71	12	28
6. Per cent that number of students taking vocational training is of number of secondary students	7.82	0–25.4	7.5f	17	28

TABLE 81 (Continued)

Factors	Average for China	Range	Hupeh	Rank	No. of Admin. Units Reporting
7. Number of social and adult educational institutions per 1,000,000 population	23.4	.96–324	4.8f	23	28
8. Per cent increase in elementary school enrollment, 1929 over 1912	316.	.69–690	.69	25	25
9. Per cent increase in secondary school enrollment, 1929 over 1912	348.	160–550	240	21	24
II. Financial Factors:					
1. Total educational expenditure per capita of population	$ .343	$.005–$4.89	.184	27	36
2. Elementary expenditure per capita of population	$ .17	.03–1.12	.07	23	26
3. Elementary expenditure per pupil enrolled	8.15	4.1–93.95	7.9f	19	28
4. Secondary expenditure per capita of population	.077	.015–1.06	.049	22	26
5. Secondary expenditure per pupil enrolled	105.52	56–786	129.07	12	36
6. Per cent of increase in secondary expenditure, 1929–30 over 1912–13	565%f	170–1270	550f	10	24
7. Per cent that expenditure for social and adult education is of total educational expenditure (1930–31)	8.66%*	.49–20	7.7	10	26
8. Per cent that provincial educational expenditure is of total provincial government expenditure (1931–32):					
A. Budget	18.05%f	2.02–20.5f	17.8f	4	20
B. Actual or closed account	—	—	9.75f		
9. Extent that educational expenditure is obstructed by military expenditure, or per cent that the latter is of total governmental expenditure (1931–32), negative ranking:					
A. Budget	24.1%f	2.1–30.6f	29.6	19	20
B. Actual	—	—	24		

Appendix

TABLE 81 (Continued)

Factors	Rank	No. of Admin. Units Reporting
III. Factors of Gross Nature Not Strictly Comparable:		
1. Number of elementary schools and kindergartens	18	35
2. Number of elementary teachers and officials	14	28
3. Amount of revenue for elementary education	14	28
4. Amount of expenditure for elementary education	14	28
5. Number of secondary teachers and officials	17	36
6. Amount of secondary school expenditure	12	36
7. Number of vocational students on secondary level	15	28
8. Number of students enrolled in colleges in all China	13	30
9. Number of social and adult education institutions	17	30
10. Number enrolled in adult and continuation schools	19	29
11. Amount of expenditure for social and adult education	10	30
12. Total amount of educational expenditure	13	36
IV. Conditions in 1907:		
1. Amount of total revenue for education	1	23
2. Amount of total expenditure for education	2	23
3. Total number of students enrolled in all schools	4	23
4. Number of vocational students	4	23
5. Number of normal school students	5	23
6. Number of college students	7	23
7. Value of school property and school funds	5	23

*1929.

f. Freshly computed from raw data in J1, J2, J4. In order to ascertain the rank of Hupeh, much labor has been spent in computing comparable figures for other administrative units. For Hupeh in Items 1 and 2, the enrollment figure is taken from the writer's own calculation.

IV, from statistical source A.

Table 81 shows that under the impetus of the great leader, Chang Chih Tung, Hupeh once (1907) ranked first or second in the amount of educational finance provided among the provinces, and fifth in the value of school property. This province ranked from fourth to seventh in number of students. Since that time it has lost ground. Both educationally and financially, she ranks on the average below the lowest decile of the total number of provinces and municipalities reporting, with the exception of the percentage that the provincial educational budget is of the total governmental budget. (The actual educational expenditure would surely lower her rank to several places below fourth.) A comparison of this Table and Table 89, on the rank of Hupeh in economic ability, would convince one that Hupeh during the two decades preceding the flood disaster did not expend an effort commensurate with her ability, which easily ranks fifth or sixth among all the provinces. No more accurate measurement is needed to establish this fact.

The Cost of the Present Program and Trends in Total and Per Pupil Expenditure

The cost of the present educational program, the trends in total and per pupil costs are shown in Tables 82 and 83, following consecutively. It must be borne in mind that these cost figures represent only the reported expenditures of individual schools and institutions, that is to say, not including overhead costs of administration.

TABLE 82

TREND IN TOTAL ACTUAL EDUCATIONAL EXPENDITURE, PUBLIC AND PRIVATE, PROVINCIAL AND LOCAL, INCLUSIVE, IN HUPEH

Year	Total Educational Expenditure (1)	Index of Wholesale Prices (2)	Real Trend in 1913 Dollars (3)	Index (4)	Funds and Value of School Property (5)
	$		$		$
1907	1,877,140	104			2,561,049
1908	1,740,136	110			3,303,569
1909	1,868,940	111			5,208,519
1912	1,074,139	106			1,665,192
1913	1,377,325	100	1,377,325	100	1,736,781
1914	1,240,577	100			1,925,866
1915	1,200,152a	116			2,206,540
1916	1,394,404b	120			2,342,207
1922	1,748,220c	136			
1929	4,600,241d	161			
1930	5,693,444d	177			
1931	5,915,498d	195			
1932	4,715,238	173	2,725,571	198	4,212,497a

TABLE 83

TREND IN PER PUPIL EXPENDITURE IN HUPEH PROVINCE, CHINA

Year	Kinder-garten Cost	Elementary School Cost			Second-ary Cost	Normal Cost	Vocational Cost		Higher Cost
		Lower	Higher	Total			Second-ary	Elemen-tary	
	$	$	$	$	$	$	$	$	$
1907	2.67	6.67	63.50		93.54	86.82	121.79		137.79
1908	1.34	7.05	49.12		71.61	115.44	132.46		278.21
1909	16.34	5.41	32.89		84.59	99.29	111.94		208.75
1912		2.53	17.59		86.72	43.89	70.95	23.95	132.10
1913		2.92	16.90		52.84	56.26	71.06	22.70	145.08
1914		2.93	10.70		36.13	117.69	119.75	14.36	193.36
1915		3.05	19.24		56.77	61.17	101.72	22.54	117.37
1916		3.36	19.25		87.72	123.66	93.73	26.98	145.11
1922		2.35	17.36		64.61	111.59	76.26		180.69
1929-a	62.43	13.36a	34.35	16.13	129.07b	309.48	150.17c		886.87f

		Lower	Complete	Total					
1929b*									
County only		5.25f	23.79f	8.48f					
1931:									
Provincial f		28.53	66.05	48.12	145.20	351.12	373.66		2,450.52
County f	11.07	5.16	21.95	8.49	35.00				
Private } f				29.94	129.24				
Municipal }									
County					158.16		157.62d		
All f		7.11	39.35	14.59	137.55				

**1929 Per pupil cost in continuation and mass education school: $3.04f
***1931 Per pupil cost in continuation and mass education school: Monthly $3.45
Yearly $41.40f

a. This is due to the low figure for elementary roll, 111,662, given by the Ministry of Education. The figure should be at least 136,952 according to the writer's computation. For lower elementary roll, it is at least 113,074 instead of 97,942.
b. Junior High School figures: Provincial, $77.12; County, $40.51.
c. Provincial, $237.85; County, $22.38.
d. Elementary.
f. All freshly computed.
*Computed from writer's own figures; see Table on enrollment.
**It is yearly according to data in the official report of Ministry of Education which gives $2.40 yearly for mass schools (writer's own computation is $2.50). Writer's computation for vocational continuation school is $5.62. The unusual discrepancy may be explained by the error of the official report in dividing total expenditure by total enrollment, the major part of which has no expenditure reported, as the case in 1931.
***By taking only those schools that have data on both enrollment and expenditure. Separately, the figure is $23.28 for mass schools and $47.88 for vocational schools.

Sources of Data for Table 82:
(1) Actual expenditure.
(4) 1912=100 in order to compare with the trend of school enrollment since 1912.
(5) From the same sources of school enrollment.
   a. Another table gives $1,200,152.
   b. Another table gives $1,394,404.
   c. By adding expenditure for all levels of schools from I.
   d. Partly from *Report of Public Finance in Hupeh, 1932.*
   1932 figures—See Table 80, Source for 1932 (including social education expenditure $5,618,060).
      Total private expenditure=$2,418,657—43 per cent.
      Total public expenditure=$3,199,403—57 per cent (12 cents per capita of population).
*Elementary only.
Remarks: The provincial budget, 1931, is $4,998,862; the allowed budget is $3,787,671; but the actual expenditure is only $2,389,759, which is only 48 per cent of the budget. Therefore, the figures given for 1929, 1930, 1931 budgets are not real and so are not used here. Actual expenditures might be only about one-half of the budgeted amounts.

Table 82 shows that the total actual expenditure of all levels of education both public and private has increased steadily from $1,877,140 in 1907 to $5,618,060 in 1932. The actual increase in equal value of the dollar in 1932 over 1913 was 198 per cent, but the enrollment in 1932 had decreased 32 per cent below that of 1913, as shown in Table 80. This may indicate a considerable waste of money or it may mean that the cost of the present program can care for at least twice the enrollment of 1913 without an increase in the total budget. This situation is also revealed by the trend in per pupil expenditure (see Table 83). The cost of educating one lower primary pupil in 1913 was $2.92, while in 1931 it was $7.11, or 244 per cent more costly. The cost of educating one higher elementary or complete elementary school pupil was $16.90 in 1913, while in 1931 it was $39.35, or 232 per cent more costly. The cost of educating one secondary school pupil in 1913 was $52.84, while in 1931 it was $137.55, or 260 per cent more costly.

From Diagram 4, opposite p. 118, it is seen that at present an approximate sum of $5,904,679 is spent each year for the educational program in Hupeh. Of this sum, about $800,000 to $1,000,000 ($1,355,671 actual for 1931-32) is paid by the Central Government for the National Wuhan University. The Provincial Government spends $2,424,459, and the county governments spend $1,160,000. Private schools and institutions expend $2,680,220. The actual sum spent in 1932–33 as reported by the Department of Education was $5,618,060, including social education expenditure and excluding the expenditure for National Wuhan University.[3] Of this sum, $2,418,657, or 43 per cent, was derived from private sources. The public spent only $3,199,403, or 57 per cent of the total. Of the latter, only $953,651, not including the expenditure for social education, was provided by the county treasuries.

It is clear that even if the government subsidy to private schools is excluded, educational finances are derived at least two-thirds from private sources, and local public support has not the significance it should have.

TRENDS IN THE EXPENDITURES OR COSTS OF PROVINCIAL AND COUNTY EDUCATION

The trend in the total educational expenditures provided by the provincial government is shown in Table 86, presented later in this study (see p. 241). It shows both the total provincial government revenues and expenditures in relation to educational expenditure with percentage ratios. The provincial government educational expenditure was $500,000 in 1914–15 and had increased very slowly to $1,000,000 in 1925–26. After the establishment of the Nationalist Government, the increase has been more than twofold. Between 1928 and 1933, the Hupeh provincial government spent each year

[3] Hupeh Department of Education, *Hupeh Educational Status and Statistics*, 1933–34, p. 13.

Appendix 235

more than $2,000,000 for education. The peak year was 1930–31, with an expenditure of $3,146,932. However, in percentage comparison with other government expenditure, education falls far behind military functions and general administration as a whole. The proportion that educational expenditure is of total government expenditure ranged from 5.9 per cent to 10.2 per cent between 1914 and 1924. The figure for 1925–26 does not reveal the true situation, as the total expenditure for all purposes is questionable. After 1927, the percentage increased markedly; it ranged from 9.8 per cent to 16.3 per cent between 1927 and 1932, but is still far below the 30 per cent provided by the Draft Constitution. Military expenditure which consumed more than 50 per cent of the total before 1925 has decreased notably in recent years, to about 25 per cent of the total in the last few years.

The trend in county educational expenditure, including private school expenditure and its variation, is shown in Table 84.

TABLE 84

THE VARIATION OF TOTAL COUNTY EDUCATIONAL EXPENDITURES

Level of Expenditure	1913	1914	1915	1916	1931	1932 Actual
$61,000 and above	1				3	1
$59,000		1				
57,000				1		
55,000						1
53,000			1			1
51,000						
49,000		1			1	1
47,000						
45,000						1
43,000				1	1	
41,000						1
39,000		1		1	2	1
37,000				1	1	1

236 *The Financing of Public Education in China*

TABLE 84 (*Continued*)

Level of Expenditure	1913	1914	1915	1916	1931	1932 Actual
$35,000		1	2		1	
33,000	1	1			1	
31,000	1	1			2	1
29,000	2	1			2	1
27,000	1	1	2			2
25,000		1	4	3	4	2
23,000	1	2	1	2	1	2
21,000	3		1	2	3	5
19,000	3	1	4	1	6	3
17,000	4	2	2	2	3	4
15,000	6	3		1	3	3
13,000	3	3		3	5	5
11,000	5	6	2	4	3	6
9,000	5	3	5	7	4	6
7,000	5	13	9	10	10	5
5,000	8	9	17	8	4	2
3,000	12	10	8	10	3	1
$1,000–$3,000	6	7	9	6	3	3
Less than $1,000						1
Number of Counties	68	68	67	63	66	60
Median	$10,200	$8230.77	$6941.8	$7,700.00	$16,334	$15,667
(in 1913 Dollars).	10,200	8230.77	5984.2	6,416.7	8376.4	9,056

Sources:
1. E. F. G. H.
2. *A Glimpse of Recent Educational Statistics in Hupeh*, 1932.
3. *Hupeh Educational Status and Statistics*, 1933.

Table 84 shows that there is a wide variation of county educational expenditures. This variation has been pictured in Map. 1, together with the extent of educational opportunities for purposes of comparison. (See page 274.) Only one county had an expenditure of more than $61,000 and only five had more than $41,000 in 1932, while the median expenditure was $15,667. The median current educational expenditure was $10,200 in 1913, but had decreased steadily to $7,700 in 1916. Then it increased to $16,334 in 1931, but again decreased in 1932. In terms of 1913 dollars, the median in 1932 showed no significant increase over the preceding years. It was actually less than the median of 1913.

The Support for the Educational Program of Hupeh

School Support in the Past

Although the government school for scholars was known to have existed in the Han Dynasty (206 B.C. to 219 A.D.), all government historical records show that the real beginning of schools was in the year 1044 A.D., the Fourth Year of the Reign of the Emperor Chin Li, of the Sung Dynasty.[4] The writer spent two months in the Library of Congress, Washington, D. C., in surveying the *General Historical Records of Hupeh Province*, published in 1803 and 1922, the historical records of ten prefectures and those of 69 counties,[5] and found that schools before the establishment of modern schools were supported by school lands and funds contributed predominantly by the people of the local communities and secondarily by the government officials. The total amount of school land established on record since 1355 A.D. was estimated to be 96,394.47 mow, plus 1,896 pieces unmeasured, and the total amount of school funds was 82,120.312 taels and 5,109,719.965 chuans. However, the actual amount existing at the beginning of the Republic could not be ascertained from these records.

These figures are summarized and tabulated on Table 85 following. Detailed tables are on file.[6]

Table 85 shows that there were very few cases of endowment directly by taxation and appropriation. The revenue directory shows that all districts paid quotas of taxes totaling 1,900,354.113 taels of silver, while the appropriation allowed for the salaries and expenses of all educational officials and for ceremonial

---

[4]Chang Chung-chi, Compiler, *General Historical Records of Hupeh Province*, Volume 55, Section 1, p. 1, 1921.
[5]Unpublished Document No. 20, Bibliography on Hupeh Provincial, Prefecture and County Historical Records.
[6]Unpublished Document No. 21.

TABLE 85

SUMMARY OF STATISTICS CONCERNING SCHOOL LANDS AND FUNDS IN HUPEH PROVINCE, 1355–1896

	Years Established	Amounts
I. Land and Buildings:		
1. School land, irrigated and non-irrigated	1355–1896	59,544.39 mow; 9,212.52 Tan (4 mow); 1,896 pieces unmeasured; Estimated total mow—(unmeasured excluded)—96,394.47
2. Buildings	..	250 houses and 542 halls and rooms
II. School Funds	1733–1896	82,120.312 Taels and 5,109,719.965 Chuans

III. Sources of School Lands and Funds, by Number of Cases of Donation:

1. Government treasury . . . . 15 cases
2. Public funds . . . . 6 ,,
3. Taxes, title deeds tax, charcoal tax, salt tax, mow tax on land, likin, and poll . . . . 10 ,,
4. Central government officials, including 1 case by the Emperor 3 ,,
5. Provincial officials . . . . 15 ,,
6. Prefect officials . . . . 49 ,,
7. District officials, the magistrates, including 15 cases by local education officials . . . . 97 ,,
8. Local gentry . . . . 273 ,,
9. People of local communities, including 33 cases by women and 5 cases by people of other districts . . . . 381 ,,
10. Temple property . . . . 52 ,,
11. Ancestral shrine property . . . . 7 ,,
12. Confiscated property of rebels, deserted and heirless homes, disputed land, and fines . . . . 127 ,,

IV. Original purposes of the donations in Lands and Funds:

1. Upkeep and sacrificial ceremonies of Confucian temples . . 123 ,,
2. Current expenses of Shu Yuan or Colleges . . . . . . 536 ,,
3. Stipends of college scholars . . . . 451 ,,
4. Yi Hsueh or publicly supported primary schools . . . . 171 ,,
5. Traveling expenses of examination candidates . . . . . 305 ,,
6. Examination expenses including paper and halls . . . . 39 ,,

Sources of data for Table 85:
Original sources—*General Historical Records of Hupeh Province,* 1921, Volume 62, Section VII, as chief basis of information, with additions and corrections from 10 Prefecture Histories and 69 District Histories, with publication dates ranging from 1614 to 1896.

Secondary sources—See separate list of references, separate tables of school lands and funds tabulated by writer for each county. These are now on file.

and examination expenses was only 22,633.759 taels, or 1.19 per cent of the total taxes paid.[7] The original purposes of endowment of land and money were, in order according to the number of cases:

1. Current expenses of colleges.
2. Stipends of college scholars.
3. Traveling expenses of examination candidates.
4. Publicly supported primary schools.
5. Upkeep and sacrificial ceremonies of Confucian temples.
6. Expenses of examination papers and of halls.

The endowments for each institution or purpose were controlled by a board of directors elected from the gentry of the community. It may be seen that there is in Hupeh a tradition of local support for schools with local control which has been in existence for centuries. The meager amount of land and money endowed, the current government appropriation, and the purposes of the endowments indicate that the maintenance of schools was not encouraged in the modern sense and that they existed for only the selected few.

The Support for the Modern Schools

Hupeh was the first among all the provinces to establish modern government schools.[8] The establishment of

[7]Lin Yuan-tsung and Wang Shiao-lien, Editors, *The Land-capitation and Grain Tribute Directory and Water Control Directory of Hupeh Province,* 1875. All totals freshly calculated.
See Unpublished Document No. 23 for calculation tables.
[8]Hupeh Department of Education, *A Glimpse of Recent Education in Hupeh,* Wuchang, 1932. Section 11, p. 1.

the Mining and Engineering College by Viceroy Chang Chih Tung in 1892 represented the heyday of modern education in Hupeh.[9] Under the Viceroy's leadership, modern schools on all levels increased by leaps and bounds, and Hupeh led almost all the provinces in number and influence until the last years of the Ching Dynasty. These schools paved the way to the success of the revolution started in Wuchang in 1911.[10]

In the beginning, Viceroy Chang turned the endowments of the old-style colleges and the taxes for Hupeh's share of the Boxer Indemnity to the support for modern schools, and used Buddhist temples and ancestral shrines for schoolhouses. Later, however, the current revenues for local schools were chiefly dependent upon the land surtaxes in the counties or districts, supplemented by multifarious petty taxes.[11]

The Sources of Educational Revenue

The educational budget of the provincial government in 1911 reached the amount of 820,000 silver taels of which 75 per cent came from the earmarked salt tax and the remainder from the so-called 5-5 and 9-9 school taxes. In 1912 the salt tax was taken over by the Central Government. From that time on, the provincial government schools have been financed under the appropriation policy. [12]

The sources of revenue of the provincial government are shown in Table 86. For comparison, the various provincial government expenditure items are also included.

---

[9]*Ibid.*, Section 11, p. 1.
[10]*Hupeh Education Monthly*, Volume 1, No. 1, September, 1933. Introduction by Chang Chun, Chairman of Hupeh Provincial Government Council.
[11]Hupeh Department of Education, *Op. cit.*, Section 11, p. 31.
[12]*The First Education Year Book of China*, 1934. Section C, p. 221.

TABLE 86

HUPEH PROVINCIAL GOVERNMENT REVENUE FOR FISCAL
YEARS 1914–15 to 1932–33
(1927–33 actual)
Corrected and Redistributed According to Sources for Purposes of
Comparison

Year	Land Tax		Consolidated Commodity Tax		Business Tax, Business Middleman License, Butchery Tax, and Pawnshop Tax	
	Amount	% of Total	Amount	% of Total	Amount	% of Total
	$		$		$	
1914–15	2,400,000.00	32.79	4,020,000.00	54.92		
1915–16	4,130,000.00	33.99	5,400,000.00	44.44		
1916–17	3,720,000.00	31.37	5,380,000.00	45.36		
1917–18	2,300,000.00	28.54	3,910,000.00	48.51		
1918–19	3,380,000.00	31.65	4,340,000.00	40.64		
1919–20	2,530,000.00	28.02	3,480,000.00	38.54		
1920–21	2,490,000.00	28.49	3,090,000.00	35.35		
1921–22	2,020,000.00	31.76	2,340,000.00	36.79		
1922–23	2,050,000.00	28.79	2,620,000.00	36.80		
1923–24	2,000,000.00	28.45	2,710,000.00	38.55		
1924–25	900,000.00	24.73	1,170,000.00	32.14		
1925–26	280,000.00	22.22	280,000.00	22.22		
1926–27	Bookkeeping incomplete					
1927–28	420,164.25	6.66	3,202,567.66	50.74		
1928–29	861,023.20	5.17	11,353,324.86	68.23	730,368.29	4.39
1929–30	930,731.82	6.51	9,236,188.43	65.00	424,273.10	2.97
1930–31	760,145.65	3.52	5,839,866.05	27.05	290,313.62	1.34
1931–32	1,025,785.70	4.20	444,215.76	1.82	1,342,783.26	5.50
1932–33	644,733.37	2.70	Abolished		2,447,480.17	10.26
1933–34						

Sources: 1. Article on Report of Hupeh financial conditions since 1914, *Hupeh Public Finance Monthly*, Volume V, Nos. 3 and 4, pp. 225–28.
2. *Report of Public Finance in Hupeh*, 1932. Tables, pp. 30–31.
3. *Report of Public Finance in Hupeh*, March–June, 1933, Appendix.

Note: 1. The column on Unclassified Revenue includes all sources except land and consolidated taxes. No data are available for segregation of these.
2. Figure for revenue from public loans is not separately available except in the year 1932–33, with different figures for a loan of $1,631,467.15.
3. Source 1 gives the total revenues and expenditures of 1927–28 and 1931–32, with a discrepancy ranging from $1,000,000 to $7,700,000.

TABLE 86, SECTION I (*Continued*)

Year	Title Deeds Tax, House Tax		Miscellaneous Surtaxes for Bandit Suppression, Public Loans and Tax Revenues from Hankow		Administrative Revenues and Revenues from Public Property and Enterprises	
	Amount	Per Cent of Total	Amount	Per Cent of Total	Amount	Per Cent of Total
(Data unclassified, 1914-15 to 1927-28, inclusive)						
1928–29	$ 730,982.76	4.39	$ 2,513,532.64	15.11	$ 449,781.21	2.70
1929–30	629,363.01	4.40	2,208,557.61	15.45	869,369.48	6.08
1930–31	390,426.99	1.81	6,765,172.99	31.34	2,425,453.34	11.24
1931–32	1,586,610.79	6.49	10,611,955.34	43.43	1,414,922.48	5.79
1932–33	623,558.31	2.62	11,250,539.05	47.18	1,727,619.18	7.25

Year	Unclassified, 1914–1928 Central Aid, 1930–1933		Total—100 Per Cent
	Amount	Per Cent of Total	
1914–15	$ 900,000	12.30	$ 7,320,000
1915–16	2,620,000	21.56	12,150,000
1916–17	2,760,000	23.27	11,860,000
1917–18	1,850,000	22.95	8,060,000
1918–19	2,960,000	27.72	10,680,000
1919–20	3,020,000	33.44	9,030,000
1920–21	3,160,000	36.16	8,740,000
1921–22	2,000,000	31.45	6,360,000
1922–23	2,450,000	34.41	7,120,000
1923–24	2,320,000	33.00	7,030,000
1924–25	1,570,000	43.13	3,640,000
1925–26	700,000	55.56	1,260,000
1926–27			
1927–28	2,688,431.94	42.60	6,311,613.85
1928–29			16,639,012.96
1929–30			14,298,483.45
1930–31	5,115,000.00	23.70	21,586,380.64
1931–32	8,010,000.00	32.78	24,436,273.33
1932–33	7,150,000.00	29.99	23,843,930.08

TABLE 86 (Continued)
HUPEH PROVINCIAL GOVERNMENT EXPENDITURE (Actual)
1914-1933
II

Year	Education		Party Expenditure		General Administration		Military	
	Amount	% of Total	Amount	% of Total	Amount	% of Total	Amount	% of Total
1914-15	$ 500,000	6.2			$ 2,490,000	32.0	4,530,000	57.3
1915-16	560,000	5.9			3,040,000	32.0	5,360,000	56.5
1916-17	580,000	5.9			3,440,000	34.5	5,350,000	54.3
1917-18	650,000	7.1			2,490,000	27.0	5,560,000	60.0
1918-19	670,000	7.1			2,790,000	29.4	5,200,000	55.0
1919-20	760,000	9.1			2,740,000	33.0	3,950,000	47.5
1920-21	590,000	7.6			2,810,000	36.0	3,720,000	47.5
1921-22	530,000	7.0			2,370,000	31.0	4,350,000	57.0
1922-23	600,000	8.2			1,970,000	27.0	4,280,000	58.6
1923-24	860,000	10.2			1,820,000	21.6	5,250,000	62.5
1924-25	600,000	9.6			1,650,000	26.6	3,500,000	56.5
1925-26	1,000,000	21.0			1,600,000	34.0	1,770,000	38.0
1926-27			Bookkeeping incomplete					
1927-28	795,150.84	14.7	285,313.45	5.1	1,969,984.99	35.6	480,000	8.6
1928-29	2,376,832.50	13.7	970,804.27	5.6	3,936,742.29	22.6	4,235,838.33	24.4
1929-30	2,487,630.59	16.3	576,552.28	3.8	4,752,838.46	31.1	804,806.66	5.3
1930-31	3,146,932.06	14.5	420,216.60	2.0	6,025,573.41	27.9	4,271,468.99	19.8
1931-32	2,389,759.46	9.8	252,965.60	1.0	3,912,681.28	15.9	5,921,036.40	24.2
1932-33	2,414,459.10	10.2	205,405.52	0.9	2,854,205.70	12.0	6,297,264.06	26.5

TABLE 86, SECTION II (Continued)

Year	Justice		Economic Reconstruction		Other Expenditures		Total
	Amount	Per Cent of Total	Amount	Per Cent of Total	Amount	Per Cent of Total	100 Per Cent
	$		$		$		$
1914–15	280,000	4.0	120,000	.5			7,920,000
1915–16	380,000	4.0	160,600	1.6			9,500,000
1916–17	350,000	3.6	170,000	1.7			9,890,000
1917–18	330,000	3.6	190,000	2.3			9,220,000
1918–19	310,000	3.2	510,000	5.3			9,480,000
1919–20	300,000	3.6	570,000	6.8			8,320,000
1920–21	260,000	3.3	440,000	5.6			7,820,000
1921–22	260,000	3.0	150,000	2.0			7,660,000
1922–23	200,000	2.7	260,000	3.5			7,310,000
1923–24	210,000	2.4	280,000	3.3			8,420,000
1924–25	170,000	2.7	280,000	4.6			6,200,000
1925–26	120,000	3.0	200,000	4.0			4,690,000
1926–27	Bookkeeping incomplete						
1927–28	352,019.17	6.4	645,982.84	11.6	1,005,182.83	18.0	5,533,634.12
1928–29	1,132,258.89	6.5	1,534,007.58	8.8	3,200,770.91	18.4	17,387,254.77
1929–30	1,304,051.88	8.6	966,293.47	6.3	4,355,456.92	23.6	15,247,630.26
1930–31	1,523,859.69	7.0	838,392.57	3.8	5,391,745.47	25.0	21,611,188.79
1931–32	1,273,318.93	5.2	1,657,187.15	6.8	9,095,107.32	37.1	24,502,056.14
1932–33	972,809.21	4.1	750,736.98	3.2	10,201,085.47	43.1	23,695,966.04

1. Civil Administration includes civil affairs, finance, and provincial government administration. Expenditure for foreign affairs is included for 1914–15.
2. Other Expenditures includes debt service, public health, local grant, reserve, expenditure for public enterprises and exchange charges, contributions to central government, 1929–31, etc.
3. Military Expenditure might not be included in total expenditure for 1927–28, except for a small amount.

Table 86 shows that the revenue of the provincial government has increased gradually from $7,320,000 in 1914–15 to $23,843,930 in 1932–33, an increase of more than 300 per cent. Up to 1926, the sources of revenue were (1) commodity taxes which constituted 22.22 per cent to 54.92 per cent of the total revenue, (2) land tax which constituted 22.22 to 33.99 per cent of the total revenue, (3) title deeds tax, butchery tax, business middleman license tax, pawnshop tax, and other nontax revenues which constituted 12.30 to 55.56 per cent of the revenue. The land tax has gradually decreased in importance since 1926. It yielded only 2.7 per cent of the total revenue in 1932–33. Following the abolishment of the commodity tax, or likin, the business tax became more important. The deficits have been made up by Central aid (23.70 per cent to 32.78 per cent of the revenue) and through borrowing ($1,866,843, or 11 per cent of the revenue of 1932-33).[13]

The status for 1932–33 has been illustrated in Diagram 4 presented in Chapter VII (see page 118). In 1932–33, provincial education funds were appropriated from the provincial treasury, which derived its income from miscellaneous taxes and public revenue from Hankow municipality (40.38 per cent), Central aid (29.99 per cent), business taxes including license tax and butchery tax (10.26 per cent), public loans (6.8 per cent), land tax (2.7 per cent), title deeds tax and house tax (2.62 per cent), and other nontax revenues (7.25 per cent).

The status of fiscal control and the sources of county educational revenue have been shown in Table 41 and Diagram 5 in Chapters VI and VII (see pages 119, 169).

The Tax Burden and the Burden of School Support

Table 87 shows that the people of Hupeh Province pay on the average annual taxes amounting to $37,000,000 to the National treasury, or $1.386 per capita; $14,700,000 to the provincial treasury, or $0.55 per capita; and $7,000,000 to the county treasuries, or $0.264 per capita. The total tax burden is around $59,000,000, or $2.20 per capita. Although most of the national revenue derived from indirect taxation is collected from Hankow, Shasi, and Ichang, and hence the burden must be shared by the people of surrounding provinces, yet if the theory

[13] *Shun Pao Year Book*, 1934, p. 456.

TABLE 87

TOTAL TAX BURDEN OF PEOPLE OF HUPEH PROVINCE
(Estimated)

Tax	Amount	Remarks
National Tax Burden		
Custom Revenue	$13,331,958.23	Actual, average of 2 years, 1930-32, converted from HK Taels at .715 Tael per $1.
Salt Revenue	11,000,944.06	Actual, average of 5 years, 1927-31.
Stamp Taxes	1,141,494.00	Actual, average of 4 years, 1928-31.
Wine and Tobacco Taxes	805,255.25	Actual, average of 4 years 1928-31.
Consolidated Taxes: Rolled Tobacco, Cotton Yarn, Flour, Matches, and Cement	2,400,000.00	Budgeted receipts, 1931-32, after abolishing likin.
Estimated yearly increase of yield in Custom Duty, Salt Tax, and Consolidated Tax	8,400,000.00	
Total	$37,079,651.54	Excluding Anti-opium tax, a temporary measure.
Per Capita		$1.3863

Provincial Tax Burden (including future tax burden in the form of public loans, excluding nontax revenue)
1928-29 (actual)	$16,189,231.75
1929-30 („)	13,429,113.87
1930-31 („)	14,045,927.28
1931-32 („)	15,011,351.45
1932-33 („)	14,966,310.89
Total	$73,641,935.24

Average burden (average of 5 years) 1928-33 $14,728,387.05
Per Capita . . . . $.55

Local Tax Burden
57 budgets for 1932-33	$ 6,377,661.00
1 budget for 1931	158,579.00
Estimate for 10 districts not reporting	666,457.00
Total	$ 7,202,697.00

Per Capita . . . . $.264

Total Tax Burden (Central, Provincial, Local) . . . $58,997,935.69
Total Per Capita (Central, Provincial, Local) $2.2
(Population, 26,739,800)

(Estimated Real Burden x 4 = $8.8)

Source: **Department of Finance,** *A General Survey of Taxation in Hupeh,* September, 1932, Wuchang, pp. 207-212.

TABLE 89

RANK OF HUPEH PROVINCE IN ECONOMIC ABILITY IN NORMAL YEARS

Factors Considered	China	Range of Provinces Reporting	Hupeh	Rank of Hupeh	Number of Provinces Considered
I. Comparable Factors:					
1. Population per square mile, 1933, among 12 most prosperous provinces, assuming that the less dense, the more tendency to prosperity—negative ranking	113	194–832	380	4	12
2. Per cent that farm population is of total population, assuming that the less farm population, the more industrial wealth—negative ranking	74.8	58–90	67	6	25
3. Per cent of total area cultivated, or cultivation index, 1928 (1930)	15	0.4–46.5	46.5 (19)	1 (8)	19 (25)
4. Per cent that crop acreage is of total cultivated acreage, 1930			144	2	25
5. Per capita cultivated land	3	0.7–6.8	5.4	3	19
6. Per cent that value of mining output is of total value of mining output in China, 1927	100	?–29.2	1.8	6	?
7. Per cent that value of coal output is of total in China, 1928	100	?–33	1.1	4	?
8. Per cent that value of iron output is of total in China, 1928	100	?–32	31.6	2	?
9. Per cent that cotton manufacture is of total in China, 1930	100	?–66.4	7.7	3	?
10. Per cent that export value of silk filature is of total in China, 1929	100	?–44.2	0.1	5	?
11. Per cent that power capacity of electricity is of total in China, 1929	100	?–42.2	3.9	4	?
12. Per cent that value of whole trade is of total in China, 1929	100	?–30.8	8.7	5	?
13. Per cent that value of foreign trade is of total in China, 1929	100	?–43.7	2.7	5	?
14. Per cent that length of railway is of total in China, 1924	100	?–21.7	2.4	6	?
15. Per cent that length of motor highway is of total in China, 1930	100	?–11.2	2.9	6	?
16. Per cent that length of telegraph lines is of total in China, 1928	100	?–10.8	4.5	5	?
17. Per cent that value of farmers' subsidiary industrial products is of that of regular farm products, 1930	?	3.76–250.7	58.34	6	21
II. Factors of Gross Nature not Strictly Comparable:					
1. Provincial government revenue in millions of dollars, 1931–32	383.6	0.2–38	23.6	7	25
2. Total food production of 17 chief food crops in million catties of rice-equivalents	?	?	11,602	4	14
3. Amount of deficiency in food requirement of total population in million catties of rice-equivalents (11,606–11,741)—negative ranking, the less deficiency, the high rank, 1929–30	?	?	−139	6	14
4. Amount of net savings deposits in Post Office Savings Banks, in millions of dollars, 1932	25	0.5–5.5	1.7	4	20

Sources and explanation:

I. 1. Area from latest estimate, *China Year Book*, 1933, p. 4; population from latest report, *Shun Pao Year Book*, 1933, p. D4.

2. From C. C. Chang, *An Estimate of China's Farms and Crops*, p. 11, Table III.

3. Corrected figures from "D. K. Lieu: China's Farm Statistics." The Chinese Economic Society, *Chinese Economic Problems*, p. 36. According to C. C. Chang, the figure for Hupeh is 19 per cent with a rank of 8 among 25. His data is based upon the report of 37 (out of the 68 districts) with only 33 million mow. His estimate for all districts with 61 million mow is too low compared with Lieu's figure, 154.5 million mow.

4. From C. C. Chang, *Op. cit.*, Table II.

5. Corrected figure from D. K. Lieu, *Op. cit.*, p. 51.

6–16. From Fong, H. D., *China's Industrialization, A Statistical Survey*, p. 31, Table Va.

17. From *Ministry of Interior Bulletin*, Volume V, Nos. 10–11, March 11, 1932. The value of subsidiary industrial products including cattle, poultry, sericulture, etc., is $106,913,152 for Hupeh and $2,239,946,968 for China.

II. 1. From the *Budget Estimates of the Provinces and Municipalities for the Twentieth Fiscal Year, 1931–32*. The Directorate of Budgets and Statistics, Nanking, 1932, pp. 1–3.

2 and 3. From Lasker, Bruno, Editor, "Problems of the Pacific." *Proceedings of the Institute of Pacific Relations*, Hangchow, 1931, p. 79 sqq. Tables III and IV.

4. *China Year Book*, 1933, p. 341. Table on General Statement of Deposits, Withdrawals, etc., During 19th Fiscal Year M. K. (up to June 30, 1931).

that the tax leak is three times the taxes collected is accepted, the actual burden of the people of Hupeh must be much more than this amount.[14]

On the average, each head of the population pays only $0.05 for county education (see Table 88 and Table 90, Column 38), $.089 for provincial education, and $.025 for central education, making a total of $.164, or 16.4 cents. This is but 7.5 per cent of the total tax paid per head to all government levels.

In 40 counties, each head pays less than 5 cents for education; in 9 counties each head pays more than 8 cents. In Yeng-Cheng the per capita cost is highest, being 25.4 cents, while in Fang-Hsien it is lowest, being only 1 cent. These estimates are based on total expenditure. Hence, they indicate the effort made by the counties as well as the burdens they bear. Tables 88 to 90 show—

TABLE 88

EDUCATIONAL EXPENDITURE PER CAPITA OF POPULATION IN HUPEH PROVINCE

Expenditure in Cents	Frequency by Counties	
	1931	1932
33–33.9		1
⋮		
25–25.9	1	
⋮		
16–16.9	1	
⋮		
11–11.9	1	
10–10.9	2	1
9– 9.9		3
8– 8.9	4	4
7– 7.9	2	6
6– 6.9	7	3
5– 5.9	8	15

[14] See page 202 of this study.

TABLE 88 (Continued)

Expenditure in Cents	Frequency by Counties	
	1931	1932
4- 4.9	17	16
3- 3.9	13	12
2- 2.9	4	3
1- 1.9	6	3
Local Mean	N=66 5	N=67 5
Provincial Mean	8.9	9.5
Central Mean (estimated)	2.5*	4.4**
Total	16.4	18.9

*Actual; **Budget.
Source: See Table 90, Columns 36 and 37.

The Cost of Expansion of the Educational Program

Hupeh, more particularly in the bankrupt counties, cannot afford to expand the present educational program to any appreciable extent in the immediate future unless national aid is given. However, when peace and order are restored, additional budgets must be provided to launch the needed program.

The population of Hupeh comprises approximately 6 per cent of the total population of China. Since the basis of estimate of the cost of the total program of expansion and improvement of all China (see Table 58) was partially school population as constituting 10 per cent of the total population and partially an illiteracy percentage of 80 per cent of the total population, it is not inaccurate to take 6 per cent of the estimated cost, excluding those items to be entirely financed by the Central Government, as the approximate cost of a similar program needed in Hupeh Province alone. Moreover, the unit cost of $7 used in that estimate corresponds closely to the average per pupil cost of $7.82 in all counties of Hupeh, as shown in Table 90, Column 36. The average percentage of children of school age in school as adopted in that estimate must be far higher than the same percentage in Hupeh, since she ranked among the lowest in this respect, as shown in Table 81, Row 1. Six per cent of the estimated cost, therefore, would be much less than what is actually needed. Nevertheless, it is used in this study, pending more accurate estimate.

The writer has made an estimate of the cost of the obligatory education program for the next twenty years and found it to be $178,000,000.[15]

Using 6 per cent as a basis, the cost of the entire program of expansion and improvement in Hupeh for the next twenty years totals at least $336,120,180, distributed as follows:

1. Obligatory education and teacher-training . . $239,160,000
2. Adult continuation education and removal of illiteracy 20,371,500
3. Annual salary increase for elementary school teachers 15,900,000
4. Expansion and improvement of secondary education 12,329,640
5. Improvement of social education 48,359,040

TOTAL $336,120,180

The provincial treasury would have to pay $49,478,700, or $2,474,000, a year; the local county treasuries, $144,911,000, or $7,245,500 a year; and the Central treasury, $141,731,000, or $7,086,500, a year. It must be borne in mind here that the dollar is assumed to be of equal value for all years.

[15]The detailed work leading to this estimate is on file in the office of Dr. George D. Strayer, Teachers College, Columbia University, New York, N. Y.
See Unpublished Document No. 24.

250 *The Financing of Public Education in China*

Can the people of Hupeh Province afford to provide such a program gradually? This question may be answered in the affirmative only when peace and order are completely restored.

THE ABILITY OF HUPEH TO SUPPORT EDUCATION

Hupeh Compared with Other Provinces

The rank of Hupeh Province in economic ability in normal years is shown in Table 89 following.

Table 89 shows that Hupeh ranks ninth in density of population among all provinces of China. But among the twelve most prosperous provinces and at the same time densest in population, Hupeh ranks fourth in having less pressure of population. Hupeh ranks first or eighth in the proportion of land cultivated according to two estimates. In trade she ranks fifth, in mining output and cotton manufacture third, and in provincial government revenue seventh. In a word, Hupeh easily ranks fifth or sixth among all the provinces in economic and financial vigor in normal years. It is reasonable to expect that her effort in support of education should not fall below this rank.

The Extraneous Factors in the Present Economic Crisis

The general economic crisis in China has been described in Chapter IX. Although all the provinces are affected, Hupeh and her neighboring provinces have suffered more severely because of certain extraneous factors. Hupeh was more vulnerable to the prey of the war lords than most provinces. The losses due to frequent internecine warfare since 1912 have been colossal. Natural disasters affecting wide areas have occurred almost every year. After the success of the Northern Expedition, the situation became aggravated by two unprecedented events:

1. *The Flood of 1931.* Forty-eight out of 68 counties and 28.7 per cent of the total land area were inundated, with a loss of $518,434,900 in property and $84,220,000 in crops. A total of 8,263,577 became refugees and 54,807 lost their lives.[16]

2. *The Spread of Communist Banditry.* Nine counties were disastrously ravaged, 23 were severely affected, and 25 were comparatively less affected. There were 264,551 casualties, and 946,114 persons became refugees in 1932. The total loss of property was $477,033,880. In the counties of Li-Shan, Hwang-An, Ma-Cheng, Yin-Shan, Hwang-Pei, Lo-Tien, Hwang-Kang, Siao-Kan, and Yen-Shan 6 to 60 per cent of the farm land was left in ruin.[17] Fortunately, these counties were gradually restored to peace and order, but the conditions prevailing in some of the northwest and western counties are still dubious.

In March, 1933, the National Government Relief Commission reported that there were 9,000,000 refugees in Hupeh, a number second only to Honan among 14 provinces reporting.[18]

With one third of the population in want and a loss of wealth amounting to more than $1,000,000,000, Hupeh's immediate problem is to feed, clothe, and shelter her people. There is little hope of extending educational opportunities in the immediate future, unless the National Treasury comes to her aid.

As the facts collected in this study concerning Hupeh's economic status in the various counties refer to normal years, certain conclusions are, therefore, not applicable at present.

[16] *Shun Pao Year Book,* 1933, pp. 70–72.
[17] *Shun Pao Year Book,* 1933, p. 75, and *Current Events Monthly,* Volume IX, No. 5, November, 1933, pp. 171–73.
[18] *Shun Pao Year Book,* 1934, p. 1022.

Ability of the Counties to Pay for Education in Normal Years

Important observations from Table 90:

1. Two new counties, Ying-Shan and Li-Shan, were added to Hupeh in 1933, making a total of 70 counties. As there are no data available concerning these two counties, they are excluded from consideration in this study. The density of population varies from 42 per square mile in Ho-Feng to 1,036 per square mile in Yun-Mang, with an average of 363 per square mile for the province. Twelve counties are comparatively sparsely populated, having densities of less than 200 per square mile (Column 4).

2. The percentage of land cultivated is an indication of economic ability and show wide variation. It ranges from 2.41 per cent in Tung-Cheng to 59.64 per cent in En-Shih, with an average of 19.95 per cent for the province as a whole. Thirteen counties have less than 10 per cent of their land cultivated (Column 6).

3. The proportion of farm population ranges from 26.9 per cent in Wuchang to 95 per cent in Sien-Feng. In 43 counties farm population constitutes more than 70 per cent of the total population (Column 7).

4. The total value of cultivated land in Hupeh is estimated to be about $2,212,993,000 (Column 9). It ranges from $5.83 per capita of farm population in Tung-Cheng to $500.98 in En-Shih. Only 35 counties have more than $100 per capita valuations for farm population (Column 11).

5. The total value of production in ten crops in Hupeh is estimated to be $644,881,735. It ranges from $2.25 per capita of farm population in Tung-Cheng to $151.76 in Shih-Show. Only 13 counties have valuations of more than $50 per capita of farm population (Column 14).

Appendix

6. By combining land value and value of production, the 68 counties were ranked according to their economic ability, especially with reference to the farm population, as shown in Columns 15–18. This ranking excludes the consideration of the income of the respective counties from subsidiary agricultural industries, which constitutes 68.34 per cent of the regular farm production for the province as a whole (see Table 89, Row 17), since no data are available for the separate counties. Nevertheless, these two factors should be closely correlated. Since the income and wealth of the urban population from business and industry cannot be determined, and hence are excluded from consideration, this ranking does not indicate the ability of the total population of the counties. There are two reasons why this ranking should be fairly indicative of the comparative ability to support education:

(1) It is the farm population who pay the most (more than 80 per cent of the cost) for education.

(2) The item of land constitutes 82 per cent of the total estimated wealth of China (see page 170).

The above-mentioned procedure gives a better measure of the counties than is found in the present practice of classification by the provincial government based on size, population, and tax revenue. It is statistically valid, since correlations may be found between Columns 15 and 16 and between Column 11 (value of land) and Column 27 (amount of tax revenue).

The following formula for computing the product moment "r" is used:

$$r = \frac{X \cdot Y - N \cdot \overline{X} \cdot \overline{Y}}{\sqrt{X^2 - N \cdot \overline{X}^2} \cdot \sqrt{Y^2 - N \cdot \overline{Y}^2}}$$

Where $\overline{X}$ is average of X; $\overline{Y}$ is average of Y.

The coefficient of correlation between per capita (of farm population) land value and per capita production value in percentum is +.3939, which is high and therefore significant for combining these two columns in ranking the counties. If the per capita of total population is used instead, the coefficient is found to be +.59, which is even higher. The coefficient of correlation between land value per capita of farm population and the amount of land tax paid per capita of farm population is —.1495. This indicates that there is a negative correlation between the two factors. Therefore, the amount of tax revenue does not measure the comparative ability of the counties, and this traditional basis for classifying the counties should be discarded.

The complete process of calculating these correlations is on file for reference upon request.[19] Space does not allow its inclusion here.

7. Legally, the people of Hupeh should pay about $4,200,000 of land tax to the county governments and $2,800,000 to the provincial government (Columns 19, 20, and 21). Actually, land tax collections have declined sharply in recent years. In the province as a whole, 64.66 per cent of the county government revenue is derived from the land tax. It varies from 10.53 per cent in Ichang to 89.42 per cent in Kien-Shih, with extraordinary conditions in four counties excluded. In 49 of the 58 counties it amounts to more than 50 per cent. In 33 counties it amounts to more than 60 per cent (Column 22).

8. Land tax as a source of school revenue. As a whole, 40.03 per cent of the county land tax revenue is paid to education. This proportion varies from 13.51 per cent in En-Shih to 72.92 per cent in Mien-Yang. Twenty-six of the 58 counties devote more than 40 per cent of their land tax revenue to education (Column 24).

[19] Unpublished Document No. 25.

Appendix 255

9. An attempt to measure the tax burden of the people. The traditional practice of measuring the tax burden per mow of land is not reliable because (1) the size of the mow varies. According to the research of Chen Han-sen and others, the size of the mow in the county of Wu-Shih in Kiangsu Province varies from 2.5 to 8.5 ares, with a total of 173 different sizes.[20] (2) The value of each mow according to fertility also varies widely. It is found that each inhabitant pays about 27.2 cents of land tax in Hupeh (Column 26), or, on the basis of farm population, each farming inhabitant pays about 53.2 cents of land tax (Column 27). In the counties, the latter figure varies from 6.6 cents in Ichang to $1.74 in Itu. This is inequitable, because one citizen pays 28 times more land tax than another, but the inequality is not valid when considered in relation to other taxes paid and to the total ability of each citizen. Hence, a better measure of the land tax burden is the amount of land tax per unit of the value of land. Here the mill measure is used, referring to the number of dollars of tax per $1,000. In the absence of accurate assessed valuation figures, the estimated price of land in Column 8 is used as a basis. Hence the result must be only a rough guess.

10. The variation of land tax burden (Columns 28 and 29). The average land tax burden is 4.32 mills. The burden in 30 counties rises above this figure. The highest is 31.62 mills (in Lo-Tien) and the lowest is .33 mills (in Ichang), one being almost 100 times as great as the other. This stark inequality is the chief cause of the cry that farmers are paying land taxes beyond their endurance. The per capita land tax of 53.2 cents appears low. This inequality and the belief that the tax leak is three times the amount of taxes received in the treasury have brought about the suffering of the farmers.

[20]Chen Han-sen and Others, *The Variation of Mow*. Nanking: Academia Sinica, 1929, *passim*.

If measured on the basis of the production value, which is indicative of the income of the farmers, the land tax burden is 14.75 mills or $14.75 per $1,000 of production, on the average. Only 27 of 58 counties fall below this average. The highest, 288.89 mills, occurs in Tung-Cheng, and the lowest, 1.34 mills, in Ichang, the former being 130 times the latter.

11. The estimated county revenues of the 68 counties total about $7,202,697. An average of only 18.77 per cent of this amount is devoted to education. Fourteen counties fall below this average. The 35 to 40 per cent proposed on page 89 is reached by only 5 counties and is surpassed by only 7 counties (Column 31).

The percentage that military expenditure is of the total county budget is, on the average, 54.73 per cent. Thirty of the 68 counties assign more than 50 per cent of their budgets to this item. This is an abnormal situation. It is suggested that when peace and order are restored, this item be diverted to education.

MAJOR PRACTICAL PROBLEMS IN THE RECONSTRUCTION OF THE SYSTEM OF PUBLIC SCHOOL SUPPORT IN HUPEH

The writer will refrain from making definite recommendations concerning the reconstruction of public school support in Hupeh, owing to his long absence from the actual scene and to the fact that practicable or workable schemes must be based upon more comprehensive data and the outcome of further research.

The most pressing problems that await solution in Hupeh appear to be the following.

I. Problems That Are Closely Related to School Finance:

1. An economic and social survey.

a. Census. What is the actual number of the population and the population in each geographical area, under each age group and in each occupation?

b. Wealth and income. What is the total wealth and income of the people and how is it distributed?

c. What is the status of agriculture, industry, and trade?

These problems should be taken up by the provincial government, and the Department of Education should see to it that the data from the point of view of education are adequately covered. The Ministry of Industry is financing this kind of project, and full coöperation should be given.

2. A scientific school survey in addition to the survey of school finance:

a. Does the traditional administrative set-up insure efficiency and fit practical needs?

b. What is the quality of instruction?

c. What is the quality of the products of the school system?

d. How well are the educational workers trained and safeguarded?

e. How can productive and rural education be effectively carried out and what is the prospect of a coördinated program with the department of reconstruction?

II. A Survey of School Finance:

1. Fiscal independence.

a. What is the most effective administrative set-up for the control of school finance? A study is needed to reveal the high and low spots of the present set-ups in Hunan, Kiangsu, and so forth.

b. Which is the best tax as a source of educational revenue, measured by the criteria of a good tax according to tax experts? How does the salt tax compare with the tobacco and wine tax, the title deeds tax, the rolled tobacco tax, the business tax, the butchery tax, and so forth, in the immediate future in the light of the principle of stability and adequacy in relation to the principle of ability? What is the prospect of using the land value tax, the income tax, and the inheritance tax as sources of educational revenue in the distant future or in the long run?

c. What is the practical approach in the light of the existing legal provisions of the National Government?

2. Local initiative versus centralization of control.

a. What are the causes of lack of local initiative in public school support, besides poverty?

b. Shall the county be a unit of school support or shall it be centralized in the provincial Department of Education?

3. National aid and provincial aid.

a. How much can Hupeh expect from the Central Government in aiding her schools both theoretically and practically?

b. What is the practical plan for relief in public education in the counties restored from bandits?

c. The equalization of burden. What is the most accurate measure of the ability and burden of the counties in school support? How can an equalization program be worked out in Hupeh?

4. Reconstruction of the tax system as a whole.

a. It is estimated by the Department of Civil Affairs that after a cadastral survey of land is made, the levy of the land value tax would yield $47,000,000 a year.[21] Can this tax be partially allocated to education to take the place of the land surtaxes and petty taxes which are to be abolished very soon, as recommended by the Second National Conference on Finance in May, 1934?

b. What should educators do in anticipating the educational use of income and inheritance taxes which are now included in the Draft Constitution to be adopted in 1935?

c. What is the immediate plan of financing the local schools after the multifarious "miscellaneous surtaxes and petty taxes" are abolished?

d. Before they are abolished, how can the various sources of school revenue in the counties be simplified? Will many sources insure stability better than a single source? Can the tax rates be made more simple and just? What is their relationship to the cost of collection and the efficiency of administration?

5. Equalization of opportunity.

a. Since Hupeh in the immediate future cannot afford to educate all children of school age, can a plan be set up to educate a selected group of gifted ones to insure better returns for the money spent before universal education is finally practicable? Would a fair sampling of the population remove the charge of a violation of the principle of democracy? To what extent will the measurement techniques aid in the solution of this problem?

b. Shall the rich continue to pay higher tuition and the poor be exempted? How can the economic status of the students' families be accurately and justly appraised? Can the provincial scholarship fund for gifted but poor students be increased, and can the counties also adopt the same plan?

[21] See Chapter X, p. 201.

c. What is the practical plan of equalizing the educational opportunities of the farmers' children and those of the owners of urban wealth? Can the idea that Hankow owes part of its wealth to the people of the entire province be instilled in the minds of the people?

6. School land.

a. An investigation of school land and other property in certain counties, under supervision of the Department of Education, is now being carried on. What is the best plan of control? How much can the schools expect from this source of revenue?

b. Can the millions of mow of waste land and forest land be diverted to establish schools of agriculture and forestry?

c. How much is the wealth of the Buddhist temples in Hupeh, and what is the practical plan for diverting it in part or in whole to school uses?

d. What is the practical plan for diverting part of the wealth of the ancestral shrines for education?

7. Certain legitimate incomes to be claimed for the school system of Hupeh.

a. How much can Hupeh expect from the Boxer Indemnity? Can 6 per cent of the total suggested by Dr. Y. T. Hoh for rural education be returned to Hupeh?

b. The Rice Tax Public Bonds for the original use of the railways and the overdue debts of the Ministry of Communications, due to Hupeh—the principal and interest of the former up to 1930 amounted to $2,051,000. It has been deposited under the control of the Ministry of Finance for financing public enterprises in Hupeh. The overdue debts in 1930 amounted to $708,000 in principal and interest. Both these funds have been set aside by the provincial government for educational endowment. What are the obstacles in the way of returning them to the school system? What is the practical plan of action?[22]

8. Publicity campaign. How can the public interest be aroused for securing better school support? Can an experimental district like Tien-Hsien of Hopei Province be set aside in Hupeh for demonstrating to the people the productivity of modern education?

9. Safeguarding teachers. What is a scientific salary schedule for educational workers in Hupeh?

[22] Hupeh Department of Education, *A Glimpse of Recent Education in Hupeh*. Wuchang: The Department, 1932, p. 24.

10. Education cannot wait. Can money be borrowed through the issuance of bonds secured on some stable taxes? To what extent can the farmers' bank and the coöperative societies aid in the financing of education?

11. How shall waste in educational expenditure be eliminated? What is true economy in the light of the actual situation in Hupeh?

There are numerous problems in connection with school expenditure. Space and time prohibit the writer from mentioning them all.

All the above issues are paramount at present. The data collected by the writer so far are inadequate for arriving at workable recommendations. The reason for the failure of so many paper schemes in the past is the fact that they do not penetrate to the very root of the problems in hand and are sometimes too idealistic for practical consideration. It is hereby suggested that the Department of Education of Hupeh Province set aside a fund adequate to make a scientific study of the problem of support as well as of other related problems. Financial and technical aid can reasonably be won from the National Government as well as from the National Economic Council. A staff of educational and tax experts should be appointed to make an inquiry into the problems listed above. It is the belief of the writer that in the long run this project will pay rich dividends. Otherwise, vague proposals or paper plans and mere clamor; drift and despair will be the result. The same vicious circle will turn indefinitely round and round like the Cycle of Cathay. "There are no gains without pains," said the great Franklin. "Poverty we think it no disgrace to acknowledge, but a real disgrace to make no effort to overcome!" says the great Pericles. Now, this moment, is the time to begin action.

DIAGRAM 7
SHOWING METHOD OF ESTIMATING THE PROPORTION OF CHINESE POPULATION IN EACH AGE GROUP

Age group on scale

	Age group scale: 0-1, 5, 10, 15, 18, 20, 25, 30, 35, 40, 45, 50, 55, 60 & above
1. Median of all countries: N=94.5	A: 11.24, 10.6, 10.46, 9.7, 45.9, 3.59, 8.5 B: 13.4, 12.5, 15, 12.1
2. Median of 22 countries: Census of children, 6-14	A: 12, 15.5, 8.64 B: 13.32, 10.82
3. Average of all provinces, China, 1912 census	A: 6.74, 6.8, 6.72, 7.88, 8.03, 9.53, 9.71, 9.61, 7.93, 7.12, 5.85, 4.36, 1.65+ B: 8.144, 11.684, 8.73, 53.142, 19.284
4. Average of 62 villages, Tien Hsien Survey	A: 15.21, 10, 10.2, 9.82, 40, 14.64 B: 17.21, 12.08, 15.76
5. 1924 census, Kiangsu Province	A: 6.9, 6.5, 11.82, 6.6, 7.2, 48.6, 19.5 B: 7.82, 11.04, 48.68, 20.86
6. 1925 census, Shansi Province	A: 8.5, 6.7, 8.28, 6.5, 8.2, 50.2, 19.4 B: 8, 11.76, 50.6, 20.64
7. 1912 census, Hupeh Province	A: 5.1, 3.25, 8.78, 6.06, 6.77 B: 6.7, 10.26, 4, 55.63, 22.45
8. Estimated basis used by Ministry of Education	10, 10, 7.7, 66.67, 13.32
9. Kiangsu—actual census	14.1
10. Honan—actual	9.1
11. Shantung—actual	12.4
12. Liaoning—actual	11.5
13. Chahar—actual	10.5
14. Nanking—actual	A: 9.2
15. Nanking, 1930 survey	C: 10.6
16. Tsingtao—actual	9.5
17. Average of %'s, 1-7	9.608, 9.81, 9.74, 62.252, 18.53
18. Average of %'s, 9-13	11.1
19. Average derived from aggregated data, 9-16, except 15C	12.1
20. Average of %'s, all China, except 8 and 19	10.08
Figures accepted for China	↓School age↓ 10, 10, 10, 62, 18

Sources:

1. League of Nations' *International Statistical Yearbook*, Geneva, 1933, Table 3, p. 30.

2. Percy, Lord E., *The Yearbook of Education*, 1933. London: Evans Brothers, p. XCVIII.

3 and 7. *Statistical Monthly*, Volume III, No. 3, March, 1931, p. 27.

4. Advanced sheet of the Tien Hsien Survey, by courtesy of Mr. F. V. Field of the Institute of Pacific Relations.

5 and 6. *Chinese Labour Yearbook*, 1928. Peiping: Institute of Social Research, p. 5.

9 and 16. J-1, Table 3.

TABLE 91
POPULATION OF HUPEH PROVINCE

Year	Population	Sources
1812	27,370,098	(From records of Board of Revenue, 17th Year of Chia Ching.)
1842	28,584,564	(Tao Kwang, 22nd Year.)
1885	28,600,000a	(33,600,000, Census, *China Year Book*, 1933, p. 2.)
1909	24,331,796	(Bureau of Statistics, State Council; *First Year Book*, p. 50.)
1910	24,900,000	(Minchengpu Census; China Year Book, 1933, p. 2.)
1912	29,590,308	(*Statistical Monthly*, November and December, 1931, pp. 19-38, Census.)
1915-16	27,245,000	(Census; D. K. Lieu, *China's Industries and Finance*, p. 86.)
1918	28,574,000	(C. C. C. Survey from Howard.)
1921	24,977,000	(Maritime Customs Estimate; *First Year Book*, p. 50.)
1923	27,167,244	(1922 P. O. Estimate; *First Year Book*, p. 51; 1920, P. O. Shun Pao, D7.)
1926	28,616,576	(*P. O. China Year Book*, 1933, p. 2; *Shun Pao* says 1928, D7.)
1928	26,699,126b;	26,939,444c; 26,695,231d; 26,696,253 (Shun D2); 26,763,091e.
1931	26,883,962	(Maritime Customs Estimate, plus Hankow, 777,-993.)
1932	26,739,800	(*Shun Pao Yearbook*, 1933, p. D4, survey made by *Shun Pao*.)
1933	32,306,313	(*Shun Pao Yearbook*, 1934, p. 168, survey made by *Shun Pao*, excluding Hankow.

a. Corrected figure based upon Census of Households.
b. **Figure used by Ministry of Education, plus Hankow, 616,174;** *Shun Pao,* **same, D3.**
c. 26,232,270, plus Hankow, 616,174. Report of Commissioner of Civil Administration, *Lei Chen Kung Pao*, Volume III, No. 2, March, 1930.
d. 26,695,231, **including Hankow, 569,444.** *Two Years of Nationalist China*, p. 413. (Population of Hankow may be taken from reports of different months of 1928 by the two sources.)
e. Almost the same as "c"; may be due to variation of Hankow's population. Department of Education: *A Glimpse of Recent Educational Status in Hupeh*, p. 2, Section I.

BIBLIOGRAPHY

(* indicates sources written in Chinese.
† indicates sources written in Japanese.)

I. Bibliographies

1. ALEXANDER, CARTER, COMPILER. *Bibliography on Educational Finance.* Publications of the Educational Finance Inquiry, Volume IV. New York: Macmillan Co., 1924.
2. ALEXANDER, CARTER, AND COVERT, TIMON, COMPILERS. *Bibliography on School Finance, 1923–31.* The National Survey of School Finance. Washington, D. C.: U. S. Government Printing Office, 1932.
*3. TAI, S. C., AND OTHERS. *Bibliography on Education, 1909–1929* (Revised and enlarged edition). Shanghai: Min Chih Book Co., 1932.
4. Periodical Index in *Human Culture Monthly.* Shanghai: The Human Culture Monthly Society, Volume I-V to date.

II. Yearbooks

1. *Chicago Daily News Almanac and Year Book, 1933.* Chicago: Chicago Daily News, p. 276.
*2. *China Year Book, or The First China Year Book, 1925.* No. 1, pp. 82–145, 587–588, 622. Shanghai: Commercial Press.
†3. *Ji Ji Year Book, 1933.* Tokyo, Japan.
4. LEAGUE OF NATIONS. *Armaments Year Book, 1933.* Geneva.
5. PERCY, LORD EUSTACE. *The Year Book of Education.*

Table 59, pp. XCIX, C, Table 58, pp. XCVIII. London: Evans, 1933.
*6. *Shun Pao Year Book,* for the Years 1933, 1934. Shanghai: The Shun Pao.
7. *Statesman's Year Book, 1932.* New York: Macmillan:
8. WOODHEAD, H. G. W., EDITOR. *The China Year Book,* for the years 1921–22, 1923, 1925, 1926, 1927, 1928, 1929–30, 1931, 1932, and 1933. Tientsin and later Shanghai: The North-China Daily News and Herald, Ld.
9. *World Almanac, The, 1933.* New York: The World-Telegram.
*10. MINISTRY OF EDUCATION. *The First Education Year Book of China.* Shanghai: Kai Ming Book Store, 1934.
*11. HSU HSING-CHENG. *Educational Directory of China,* for 1925 and 1926. Shanghai: Commercial Press.

III. Primary Sources of Data

A. Sources of Educational Statistical Data

The earliest school statistics so far discovered from government documents can be traced in the "History of Yuan Dynasty," according to Dr. Huang Yin-pei, founder of the Chinese National Vocational Education Association. It was recorded in Volume XIV that there were 20,166 schools in 1286 A. D. Volume XV gives 24,400 schools throughout the empire in 1288 A. D. Volume XVI gives 21,300 for the year 1291 A. D. Since the establishment of the modern school system, the government published the following statistics concerning schools, except I:

*A. 1907 *The First Report of Educational Statistics and Charts.*
*B. 1908 *The Second Report of Educational Statistics and Charts.*
*C. 1909 *The Third Report of Educational Statistics and Charts.*

*D. 1912–13 (The First Year of the Republic of China) *The First Report of Educational Statistics and Charts.*
*E. 1913–14 *The Second Report of Educational Statistics and Charts.*
*F. 1914–15 *The Third Report of Educational Statistics and Charts.*
*G. 1915–16 *The Fourth Report of Educational Statistics and Charts.*
*H. 1916–17 *The Fifth Report of Educational Statistics and Charts.*
*I. 1922–23 CHINESE NATIONAL ASSOCIATION FOR THE ADVANCEMENT OF EDUCATION: *Statistical Summaries of Chinese Education (1922–23)*, Bulletin 16, Volume II, Peking, 1923.
*J. 1929–30 1. *The Status of Elementary Education, 1929–30 in All China.* Nanking: Ministry of Education, April, 1932.
2. *The Status of Secondary Education, 1928–29 in All China.* July, 1932.
3. *Higher Education Statistics in All China, 1928–29.* November, 1931.
4. *Status of Social Education in All China, 1928–29.* August, 1931.
K. 1931–32 *Higher Education Statistics in All China, 1931–32.* July, 1933. (Other statistics for 1930–31 not available.)

B. Unpublished Documents and Odd Data from Correspondence, Replies to Questionnaire and Calculation Tables

1. Table on Number of Magazine Articles Written on Educational Finance in China Since 1909.
2. Table Showing Some Outstanding Books on Educational Administration and Their Relative Emphasis on the Subject of Educational Finance.

3. Tabulation of political, military, and financial events that have been paramount in causing slow educational progress, since 1912.
4. Sources of data concerning the evidences and causes of inadequate and unstable educational support. (See footnotes.)
5. Method of estimating the cost of sending students abroad.
*6. Data on the index of the wholesale prices in China and some cities since 1900.
7. Calculation table on educational budgets and general budgets of 20 provinces and 5 special municipalities for the fiscal year 1931–32.
8. "Chart Your Budget Here." Compliments of A. J. Nystrom and Co., Chicago, Ill., U. S. A.
9. Tabulation of teachers' salary schedules in China from available data.
10. Frequency distribution of monthly salaries and wages of educational workers in the Hupeh Provincial Schools, 1933–34.
11. Percentage analysis of the budget of Hupeh Provincial Department of Education for the fiscal year 1933–34.
12. A. Calculation tables on the percent that educational and military expenditures are of the total national budget in 62 countries.
   B. Exchange rates issued by the U. S. Federal Reserve Board, October 10, 1933.
   C. Exchange rates of Chinese Mexican dollars in U. S. cents.
13. Diagram showing the proportion of educational task in regular schooling and social adult education in removing illiteracy in China, based upon 1929–30 data.
*14. Reply and data from the Department of Education of Shensi Province, December 17, 1932.
*15. Reply of the Department of Social Education of the Ministry of Education: The educational budgets of the Central Government, 1928–34. November 2, 1933.

*16. Budget Estimates of the National Government of China, 1933–34, compared with 1932–33.
17. Sources of data on the battle for fiscal independence under professional leadership in China. See Footnotes.
18. Calculation table of China's indebtedness since 1912 with sources of data.
19. CHENG, RONALD Y. S. *Technical Education or Education for Industry in England and Its Lesson for China.* Term paper, Summer, 1932.
20. The Cost of the U. S. Federal Government in seven charts, courtesy of the National Association of Manufacturers, Summer, 1933.
*21. Bibliography in Chinese on the Historical Records of Hupeh Province, the Ten Prefectures and 69 Counties, available in the Library of Congress, Washington, D. C.
22. Separate tables on school funds and lands in Hupeh in the past.
*23. Calculation table, county revenue and expenditure of Hupeh, Manchu Dynasty.
24. Budget estimate of 20-year program of obligatory education for Hupeh.
25. Data showing the calculation of coefficient of correlation in Table.
26. Calculation table on the value of production in all counties of Hupeh.
27. Questionnaire blank used for this study.

C. Official Reports and Bulletins

*1. ANHWEI PROVINCIAL DEPARTMENT OF EDUCATION. *One Year of Education in Anhwei.* Anking, 1930. Section III and pp. 3–4.
*2. *Budget Estimates of the Provinces and Municipalities for the Twentieth Fiscal Year, 1931–32.* Nanking: The Directorate of Budgets and Statistics, 1932.

*3. CENTRAL EXECUTIVE COMMITTEE. *A Survey of Party Members Sent Abroad.* Nanking: Central Party Headquarters, 1931.

*4. CHANG, CHUNG-CHIH, EDITOR. *General Historical Records of Hupeh Province.* Wuchang: Hupeh Government Publication Bureau, 1921. Volume 62, Section VII, etc.

*5. CHEKIANG PROVINCIAL DEPARTMENT OF EDUCATION. *Three Years of Education in Chekiang Province.* Hangchow: The Chekiang Department of Education, 1933, pp. 21–32.

*6. CHIANG WEI-CHIAO. *Status of Educational Administration in Kiangsu.* Shanghai: Commercial Press, 1924, 73 p.

*7. CHINA INSTITUTE OF GEOLOGICAL SURVEY. *Second, Third and Fourth Reports of the China Institute of Geological Survey, up to 1932.* Peiping.

8. *Chinese Maritime Customs Annual Reports, The.* Shanghai: The Chinese Maritime Customs House, 1895–1933.

9. COMMISSION OF FINANCIAL EXPERTS. *Report on Revenue Policy.* Nanking: Ministry of Finance, 1929 (in mimeograph form).

*10. FANG, YUAN-TSUNG, AND OTHERS, EDITORS: *Directory of Land-Capitation Tax and Grain Tribute in Hupeh Province, 1875.* "Introduction."

11. FEDERAL RESERVE BOARD. *Statement for the Press, October 10, 1933.*

*12. FIRST NATIONAL CONFERENCE ON EDUCATION, *Proceedings.* Shanghai: Commercial Press, 1928, pp. 195–96, 226, 223–292, 303, 293–302, 141, 193–209, 355–65.

*13. FUKIEN DEPARTMENT OF EDUCATION. *Report of Fukien Provincial Department of Education,* July, 1930.

*14. FUKIEN DEPARTMENT OF EDUCATION *Weekly.* Special Number of Educational Fiscal Independence. No. 10, December 11, 1928. Foochow: The Department.

*15. HANKOW MUNICIPAL GOVERNMENT. *Statistical Year Book of the Hankow Special Municipality for the Fiscal Year*

1929–30. Hankow: The Hankow Municipal Government, 1930, pp. 348, 353.
*16. Historical Records of 10 Prefects and 69 Counties, etc., 1612–1896.
17. HODGES, CHARLES. "Non-Political Factors Underlying the Chinese Problem." Preliminary Papers Solicited by the Data Committee. Paper No. VI, Conference on American Relations with China. Baltimore, September 17–20, 1925.
*18. HONAN DEPARTMENT OF EDUCATION. *Honan Educational Year Book*, 1930. Kaifeng: The Department, 1931. Section B, pp. 1–510.
*19. HONAN DEPARTMENT OF EDUCATION. *Special Bulletin on the Educational Funds and Property on Honan Province*. Kaifeng, 1930, pp. 92–96.
*20. HSU, HSING-CHEN, or SHU HSING-CHEN. *Historical Source Materials of Modern Education in China*. Shanghai: Chung Hua Book Co., 1928. In 4 volumes, 1073 p.
21. HUNAN PROVINCIAL GOVERNMENT. SECRETARIAT. *The Political Year Book of Hunan Province*, 1930. Changsha: Hunan Provincial Government, 1931, p. 419.
*22. *Hupeh Education Bulletin*. Wuchang: Hupeh Department of Education, 1929–1933.
*23. HUPEH PROVINCIAL DEPARTMENT OF CIVIL AFFAIRS. *Report of Hupeh Provincial Civil Affairs*. Wuchang, December, 1930.
*24. HUPEH DEPARTMENT OF EDUCATION. *Classified Expenditure Budget of Hupeh Provincial Education for the Fiscal Year 1933–34*. Wuchang: The Department, 1933 (December).
*25. HUPEH DEPARTMENT OF EDUCATION. *A Glimpse of Recent Education in Hupeh*. Wuchang, 1932.
*26. HUPEH DEPARTMENT OF EDUCATION. *Hupeh Education Status and Statistics for the year 1933*. Wuchang, January, 1934.

*27. HUPEH DEPARTMENT OF EDUCATION. *The Status of Education in Hupeh, 1929-30.* Wuchang, 1930.

*28. HUPEH DEPARTMENT OF EDUCATION. *Present Laws and Regulations of the Department of Education of the Hupeh Provincial Government.* Wuchang: The Department, March, 1932.

*29. HUPEH DEPARTMENT OF FINANCE. *The Consolidated Commodity Tax Laws of Hupeh Province.* Wuchang, 1928.

*30. HUPEH DEPARTMENT OF FINANCE. *A General Survey of Taxation in Hupeh.* Wuchang, September, 1932.

*31. HUPEH DEPARTMENT OF FINANCE. *Report of Public Finance in Hupeh, 1932.* Wuchang.

*32. HUPEH DEPARTMENT OF FINANCE. *Report of Public Finance in Hupeh, 1932, and March-June, 1933.* Wuchang.

*33. HUPEH DEPARTMENT OF FINANCE. *The Revenue and Expenditure Budgets of the County Local Governments of Hupeh Province for the Fiscal Year 1932-33.* Wuchang: The Department, 1932.

*34. KIANGSU PROVINCIAL DEPARTMENT OF EDUCATION. *Recent Educational Conditions in Kiangsu Province.* Nanking, 1930. Appendix, p. 1.

*35. KUOMINTANG. *The Manifesto and the Resolutions of the Third National Congress of the Kuomintang.* Compiled by the Publicity Department of The Central Executive Committee of the Kuomintang, 1928, pp. 43-44.

*36. Kwo, WEI. *A Complete Collection of the Administrative Laws of China.* Shanghai: Hwei-Wen Tong Hing-Ki Book Co., June, 1933. 2 vol., 2170 p.

*37. "Manifesto of the National Society for the Educational Independence Movement." *The New Education.* Volume IV, No. 5, May, 1922, pp. 901-03.

*38. MIAO YUEN YIAN. *An Account of the Second National Conference on Education.* Shanghai: Kiangtung Book Co., 1930, 410 p.

39. MINISTRY OF FINANCE. *Annual Report for the 18th Fiscal Year, July 1929 to June 1930.* Nanking: Ministry of Finance, 1931.
40. MINISTRY OF FINANCE. *Annual Report for the Fiscal Year, July 1928 to June 1929.* Nanking: Ministry of Finance, 1930.
41. MINISTRY OF FINANCE. *Report for the 19th and 20th Fiscal Years, July 1930 to June 1932.* Nanking: Ministry of Finance, 1932.
*42. MINISTRY OF FINANCE. *Proceedings of the National Conference on Public Finance.* Nanking: The Ministry of Finance, 1928, 616 p.
*43. MINISTRY OF FINANCE. *Proceedings of the National Economic Conference.* Nanking: The Ministry, 1928, 626 p.
*44. MINISTRY OF EDUCATION. *Bulletin of Ministry of Education,* Volume II, No. 14, April 5, 1930, p. 46.
*45. MINISTRY OF EDUCATION. *The First Education Year Book of China,* Volume I. Shanghai: Kai Ming Book Store, 1934, 558 p.
*46. MINISTRY OF INDUSTRY. *Industrial Statistics,* Volume I, Nos. 5-6, December, 1933, p. 6 *sqq.* Nanking: Ministry of Industry; also Volume I, No. 1, February, 1933, p. 12.
*47. MINISTRY OF INTERIOR. *Bulletin,* Volume III, No. 2, March, 1930.
47a NATIONAL COMMITTEE FOR ECONOMY IN GOVERNMENT. *Federal Appropriations of 1932-33-34.* Chart VI. Washington: National Association of Manufacturers, Union Trust Building, December, 1932.
*48. *The Nationalist Daily of Yunnan,* April 4, 1932. Kwun-Min, Yunnan.
*49. *The National Revenue and Expenditure Budget of the Republic of China.* Nanking: The Directorate of Budget and Statistics. Promulgated April 28, 1932.
*50. "Prices of Land in Hupeh, 1933." *Kwo Wen Weekly,* Volume XVII, No. 20, May 30, 1933.
*51. *The Quarterly Journal of Economics and Statistics,*

Volume II, No. 3, September, 1933, pp. 693 *sqq.* Tientsin: Nankai University.
*52. "Report of Hupeh's Financial Conditions Since 1914." *Hupeh Public Finance Monthly,* Volume V, Nos. 3 and 4. Wuchang.
*53. SECOND NATIONAL CONFERENCE ON EDUCATION, *Proceedings.* Shanghai: Kiangtung Book Co., 1930. Section III.
*54. *Seventh Report of the Ministry of Agriculture and Commerce.* Peking: The Ministry, 1922.
*55. SHANTUNG DEPARTMENT OF EDUCATION. *County Local Educational Budgets in Shantung for the Fiscal Year 1932-33.* 1128 p. Tsinan: The Department, 1932.
*56. SHANTUNG DEPARTMENT OF EDUCATION. *A Survey of the Educational Funds and Property of the Counties of Shantung.* Tsinan: The Department, 1932. In 4 volumes. Table following p. 4476.
*57. SHANTUNG DEPARTMENT OF EDUCATION. *A Tabular Glimpse of County School Revenues for the Fiscal Year. 1929-30.* Tsinan: The Department, 1930, 1601 p.
*58. *Shun Pao.* Educational News Section. Shanghai, June 6, 1933 and December 29, 1933.
*59. *The Statistical Monthly,* No. 9, January-February, 1933; No. 10, March-April, 1933, Volume I, No. 10, December, 1929, Table on Educational Finance of 12 Provinces. Nanking: Directorate of Statistics.
*60. *The Statistical Monthly.* Volume III, No. 2, February, 1931; November-December, 1932; January-February, 1902. Nanking: Directorate of Statistics.
*61. *Ta Tsing Educational Laws,* Volume I.
*62. TAI, HSIA. *Report of Education in Shansi Province.* Nanking: Ministry of Education, 1933, p. 1.

IV. Secondary Sources—Books and Periodicals

1. ABEL, JAMES F. *Education in Belgium.* Washington: Government Printing Office, 1932, p. 6.

2. ABEL, JAMES F. *The Effects of the Economic Depression on Education in Other Countries.* Washington: Government Printing Office, 1933, 37 p.
3. AMERICAN COUNCIL INSTITUTE OF PACIFIC RELATIONS. *Memorandum* (On Chinese Government Finances), Volume II, No. 3, February 10, 1933.
4. ARNOLD, JULEAN. *China Through an American Window.* Shanghai: The American Chamber of Commerce, 1932, pp. 25–27.
5. ARNOLD, JULEAN. *Some Bigger Issues in China's Problems.* Shanghai: The Commercial Press, 1928. Foreword, p. 1.
*6. ASIAN GEOGRAPHIC SOCIETY, THE. *Maps of the Counties of Hupeh Province.* Wuchang: The Society, 1927.
*7. *The Bankers Weekly,* Volume XVII, No. 46, November 28, 1933; No. 25, July 4, 1933. Shanghai: The Bankers Weekly Society.
8. *Biennial Survey of Education, 1928–30.* Bulletin, 1931, No. 20 (In 2 volumes). U. S. Office of Education. Washington: Government Printing Office, 1931, pp. 10–12, 26, 37, 56, 94.
9. BUCK, J. L. *Chinese Farm Economy.* Chicago: University of Chicago Press, 1930.
10. BUEHLER, A. D. *General Sales Taxation.* New York: The Business Bourse, 1932, p. 17.
*11. *Central Party Affairs Monthly,* No. 40, November, 1931, pp. 2479, 2606. Nanking: Central Party Headquarters.
12. CHANG, C. C. *An Estimate of China's Farms and Crops.* Nanking: University of Nanking, 1932, p. 11.
*13. CHANG CHIH TUNG, VICEROY. *An Exhortation to Learning* (Woodbridge, Samuel I., Translator. *China's Only Hope, An Appeal by Her Greatest Viceroy, Chang Chih-Tung.* New York: Fleming H. Revell Co., 1900, p. 6, 98–100).
*14. CHANG HSIAO-MIEN. *The Problem of Chinese Farm Land in the Different Dynasties.* Shanghai: New Life Book

Co., 1932, pp. 303–04.
15. CHANG KIA-NGAU. "Some Economic Symptoms in China." *The China Critic,* Volume V, No. 40, October 6, 1932. Shanghai: The China Critic Society.
*16. CHEKIANG INDUSTRIAL BANK. "A Survey of Special and Local Public Loans." *Shun Pao Year Book,* 1933, pp. M60–63.
17. CHEN, GIDEON. *Chinese Government Economic Planning and Reconstruction Since 1927.* Shanghai: China Institute of Pacific Relations, 1933, *passim.*
18. CHEN HAN-SENG. *The Present Agrarian Problem in China.* Shanghai: China Institute of Pacific Relations, 1933, pp. 1, 12.
*19. CHEN HAN-SENG AND OTHERS. *The Variation of Mow.* Nanking Academie Sinica, 1929.
*20. CHEN HSU-LING. *History of Education in China in the Last Three Decades.* Shanghai: Pacific Book Store, 1930, pp. 43–58, 79.
21. CHEN HUAN-CHANG. *The Economic Principles of Confucius and His School.* Faculty of Political Science of Columbia University, New York, 1911.
22. CHEN KUNG-PO. "China's Four-Year Industrial Plan." *Chinese Economic Journal,* Volume XIII, No. 3, September, 1933, p. 219.
*23. CHEN KUNG-PO. "Two Years of Observation." *The Nation,* Volume I, No. 3, March 1, 1933. Shanghai.
*24. CHEN PAO-CHUAN. *The Evolution of the Chinese School System.* Peiping: The Culture Society, 1927.
*25. CHEN PIN-HO. "Educational Fiscal Independence, An Urgent Necessity." Editorial, *Shun Pao,* 1932 (January 26).
*26. CHEN PIN-HO. "On the Fundamental Problems of Education Heretofore." Editorial, *Shun Pao,* August 20, 1931.
*27. CHEN SIANG-FAN (or SANFORD CHEN). *Educational Administration in China.* Shanghai: Commercial Press,

1930, 356 p.
*28. CHENG, CHENG-YI. "Our Business and Sales Tax Heretofore." *Chinese Economic Problems.* Shanghai: Commercial Press, 1929, pp. 103–04.
29. CHENG, RONALD Y. S. *Technical Education or Education for Industry in England and Its Lessons for China.* (In manuscript), 1932.
*30. CHIA, SHI-YI. *China's Finances, the Public Debt.* Shanghai: Commercial Press, 1930, pp. 1 sqq.; 90 sqq.
*31. CHIA, SHI-YI. *Financial History of the Republic of China.* Shanghai: Commercial Press, 1917, pp. 1182, 1202, 1164, 1179, 1548.
*32. CHIANG, CHIH, AND CHIU, CHUN. *A Study of Modern Educational Administration for China.* Shanghai: Commercial Press, 1927. 117 p.
*33. CHIANG, KUNG-CHEN. *A History of National Humiliation.* Shanghai: Chung Hua Book Co., 1927, pp. 6–7.
*34. CHIANG WEI-CHIAO. *Status of Educational Administration in Kiangsu.* Shanghai: Commercial Press, 1924, p. 17.
*35. CHINA SOCIETY OF ECONOMIC STUDY, THE. *China's Economic Problems.* Shanghai: Commercial Press, 1929, pp. 37–51–53.
*36. CHING, KIA-CHU. *Domestic Debts in China.* Peiping: Institute of Social Research, 1933, pp. 2, 41 sqq.
37. *Chinese Economic Journal.* Volume X, No. 3, March, 1932.
*38. CHU, PIAN-YUAN, AND TANG TSEH-YEN. "Ten Years of Central Finance." *Tsing Hua Research Bulletin (Tsing Hua Hueh Pao),* Volume III, No. 2, January and February, 1926, pp. 967–97. Peiping: Tsing Hua University.
39. CHU, Y. K. *Some Problems of a National System of Education in China.* Shanghai: Commercial Press, 1933, pp. 53, 110–11, 293–95, 165.
*40. CHUAN, C. H. "Thirty Years of Chinese Modern Edu-

cation." *Educational Research,* Volume II, No. 2, March, 1928. Canton: National Chung Shan University.

*41. *Chung-hua Educational Review.* Volume XVIII, No. 12, 1931, Appendix; Volume XVI, No. 13, September, 1926, News Section, pp. 5–9. Shanghai: Chung Hua Book Co.

42. CLARK, GROVER. *Economic Rivalries in China.* New Haven: Yale University Press, 1931, pp. 44–45.

43. CLARK, HAROLD F. *The Cost of Government and the Support of Education.* New York: Bureau of Publications, Teachers College, Columbia University, 1924, pp. 3–5.

44. CLARK, HAROLD F. *The Economic Effects of Education.* Bureau of Coöperative Research, Indiana University, 1928, *passim.*

45. *Complete Works of Chang Wen Hsiang Kung, The.* Volume 54: "Petition for Raising Huge Funds for Carrying Out Important Affairs." Fifth Day of Sixth Moon, 1901.

46. CONDLIFF, J. B. *China To-day, Economic.* Boston: World Peace Foundation, 1932.

*47. *Current Events Monthly,* Volume IX, No. 5, November, 1933, pp. 171–73. Nanking: Current Events Monthly Society.

*48. DEPARTMENT OF AGRICULTURAL ECONOMICS OF THE UNIVERSITY OF NANKING. *The 1931 Flood in China, An Economic Survey.* Nanking, 1932, p. 10 *sqq.*

49. DEPARTMENT OF SUPERINTENDENCE. *Twelfth Yearbook: Critical Problems in School Administration,* Chapter III, "The Financial Support of Public Education," pp. 57–90. Washington: National Education Association, February, 1934.

50. DJIANG, SIAO-MEI. *The Position of China As a Producer of Raw Materials and Manufactured Goods.* Shanghai: China Institute of Pacific Relations, 1933, *passim.*

51. DOANE, ROBERT R. *The Measurement of American Wealth.*

New York: Harper and Brothers, 1933. Table X, p 35.
52. "Draft Constitution of China, The." *Chinese Affairs*, Volume V, No. 19, March 15, 1934, p. 297. Nanking: International Relations Committee.
53. DRESDNER BANK. *The Economic Forces of the World.* Berlin: Dresdner Bank, 1930. Table 2 and pp. 169, 171, 176.
54. EDIE, L. D. *Economics, Principles and Problems.* New York: Thomas Y. Crowell, 1926, p. 273.
*55. *Educational Review, The.* Volume VI, No. 1, 1914, News Section; Volume VI, No. 3, 1914, News Section; Volume VII, No. 8, 1915, News Section; Volume XV, No. 12, 1923, News Section; Volume XVI, No. 6, June, 1923.
*56. *Education and the Masses.* Volume V, No. 6, February 28, 1934, p. 1086. Table on Provincial and Municipal Educational Expenditure for the Fiscal Year 1933–34. Wusih, Kiangsu: Kiangsu Provincial College of Education.
57. ENGELHARDT, N. L. *Planning School Building Programs.* New York: Bureau of Publications, Teachers College, Columbia University, 1930, *passim.*
58. ENGELHARDT, N. L., AND ALEXANDER, C. *School Finance and Business Management Problems.* New York: Bureau of Publications, Teachers College, Columbia University, 1928.
59. ENGELHARDT, N. L., AND ENGELHARDT, FRED. *Public School Business Administration.* New York: Bureau of Publications, Teachers College, Columbia University, 1927, pp. 219, 771.
*60. Excerpts from the Reports of Twelve National School Inspectors. News Section, *Shun Pao,* December 29, 1933. Shanghai: The Shun Pao.
61. FAIRCHILD, F. R., AND OTHERS. *Elementary Economics,* Volume II, 1926, p. 201.

62. FEDERAL BOARD FOR VOCATIONAL EDUCATION. *Principles Underlying the Distribution of Aid to Vocational Education in Agriculture.* Washington: Government Printing Office, 1923.
63. FONG, H. D. *China's Industrialization. A Statistical Survey.* Shanghai: China Institute of Pacific Relations, 1931, p. 45.
*64. FONG, H. D., and CHEN, C. M. "A Analysis of China's Industrial Difficulties." *The Economic Weekly, Ta Kung Pao,* August 23, 1933, p. 3. Tientsin: Ta Kung Newspaper.
65. GREEN, W. R. *The Theory and Practice of Modern Taxation.* New York: Commercial Clearing House, 1933.
*66. *Heng Chien Monthly, The.* "Special Number on Planning Economy," Volume II, No. 4, April, 1933, p. 99. Peiping: The Heng Chien Monthly Society.
67. HOH, YAM-TONG. *The Boxer Indemnity Remissions and Education in China.* Doctoral Dissertation (in manuscript), Teachers College, Columbia University, New York, N. Y., 1933.
†68. HOMO-LINGUISTIC SOCIETY, THE. *Geographical Survey of the Chinese Individual Provinces.* Hupeh, Tokyo, Volume 9, 1918.
69. HO, PING-YIN. "China's Industry and Commerce During 1933." *Chinese Economic Journal,* Volume XIV, No. 1, January, 1934, p. 19 *sqq.*
*70. HSIA, CHEN-FUNG. *Modern Educational Administration.* Shanghai: Chung Hua Book Co., 1932, pp. 90–141, 196–97.
*71. HSIAN, PI-HSIEN, AND OTHERS, ED. *The Second Chinese Labour Year Book,* 1932, p. 207. (See Index Number of Wholesale Prices made by the National Committee on Tax Laws). Peiping: The Bureau of Social Research, 1932.

*72. HSIAO, YI-SHAN. *General History of Manchu Dynasty*, Volume II, pp. 440–41. Shanghai: Commercial Press, 1928.

*73. HSU, HSING-CHEN. *Principles and Plans of Educational Reconstruction in China.* Shanghai: Chung Hua Book Co., 1931, 144 p.

74. HSU, LEONARD S. *Sun Yat-sen, His Political and Social Ideals.* Los Angeles: University of Southern California Press, 1933, p. 138.

75. HU, SHIH. "Which Road Are We Going?" *Pacific Affairs*, October, 1930. Honolulu: Institute of Pacific Relations.

*76. HUANG, YIN-PEI. "An Appraisal of Twenty Years of Chinese Educational Statistics." *Human Culture Monthly*, Volume IV, No. 5, June 16, 1933, pp. 1–28.

77. INTERNATIONAL BUREAU OF EDUCATION. "Inquiry into the Education Budget of Certain States." Bulletin Year VII, 4th Quarter, No. 29, 1933, pp. 160–61.

78. INTERNATIONAL LABOR OFFICE. *The Possibilities and Limitations of International Comparisons of Cost of Living and Family Budgets.* Honolulu: Institute of Pacific Relations, 1931, *passim*.

79. JOINT COMMISSION ON THE EMERGENCY IN EDUCATION. *Report of National Conference on the Financing of Education.* "School Finance Charter," p. 9. Washington: National Education Association, 1933, 78 p.

80. JOINT COMMISSION ON THE EMERGENCY IN EDUCATION. By Phi Delta Kappa Fraternity. *Evaluating the Public Schools.* Washington: National Education Association, 1934.

†81. (Japanese) DEPARTMENT OF EDUCATION. *A General Survey of Education in Japan.* Tokyo, Department of Education, 1933, pp. 62–63, 57.

*82. KAN, YU-YUAN. *County Educational Finance in Kiangsu.* Nanking: National Central University, 1928, 16 p.

*83. KU, YOU-CHUAN. "The Development of Energy Resources and the Modernization of China." *Shun Pao Monthly*, Volume II, No. 7, July 15, 1933, pp. 87–96.

*84. KWO, NAN. "A Survey and Study of the Compensation of Elementary and Secondary School Teachers and Officers." *Educational Review*, Volume XXIII, No. 1, January, 1931, pp. 121–40.

85. KWO, P. W. *The Chinese System of Public Education*. New York: Bureau of Publications, Teachers College, Columbia University, 1917, pp. 62–63, 146–47.

86. LARSON, EMIL L. *School Finance and Related Problems*. Tucson, Arizona: University of Arizona Press, 1933, pp. 7–10.

87. LASKER, BRUNO, EDITOR. *Problems of the Pacific*. Proceedings of the Institute of Pacific Relations, Hangchow, 1931. Chicago: University of Chicago Press, 1932.

88. League of Nations' Mission of Educational Experts. BECKER, C. H., FALSKI, M., LANGEVIN, P., TAWNEY, R. *The Reorganization of Education in China*. Paris: League of Nations Institute of Intellectual Coöperation, 1932, pp. 52–55.

89. LEGGE, JAMES, TRANSLATOR. *The Chinese Classics*. (Second Edition, Revised.) Oxford: The Clarendon Press, 1893. Volume I, Book IX, Chapter XIV; Chapter X, Section 7, "The Commentary of the Great Learning"; Book IV, Chapter XVI; Book XIV, Chapter I; Book XI, Chapter XVI.

*90. LIANG, CHIH-CHIAO. "A Personal View of Our Educational Policy." *The Works of Yin Pien Shih*, Volume 29.

91. LIANG, CHING-CHUN. *The Relationship Between Population and Food Supply of China*. Doctorate Dissertation in manuscript. Cambridge, Mass.: Harvard University. Summary.

*92. LI, BU-CHING. "The Problem of Financing Elementary Education." *Chung-Hua Educational Review,* Volume IV, No. 2, 1924, pp. 1-9.

*93. LI, CHUAN-SHIH. "My Views of Inheritance Taxation." *Bankers' Weekly,* Volume XVII, No. 50, December 6, 1933, pp. 1-2.

*94. LI, CHUAN-SHIH. "Ten Years of Chinese National Economy." *The World Magazine,* Tenth Anniversary Issue, August 10, 1931. Shanghai: The World Book Co., p. 90.

95. LIEU, D. K. *China's Industries and Finance.* Shanghai: Chinese Government Bureau of Economic Information, 1927.

*96. LIN, CHUAN-KIA. *Geography of Hupeh Province.* Wuchang: Chung Hua University, 1919.

97. LINN, H. H. *Practical School Economies.* New York: Bureau of Publications, Teachers College, Columbia University, 1934, p. 167.

*98. LIN, YUAN-TSUNG AND WANG SHIAO-LIEN, EDITORS. *The Land Capitation and Grain Tribute Directory and Water Control Directory of Hupeh Province.* Wuchang: Department of Finance, 1875.

*99. LI, SHIH-TSENG. "A Proposal for Educational Independence." *The Educational Review,* Volume XIV, No. 2, February, 1922, pp. 1-9.

100. LIST, FRIEDERICH. *The National System of Political Economy.* Translated by S. S. Lloyd, 1922.

*101. LIU, NAI-CHIEN. "Educational Fiscal Independence in the Provinces and Municipalities." *Current Events Monthly.* Nanking: The Current Events Monthly Society. Volume X, No. 2, February, 1934, pp. 61-64.

*102. LIU, TAO-YUAN. *Land Tax System of the Two Sung Dynasties.* Shanghai: The New Life Book Co., p. 35.

*103. LO, KIA-LUN. "The Crisis of Chinese Higher Education." *Hupeh Education Monthly,* No. 5, January, 1934. Wuchang: Hupeh Provincial Department of Education.

104. LOWE, CHUAN-HUA. *Facing Labour Issues in China.* Shanghai: China Institute of Pacific Relations, 1933. Chapter X, p. 115 *sqq.*
105. LUTZ, HARLEY L., AND CARR, W. G. *Essentials of Taxation.* Washington: National Education Association. November, 1933.
106. MCGAUGHY, J. R. *Fiscal Administration of City School Systems.* New York: Macmillan, 1924.
107. MAGILL, R. F. *Lectures in Taxation.* Columbia University Symposium, 1932. New York: Commercial Clearing House.
108. MARSHALL, ALFRED. *Principles of Economics,* 1922, pp. 42-47.
109. MATZEN, JOHN M. *State Constitutional Provisions for Education.* New York: Bureau of Publications, Teachers College, Columbia University, 1931.
*110. MA, YEN-CH'U. *The Lectures of Ma, Yen-ch'u.* Shanghai: Commercial Press, 1925. Volume II, pp. 35-43, 193 (1928 edition).
111. MAYTON, J. G. *Budgets of Far Eastern Countries.* Washington: Government Printing Office, 1927, p. 28.
*112. MINISTRY OF INTERIOR. *Bulletin,* Volume V, Nos. 10-11, March 11, 1932, "The Value of Subsidiary Industrial Products."
*113. MINISTRY OF RAILWAYS. *Railway Bulletin,* No. 255, April 19, 1932. "Table on Ten Years of Educational Expenditure of the National Railways."
114. MOEHLMAN, A. B. "Public School Accounting." *Review of Educational Research,* Volume II, No. 2. Finance and Business Administration. Washington: National Education Association, 1932.
115. MOEHLMAN, A. B. *Public School Finance.* New York: Rank McNally, 1927, p. 8.
116. MONROE, WALTER S., AND ENGELHARDT, MAX D. *The Technique of Educational Research.* Urbana: The University of Illinois *Bulletin,* Volume 25, No. 19, 1928.

117. MORRISON, H. C. *The Management of School Money.* Chicago: University of Chicago Press, 1933, p. 32.
118. MORRISON, H. C. *School Revenue.* Chicago: University of Chicago Press, 1930, p. 46.
119. MORT, PAUL R. *The Measurement of Educational Need.* New York: Bureau of Publications, Teachers College, Columbia University, 1924.
120. MORT, PAUL R. *State Aid for Public Schools in the State of New York.* Report of the Special Joint Committee on Taxation and Retrenchment of the Legislature of the State of New York. Albany: J. B. Lyon, 1925.
"Obviously it would be desirable to express such a minimum in terms of the educational product and the time may come when this will be possible. For the present, however, the best that can be done is to express it in terms of money accompanied with such prescriptions with regard to the quality of teachers, facilities and curricula as the educational authorities may find it practicable to lay down."
121. MORT, PAUL R. *State Support for Public Education.* Report of the National Survey of School Finance. Washington: The American Council on Education, 1933, pp. 12, 435.
122. MORT, PAUL R. AND OTHERS. *State Support for Public Schools in New York as Related to Tax Relief and Educational Expansion.* A Report to the New York State Tax Commission for the Revision of the Tax Laws, Memorandum No. 2, 1932.
123. MORT, PAUL R. "Teachers College Influence Upon the Financing of Public Education." A Reprint from the *Teachers College Record,* Volume XXX, March, 1929, pp. 572–77.
124. NAGANO, AKIRA. *Chinese Social Organization.* Translation by Chu, Kia-ching. Shanghai: The Light Book Co., 1930, p. 187.

125. NATIONAL ASSOCIATION OF VOCATIONAL EDUCATION. *Proceedings of the Tenth National Conference on Vocational Education.* Shanghai: The Association, 1932, 98 p.
126. NATIONAL EDUCATION ASSOCIATION, RESEARCH DIVISION. "School Revenues and New Methods of Taxation." *Studies in State Educational Administration.* Study No. 2, January, 1930. Washington: National Education Association.
127. NATIONAL TAX ASSOCIATION. "Preliminary Report of the Committee Appointed by the National Tax Association to Prepare a Plan of a Model System of State and Local Taxation." *Proceedings,* November, 1918.
128. NATIONAL TAX ASSOCIATION. *Second Report on a Plan of a Model System of State and Local Taxation.* National Tax Association, 1933.
129. NATIONAL EDUCATION ASSOCIATION. Department of Superintendence, and Research Service. Circular No. 9, September, 1933. Washington: National Education Association.
130. NEWCOMER, MABEL. *Financial Statistics of Public Education in the United States.* New York: Macmillan, 1924.
*131. *New Education, The.* Volume IV, No. 3, March, 1922, pp. 471–6; Volume IV, No. 5, May, 1922, pp. 953–58; Volume V, Nos. 1–2, August, 1922, pp. 241–43; Volume V, No. 3, October, 1922, pp. 589–91; Volume VII, Nos. 2–3, October, 1923, pp. 51–58; Volume IX, Nos. 1 and 2, September, 1924; Volume XI, No. 2, September, 1925, p. 209 *sqq.*
132. NIEH, C. L. *China's Industrial Development, Its Problems and Prospects.* Shanghai: China Institute of Pacific Relations, 1933, *passim.*
133. NORTON, JOHN K. *The Ability of the States to Support Education.* Washington: National Education Association, 1926. Table 5, p. 19.

134. NORTON, JOHN K. *Major Issues on Public School Finance* (in manuscript), 1933, pp. 6–9.
135. PEARMAN, W. I. *Support of State Educational Programs.* New York: Bureau of Publications, Teachers College, Columbia University, 1933, 141 p.
136. PITKIN, ROYCE S. *Public School Support in the United States During Periods of Economic Depression.* Brattleboro, Vt.: Stephen Daye Press, 1933, p. 135 *sqq.*
*137. "Plans for the Educational Use of the Boxer Indemnity." *Oriental Library Series,* in three volumes. Shanghai: Commercial Press.
*138. Po, MEI-CHU. *Geography of the Provinces of Hupeh, Hunan and Kiangsi, China,* Volume V. Peiping: Department of History and Geography, Peking Normal University, 1927.
*139. "Proceedings of the National Conference of the Educational Associations." In SHU HSING-CHEN: *History of Modern Educational Thoughts in China.* Shanghai: Chung Hua Book Co., 1929, p. 259 *sqq.*
*140. *The Public Forum of the Times.* Nanking: National Central University. Article by Tsang-Hwei, No. 9, 1932, pp. 6–9.
141. RAINEY, H. P. *Public School Finance.* Century Co., 1929, pp. 36–54.
142. RAMIREZ, RAFAEL. *Seminar in Mexico, A Cooperative Study of Mexican Life and Culture.* 4th Annual Edition, 1929. Mexico City, p. 7.
143. *Recent Social Trends in the United States.* Report of the President's Committee, Volume II, pp. 1324–26, 1365. New York: McGraw-Hill Book Co., 1933.
144. REEDER, WARD G. "Methods of Research in School Finance." *Review of Educational Research.* Washington: American Educational Research Association of the National Education Association, Volume IV, No. 1, February, 1934, p. 45.

145. REMER, C. F. *Foreign Investments in China.* New York: Macmillan, 1933, pp. 69, 70, 76, 145.
146. Report of the Governor's Commission. *Reconstruction of the System of Public School Support in the State of New Jersey.* Volume II, December, 1933.
147. RESEARCH DIVISION OF THE NATIONAL EDUCATION ASSOCIATION. Current Issues in Teacher Retirement. *Research Bulletin,* Volume VIII, No. 5, November, 1930, p. 230.
148. RIGNANO, EUGENIO. Translated by Josiah Stamp. *The Social Significance of Death Duties.* London: N. Douglas, 1925.
149. RESEARCH DIVISION OF THE NATIONAL EDUCATION ASSOCIATION. *Five Years of State School Revenue Legislation, 1929-1933.* Washington: The Association, 1934.
150. RESEARCH DIVISION OF THE NATIONAL EDUCATION ASSOCIATION. *State Sources of Revenue for Public Education: A Selected and Annotated Bibliography.* Washington: The Association, March, 1929.
151. RESEARCH STAFF, NATIONAL SURVEY OF SCHOOL FINANCE AND SPECIAL CONSULTANTS. *Research Problems in School Finance.* Washington: American Council on Education, 1933.
152. *Review of Educational Research,* Volume II, No. 2, April, 1932. Washington, National Education Association, p. 113.
153. RUGG, HAROLD. *The Great Technology.* New York: John Day, 1933, p. 250 *sqq.*
154. RUSSELL, BERTRAND. *Education and the Modern World.* Chapter VIII, "Education and Economics." New York: W. W. Norton, 1932, p. 191 *sqq.*
155. RUSSELL, BERTRAND. "The Problem of China." In *Education and the Modern World.* New York: W. W. Norton, 1932, p. 194.
156. SELIGMAN, EDWIN R. A. *Essays in Taxation,* Ninth Edition. New York: Macmillan, 1931.

157. SELIGMAN, EDWIN R. A. *Principles of Economics*, 1926, p. 423.
158. SCHMIDT, ARTHUR W. *The Development of a State's Minimum Educational Program*. New York: Bureau of Publications, Teachers College, Columbia University, 1932.
159. SCHULTZ, W. J. *American Public Finance and Taxation*. New York: Prentice Hall, 1931, 635 p.
*160. SHANG, TAO-CHIH. *Outline of Educational Administration*. Shanghai: Chung Hua Book Co., 1930, 2 volumes, 542 p.
161. SHAW, KINN-WEI. *Democracy and Finance in China*. New York: Columbia University Press, 1926, pp. 169–94.
*162. SHIH, TUNG. "The Status of the Russian Boxer Indemnity and Educational Finance." *Education of To-morrow*, Volume II, No. 9, May 16, 1933. Table 7, p. 13.
163. SCHULTZ, W. J. *The Taxation of Inheritance*. Houghton, 1926.
*164. *Shun Pao Monthly*. Shanghai: The Shun Pao. Volume II, No. 4, pp. 37–41; No. 7, pp. 87–96.
165. SIMPSON, A. D. *Financing Education in Connecticut. A Proposed Plan to Enable the State of Connecticut to Meet More Adequately Its Educational Responsibility*. Hartford, 1927.
166. SMITH, H. L., AND ODELL, E. A. "Bibliography of School Surveys and of References on School Surveys." *School of Education, Indiana University, Bulletin*, September-November, 1931. Volume VIII, No. 1 and No. 2, April, 1932.
167. SOCIETY OF INDUSTRIAL ENGINEERS. *The Economic Significance of Technological Progress*. New York, 1933, passim.
168. "Special and Local Public Loans." *Chinese Economic Journal*. Volume VIII, No. 5, November, 1933, pp. 60–63.

169. SPRINGFIELD, MASS., U. S. A. *Annual Report of the Springfield Public Schools.* Springfield: Board of Education, 1930, p. 59.
170. STATE PLANNING COMMISSION. *Summary of the Fulfillment of the First Five-Year Plan.* Moscow, 1933. Tables 24 and 28, pp. 286–7, 291.
171. STAUFFER, M. T. *The Christian Occupation of China.* Shanghai: The China Continuation Committee, 1922.
*172. Sun Yat-sen's "Lecture on the Analysis of Socialism." *The Complete Works of Chung Shan,* 1923.
173. STRAYER, GEORGE D., DIRECTOR OF STUDIES. *Report of the Governor's Committee on the Costs of Public Education in the State of New York,* 1934.
.174. STRAYER, GEORGE D., DIRECTOR. *Report of the Survey of the Public Schools of Chicago, Illinois.* New York: Bureau of Publications, Teachers College, Columbia University, 1932. Volume I, pp. 24–25.
175. STRAYER, GEORGE D. "The Work of the Division of Field Studies." *Teachers College Record,* November, 1931, pp. 118–22.
176. STRAYER, GEORGE D., AND HAIG, R. M. *The Financing of Education in the State of New York.* Report of the Educational Finance Inquiry. New York: Macmillan, 1923, pp. 142–45, 172.
*177. "A Summary of the Chinese Domestic and Foreign Loans and the Indemnity Funds for 1933." *Bank of China Monthly Review.* Volume XIII, No. 3, March, 1934, p. 16.
178. SWIFT, F. H. *Federal and State Policies in Public School Finance in the United States.* New York: Ginn and Co., 1931, pp. 20, 25–26, 68.
179. SWIFT, F. H. *The Financing of Institutions of Public Instruction in France.* Berkeley: University of California Press, 1933, p. 33.

180. SWIFT, F. H. *A History of Public Permanent Common School Funds in the United States, 1795–1905.* New York: Henry Holt and Co., 1911.
181. SWIFT, F. H. "Let America Study the French System of Financing Schools." *Nation's Schools,* Volume XII, No. 1, July, 1933, pp. 41–48.
182. SWIFT, F. H., AND OTHERS. *Studies in Public School Finance.* In 4 volumes. Minneapolis: The University of Minnesota, 1922 and 1923.
*183. TAI, CHI-TAO. "Chinese Economic Reconstruction and Educational Reconstruction." *The New Asia,* Volume IV, No. 3, July 1, 1932, pp. 1–9.
*184. TAI, SHUANG-CHIU. "The Movement for the Use of Temple Property in Establishing Schools, A Proposed Educational Finance Policy." *Chung-Hua Educational Review.* Volume XVII, No. 4, 1928. Appendix. Shanghai: Chung Hua Book Co.
*185. TAI, S. C. *The Problem of Using Temple Property for Education.* Shanghai: Chung Hua Book Circulating Club, 1929, 122 p.
186. TAO, L. K. *The Standards of Living Among Chinese Workers.* Shanghai: The China Institute of Pacific Relations, 1931, p. 4.
187. TAWNEY, R. H. *Land and Labour in China.* London: George Allen and Unwin, 1932, pp. 28, 90–91.
188. TAX RESEARCH FOUNDATION. *Federal and State Tax Systems.* 4th Edition. Chicago: Commerce Clearing House (205 W. Monroe St.), January, 1933.
189. TRUE, ALFRED C. *A History of Agricultural Education in the United States, 1885–1925.* Washington: Government Printing Office, 1929, 436 p.
*190. T'SAI, YUAN-PEI. "Suggestions for Educational Independence." *The New Education,* Volume IV, No. 3, March, 1922, pp. 317–19.

191. TU, TSO-CHOU. *The Principles of Educational and School Administration.* Shanghai: Commercial Press, 1930, 330 p.
192. TWISS, GEORGE R. *Science and Education in China.* Shanghai: Commercial Press, 1925. Chapter I.
193. TYAU, M. T. Z. *Two Years of Nationalist China.* Shanghai: Kelly and Walsh, Ltd., 1930, pp. 29, 32, 224–25.
194. "Unified Financial Plan." V. O. K. S. Moscow: The Soviet Union Society for Cultural Relations with Foreign Countries. Volume II, Nos. 7–9, 1931.
195. U. S. OFFICE OF EDUCATION. *The Deepening Crisis in Education.* Leaflet No. 44, 1933, p. 6.
195a U. S. OFFICE OF EDUCATION. *Leaflet No. 2,* February, 1931.
*196. WANG, CHIN-PIN, AND OTHERS, ED. *The First Chinese Labour Year Book.* Peiping: The Bureau of Social Research, 1928. Appendix II, pp. 154–56, Table on Index Numbers of Wholesale Prices of China and Other Countries, 1870–1926.
*197. WANG, HWANG-HWEI. *History of Chinese Constitution.* Shanghai: World Book Co., 1931.
*198. WANG, KWO-CHUNG. "Foreign Debts of Our Country." *Ta Kung Pao,* January 24, 1934. Tientsin: Ta Kung Newspaper.
*199. WEI, SUNG-TANG. "The Status of Chinese Public Finance and Its Future." *New China Magazine (Hsing Chung Hua),* Volume I, No. 3, February 10, 1933, pp. 1–7.
*200. WEI, TIN-SUN. "Chinese Public Finance and Permanent Educational Funds." *Chung-Hua Educational Review,* Volume XIX, No. 3, September, 1931, pp. 67–70.
*201. WEI, TIN-SUN. *The Reconstruction of Public Finance.* Shanghai: The Pacific Book Store, 1929, pp. 166–70, 15–16.
*202 WEN, KUNG-CHIH. *History of Chinese Military Strife.* Shanghai: Pacific Book Store, 1930.

203. WHITE HOUSE CONFERENCE ON CHILD HEALTH AND PROTECTION. *Special Education, the Handicapped and Gifted.* New York: The Century Co., 1931.
*204. WONG, SHEYTIN S. C. *A Treatise on Constitutional Law.* Shanghai: Commercial Press, 1927. Appendix, pp. 765–840.
205. WONG, W. H., DIRECTOR OF THE NATIONAL GEOLOGICAL SURVEY OF CHINA. *The Distribution of Population and Land Utilization in China.* Shanghai: China Institute of Pacific Relations, 1933.
206. YAKEL, RALPH. *The Legal Control of the Administration of Public School Expenditures.* New York: Bureau of Publications, Teachers College, Columbia University, 1929.

GLOSSARY OF CHINESE TITLES IN BIBLIOGRAPHY

(Numbers given in list below correspond to numbers given in above Bibliography)

I. Bibliographies

   3. Chiao Yü Lung Wen So Yin.

II. Yearbooks

   2. Ti I T'zu Chung Kuo Nien Chien.
   6. Shun Pao Nien Chien.
  10. Ti I T'zu Chung Kuo Chiao Yu Nien Chien.
  11. Chung Kuo Chiao Yu Chih Nan.

III. Primary Sources of Data

A.
  A. Ti I T'zu Chiao Yu T'ung Chi T'u Piao.
  B. Ti Er T'zu Chiao Yu T'ung Chi T'u Piao.
  C. Ti San T'zu Chiao Yu T'ung Chi T'u Piao.
  D. Ti I T'zu Chiao Yu T'ung Chi T'u Piao.
  E. Ti Er T'zu Chiao Yu T'ung Chi T'u Piao.
  F. Ti San T'zu Chiao Yu T'ung Chi T'u Piao.
  G. Ti Szu T'zu Chiao Yu T'ung Chi T'u Piao.
  H. Ti Wu T'zu Chiao Yu T'ung Chi T'u Piao.
  I. Chung Kuo Chiao Yu T'ung Chi K'ai Lan.
  J. 1. Ch'uan Kuo Ch'u Teng Chiao Yu K'ai K'uang.
     2. Ch'uan Kuo Chung Teng Chiao Yu K'ai K'uang.
     3. Ch'uan Kuo Kao Teng Chiao Yu K'ai K'uang.
     4. Ch'uan Kuo She Hui Chiao Yu K'ai K'uang.
  K. Ch'uan Kuo Kao Teng Chiao Yu T'ung Chi.

B.
   6. Chung Kuo P'i Fa Wu Chia Chih Shu.
  14. Shensi Hsing Chiao Yu Ting T'ung Hsin.

15. Chiao Yu Pu She Hui Chiao Yu Szu T'ung Hsin.
16. Kuo Chia Yu San.
21. Hupeh Hsing Fu Hsien Chih Shu Mu.
22. Hupeh Ke Hsien Hsueh K'uan Hsueh T'ien Chi San Piao.
23. Ching Tai Hupeh Ke Hsien Sui Yu Sui Ch'u Chi San Piao.

C.
1. I Nien Lai Chih Anhwei Chiao Yu.
2. Chung Hua Min Kuo Er Shih Nien Tu Ti Fang Sui Yu Sui Ch'u Yu San Chih K'ai San.
3. Tang Yuan Liu Hsueh Tiao Ch'a Lu.
4. Hupeh Hsing T'ung Chih.
5. Chekiang Hsing San Nien Lai Chiao Yu K'ai K'uang.
6. Kiangsu Chiao Yu Hsing Cheng K'ai K'uang.
7. Chung Kuo Ti Chih Tiao Ch'a So Pao Kao.
10. Ao Hsing Ting T'sao Chih Chang.
12. Ch'uan Kuo Chiao Yu Hui I Pao Kao.
13. Fukien Hsing Chiao Yu Ting Pao Kao.
14. Fukien Chiao Yu Ting Chiao Yu Chou K'an.
15. Hankow Te Pieh Shih Shih Cheng T'ung Chih Nien K'an.
16. Shih Fu Lu Shih Chiu Chou Hsien Chih.
18. Honan Chiao Yu Nien Chien.
19. Honan Chiao Yu Kuan Ch'an Te K'an.
20. Chin Tai Chung Kuo Chiao Yu Shih Liao.
21. Hunan Cheng Ch'ih Nien Chien.
22. Hupeh Chiao Yu Kung Pao.
23. Hupeh Hsing Min Cheng Pao Kao Shu.
24. Min Kuo Er Shih Er Nien Tu Hupeh Hsing Chiao Yu Wen Hua Fei Sui Ch'u Fen Lei Yu San Shu.
25. Tsui Chin Hupeh Chiao Yu I Lan.
26. Min Kuo Er Shih Er Nien Hupeh Chiao Yu K'ai K'uang T'ung Chi.
27. Hupeh Chiao Yu Hsien K'uang.
28. Hupeh Hsing Cheng Fu Chiao Yu Ting Hsien Hsing Kuei Chang.

29. Hupeh Hsing T'ung Shui Shui Tse.
30. Hupeh Shui Wu K'ai Yiao.
31. Min Kuo Er Shih I Nien Hupeh T'sai Cheng Pao Kao Shu.
32. Hupeh T'sai Cheng Ting Min Kuo Er Shih Er Nien San Yueh Chih Lu Yueh T'sai Cheng Pao Kao.
33. Hupeh Hsing Ke Hsien Er Shih I Nien Tu Hsien Ti Fang Sui Yu Sui Ch'u Yu San Piao.
34. Kiangsu Hsing Tsui Chin Chiao Yu K'ai K'uang.
35. Ti San T'zu Ch'uan Kuo Tai Piao Ta Hui Hsuan Yen Chi I Chueh An.
36. Hsing Cheng Fa Ling Ta Ch'uan.
37. Chiao Yu Ching Fei Tu Li Yun Tung Hsuan Yen.
38. Ti Er T'zu Ch'uan Kuo Chiao Yu Tui I Shih Mo Chi.
42. Ch'uan Kuo T'sai Cheng Hui I Hui Pien.
43. Ch'uan Kuo Ching Chi Hui I Hui Pien.
44. Chiao Yu Pu Kung Pao.
45. Ti I T'zu Chung Kuo Chiao Yu Nien Chien.
46. Chih Yeh T'ung Chi.
47. Lei Cheng Pu Kung Pao.
48. Yunnan Min Kuo Er Pao.
49. Chung Hua Min Kuo Er Shih Nien Tu Kuo Chia Pu T'ung Sui Yu Sui Ch'u Tsung Yu San.
50. Hupeh T'ien Chia Tiao Ch'a.
51. Ching Chi T'ung Chi Chi K'an.
52. Hupeh T'sai Cheng Yueh K'an.
54. Ti Ch'i T'zu Lung Shang Pu Pao Kao.
55. Shantung Hsing Ke Hsien Ti Fang Min Kuo Er Shih I Nien Tu Chiao Yu Fei Yu San.
56. Shantung Ke Hsien Chiao Yu K'uan Ch'an I Lan.
57. Shantung Ke Hsien Ti Fang Shih Pa Nien Tu Chiao Yu Ching Fei Sui Yu I Lan Piao.
58. Shun Pao Chiao Yu Hsing Wen Lan.
59. T'ung Chi Yueh Pao.
61. Ta Ching Chiao Yu Fa Ling.
62. Shih Ch'a Shansi Chiao Yu Pao Kao Shu.

Bibliography

IV. Secondary Sources

6. Hupeh Fang Hsien Ch'ang Tu.
7. Yin Hong Chou Pao.
11. Chung Yang Tang Wu Yueh K'an.
13. Ch'uan Hsueh P'ien.
14. Li Tai Chung Kuo Keng Ti Wen Ti.
16. Ke Hsing Shih Chi Te Chung Lei Tsai I Lan.
19. Mou Ti Ch'a I.
20. San Shih Nien Chung Kuo Chiao Yu Shih.
24. Chung Kuo Chin Tai Hsueh Chih Pien Ch'ien Shih.
25. Chiao Yu Ching Fei Chi Yen Tu Li.
26. Chin Hou Chiao Yu Shang Chi Pen Wen Ti Chih Tao Lung.
27. Chung Kuo Chiao Yu Hsing Cheng.
28. Chung Kuo Ching Chih Wen Ti.
30. Kuo Tsai Yu Chin Yung.
31. Min Kuo T'sai Cheng Shih.
32. Chung Kuo Hsing Chiao Yu Hsing Cheng Chih Tu Nien Chiu.
33. Kuo Ch'ih Shih.
34. Kiangsu Chiao Yu Hsing Cheng K'ai K'uang.
35. (Same as 28.)
36. Chung Kuo Ti Lei Tsai.
38. Chin Shih Nien Lai Chung Yang T'sai Cheng K'ai K'uang.
40. Chiao Yu Nien Chiu (Tsa Chih).
45. Chang Wen Hsiang Kung Ch'uan Chi.
47. Shih Szu Yueh Pao.
48. Min Kuo Er Shih Nien Shui Tsai Ching Chi Tiao Ch'a.
55. Chiao Yu Tsa Chih.
56. Chiao Yu Yu Min Chung.
60. Chiao Yu Pu Chuan Yuan Pao Kao—Hsing Wen.
64. Chung Kuo Kung Yeh K'un Nan Chih Feng Hsi.
66. Hsing Chien Yueh K'an.
68. Chih La Hsing Pieh Ch'uan Chih, Hupeh Hsing.
70. Hsien Tai Chiao Yu Hsing Cheng.

71. Ti Er T'zu Chung Kuo Lao Tung Nien Chien.
72. Ching Tai T'ung Shih.
73. Chung Kuo Chiao Yu Chien She Fang Chen.
76. Chung Kuo Er Shih Wu Nien Chien Ch'uan Kuo Chiao Yu T'ung Chi Ti Tsung Chien Ch'a.
82. Kiangsu Ke Hsien Chih Chiao Yu T'sai Cheng.
83. Chung Kuo Tung Li Chih Fa Chan Chi Chi Hsien Tai Hua.
84. Chung Shiao Hsueh Chiao Szu Pao Ch'ou Chih Tiao Ch'a Yu Nien Chiu.
90. Yin Ping Shih Ch'uan Chi.
92. Shiao Hsueh Chiao Yu Ching Fei Wen Ti.
93. E Tei Yu I Ch'an Shui Ti I Chien.
94. Shih Nien Lai Chih Chung Kuo Ching Chi.
96. Hupeh Hsing Ti Li Chih.
98. Ao Hsing Ting T'sao Shui Li He Pien.
99. Chiao Yu Tu Li I.
101. Ke Hsing Shih Chiao Fei Tu Li Yuen Tung.
102. Liang Sung T'ien Chih.
103. Chung Kuo Ta Hsueh Chiao Yu Chih Wei Chi.
110. Ma Yen-ch'u Yen Chiang Chi.
112. Lei Cheng Kung Pao.
113. T'ieh Tao Pu Kung Pao.
131. Hsin Chiao Yu.
137. Keng K'uan Hsing Hsueh Chi Hua.
138. Ao Hsiang Kung San Hsing Chih.
139. Ch'uan Kuo Chiao Yu Lien He Hui Li Chieh Ta Hui I Chueh An.
140. Shih Tai Kung Lung.
160. Chiao Yu Hsing Cheng Ta Kang.
162. E Keng K'uan Shih Mo Yu Chiao Yu.
164. Shun Pao Yueh K'an.
172. Chung Shan Ch'uan Shu.
177. Er Shih Er Nien T'sai Cheng Pu Hsien Fu Lei Wai Tsai K'uan Chih Ching San.

183. Chung Kuo Ti Ching Chi Chien She Yu Chiao Yu Chien She.
184. Miao Ch'an Hsin Hsueh Yuen Tung.
185. Miao Ch'an Hsin Hsueh Wen Ti.
190. T'sai Yuan-pei: Chiao Yu Lu Li I.
191. Chiao Yu Yu Hsueh Shiao Hsing Cheng Yuan Li.
196. Ti I T'zu Chung Kuo Lao Tung Nien Chien.
197. Chung Kuo Hien Fa Shih.
198. E Kuo Ti Wai Tsai.
199. Chung Kuo T'sai Cheng Hsien Chung Chi Ch'ih Ch'ien Chu.
200. Chung Kuo T'sai Cheng Yu Chiao Yu Chi Chin.
201. T'sai Cheng Kai Tsao.
202. Chung Kuo Chun Shih Shih.
204. Pi Chiao Hsien Fa.

VITA

Ronald Yu Soong Cheng was born in a mountainous village, known as Cheng Family Headland (Cheng Chia Tsui), in Chen Huang Borough, Second District, King Shan County, Hupeh Province, China, on the 7th of the 10th Lunar Month, 1903. He was taught the classics by his father, Cheng Ming-Ch'ü and his uncle, Cheng Tsung-huang, and received his modern elementary education in the North Higher Primary School, King Shan County and David Hill Memorial School, Wuchang, and his secondary education at Wesley College, Wuchang. Through the assistance of Rev. B. B. Chapman he graduated and obtained a certificate for supervisors and principals from the Philippine Normal School, Manila, P.I. in 1922 and attended the University of the Philippines during 1922 and 1925–26, and the University of California in the summer of 1929. He attended Teachers College, Columbia University, from the fall of 1929 to 1933–34 where he received the degree of Bachelor of Science in Education in 1930, and Master of Arts in 1931.

He taught from 1923 to 1924 in the City Normal School, Canton, and Central China Teachers College, Wuchang. Since that time he has held the following positions: Instructor and Proctor, Senior High School. Chinan University, Shanghai, 1924–25; Instructor in Great China University, and Librarian, Oriental Library, Commercial Press, Shanghai, 1926–27; Officer, Kwangsi Provincial Department of Education and Librarian, Chekiang Provincial Library, 1927–28; Editor, *Chung Sai Daily News,* San Francisco, 1929; Secretary of the Illiteracy Committee, World Federation of Education Associations since 1931. He held the Hupeh Provincial Government fellowship for five and a half years and the International Institute scholarship for three years and was elected to the Kappa Delta Pi in 1934.

Some of his professional publications are as follows:

"Lectures on Methods to Normal School Students," edited by Chang Hua-kung, Commercial Press, Shanghai.

"How to Study," Commercial Press, Shanghai.

"Methods of Teaching Arithmetic," Edward Evans and Sons, Shanghai.

"Methods of Teaching Geography," Edward Evans and Sons, Shanghai.

图书在版编目(CIP)数据

中国教育财政之改进＝The financing of public education in China: a factual analysis of its major problems of reconstruction:英文/陈友松著.—北京:商务印书馆,2015
（中华现代学术名著丛书.英文本）
ISBN 978-7-100-11074-7

Ⅰ.①中… Ⅱ.①陈… Ⅲ.①教育财政—研究—中国—英文 Ⅳ.①G526.7

中国版本图书馆 CIP 数据核字(2015)第 029685 号

所有权利保留。
未经许可,不得以任何方式使用。

中华现代学术名著丛书
中国教育财政之改进
（英文本）
陈友松 著

商 务 印 书 馆 出 版
（北京王府井大街36号 邮政编码 100710）
商 务 印 书 馆 发 行
北 京 冠 中 印 刷 厂 印 刷
ISBN 978-7-100-11074-7

2015年5月第1版　开本700×1000　1/16
2015年5月北京第1次印刷　印张20¾　插页14
定价:69.00元